LAME CAPTAINS AND LEFT-HANDED ADMIRALS

Peculiar Bodies: Stories and Histories

CAROLYN DAY, CHRIS MOUNSEY, AND WENDY J. TURNER, EDITORS

Lame Captains and Left-Handed Admirals

AMPUTEE OFFICERS IN NELSON'S NAVY

Teresa Michals

UNIVERSITY OF VIRGINIA PRESS

Charlottesville and London

University of Virginia Press
© 2021 by the Rector and Visitors of the University of Virginia
All rights reserved
Printed in the United States of America on acid-free paper

First published 2021
1 3 5 7 9 8 6 4 2

Library of Congress Cataloging-in-Publication Data

Names: Michals, Teresa, author.
Title: Lame captains and left-handed admirals : amputee officers in Nelson's Navy / Teresa Michals.
Other titles: Amputee officers in Nelson's Navy
Description: Charlottesville : University of Virginia Press, [2021] | Series: Peculiar bodies: stories and histories | Includes bibliographical references and index.
Identifiers: LCCN 2021018740 (print) | LCCN 2021018741 (ebook) | ISBN 9780813946726 (hardcover) | ISBN 9780813946733 (paperback) | ISBN 9780813946740 (ebook)
Subjects: LCSH: Great Britain. Royal Navy—History—19th century. | Seymour, Michael, Sir, 1768–1834. | Pell, Watkin Owen, Sir, 1788–1869. | Gordon, James Alexander, Sir, 1782–1869. | Nelson, Horatio Nelson, Viscount, 1758–1805. | Amputees—Great Britain—Biography. | Admirals—Great Britain—Biography. | Great Britain—History, Naval—19th century.
Classification: LCC DA87.1.A1 M53 2021 (print) | LCC DA87.1.A1 (ebook) | DDC 940.2/745092241—dc23
LC record available at https://lccn.loc.gov/2021018740
LC ebook record available at https://lccn.loc.gov/2021018741

Cover art: *Admiral Lord Nelson*, John Marshall, 1798. (© Trustees of the British Museum)

For Robert, always

CONTENTS

LIST OF ILLUSTRATIONS   ix
ACKNOWLEDGMENTS   xi

Introduction: Amputee Officers   1
1. Patrons and Followers   37
2. Looking Like a Hero   82
3. Love and Friendship   132
4. Becoming Victorian   174

APPENDIX: SHORT BIOGRAPHIES OF AMPUTEE OFFICERS
WHO RETURNED TO ACTIVE DUTY   207
NOTES   221
BIBLIOGRAPHY   247
INDEX   259

ILLUSTRATIONS

1. *The Battle of the Nile*, George Cruikshank 116
2. *Extirpation of the Plagues of Egypt;—Destruction of Revolutionary Crocodiles;—or, ye British Hero Cleansing ye Mouth of ye Nile*, James Gillray 118
3. Rear Admiral James Alexander Gordon, Andrew Morton 119
4. Admiral Sir Watkin Owen Pell, John Lucas 120
5. Sir Frescheville Holles and Sir Robert Holmes, Peter Lely 121
6. Captain Galfridus Walpole, Charles Jervas 122
7. Vice Admiral Horatio Nelson, Lemuel Francis Abbott 123
8. Sir Michael Seymour, James Northcote (engraved by Richard Cook) 124
9. Rear Admiral Samuel Hood, John Hoppner 125
10. Rear Admiral Horatio Nelson, Guy Head 127
11. *The Death of Nelson*, Samuel Drummond 129
12. Captain James Alexander Gordon, engraved by William Greatbatch 130
13. Lydia Gordon 153
14. Robert Heriot Barclay in oval mat 180
15. Admiral Sir Michael Seymour (wrist restored), Bart 181

ACKNOWLEDGMENTS

THIS BOOK'S ERRORS are my own, but the generosity of many stands behind its strengths. I wish to thank Chris Mounsey and Carolyn Day for their tireless support. With an enthusiasm that surprised me years ago, but that I now recognize as entirely characteristic, Chris listened to a short conference paper about representing Nelson's empty right sleeve and heard a book. Carolyn was a guiding light to relevant archives. David Gerber's commitment to bringing the history of military veterans and the history of disability rights activism into conversation with each other has been invaluable at each step of this project. I am indebted to N. A. M. Rodger's deep knowledge of the history of Admiralty and Chatham Chest pensions for wounds, and his gift for explaining the "delightful complexity" of this subject in clear and concise terms. I appreciate both the thoughtfulness and the speed of Sarah Schneewind's comments on drafts. I would also like to thank my helpful editor, Angie Hogan, the insightful readers at the University of Virginia Press, and the resourceful librarians at the National Maritime Museum's Caird Archive, the British Library, the Northumberland Archives, the National Archives, the Toronto Public Library, and Heidelberg University. In the midst of a global pandemic, George Mason University's Korea campus gave me a collegial community within which to work on this project, and talented and determined George Mason student Carolyn Klein provided essential help in manuscript editing and locating sources at a distance. My father, Dr. Edward Michals, was proud to wear the uniform of a captain in the United States Public Health service and then to make a second career in occupational medicine. My mother, Vivien Krippner Michals, poured compassion, respect, and optimism into her career as primary school special education teacher at the time when the Americans with Disabilities Act first began to build ramps and throw open classroom doors. It was not until I had nearly finished this book that I saw them both in its every page. My husband, Robert Matz, is my life's greatest pleasure. He also enables me to meet its challenges, from moving to new continents to writing new books. He combines an intellectual's joy in problematizing with a good administrator's joy in problem-solving, and there could be no better friend. This book is dedicated to him. Finally, I want to thank our children, David and Rachel, for kindly listening to more stories about the Napoleonic Wars than it was reasonable to expect them to tolerate, and to apologize for leaving them with the impression that these wars were fought entirely at sea.

LAME CAPTAINS AND LEFT-HANDED ADMIRALS

INTRODUCTION

Amputee Officers

VILLAINOUS AMPUTEES ABOUND in popular images of the Age of Sail. Robert Louis Stevenson's one-legged Long John Silver impales an enemy with his crutch. J. M. Barrie's one-handed captain swaggers about eviscerating members of his own crew with his eponymous iron hook. Although Melville's Captain Ahab does not use his prosthesis as a murder weapon, he does stamp his ivory peg leg across the *Pequod*'s quarterdeck in an unnerving manner as he drags his men to their deaths. These figures are, of course, all fictional. In creating them, Barrie, Melville, and Stevenson follow the popular literary convention of using outward deformity to signify an inner monstrous nature. Amplifying Francis Bacon's assertion in "Of Deformity" (1625) that "there is . . . consent between the body and the mind," the power of this convention is remarkable.[1] In fact, in their own time, the actual amputees who commanded tall ships were not villains. They were national heroes. Admiral Lord Horatio Nelson is the single amputee hero whose popularity can still rival the popularity of these fictional villains. Shattered by a musket ball as he led a raid at Santa Cruz de Tenerife on July 25, 1797, Horatio Nelson's right arm was amputated immediately below the shoulder. He had lost most of the sight in his right eye in combat four years earlier. That is, Nelson lost his arm well before he fought his greatest battles: the Nile (1798), Copenhagen (1801), and Trafalgar (1805). He made his most historically significant contributions to Britain's security and international power as a physically impaired officer serving on active duty—as a one-armed, half-blind admiral who was working at the peak of his administrative genius, technical expertise, and charismatic leadership. Melville's own *White Jacket* and *Billy Budd* include panegyrics to the one-armed admiral, "the greatest sailor since our world began," and monuments, film, and historical fiction still bear his imprint. In his own time, however, Nelson did not stand alone. In fact, as an amputee naval hero, he was in excellent company.

This book focuses on a group of Napoleon-era British Royal Navy officers who served at sea after they lost a limb in battle. From 1795 to 1837, at least twenty-six officers, in addition to Nelson, survived amputation of a limb and went on to further active service, including command at sea. Seven of them returned to active duty without a leg; nineteen without an arm. While Nelson was exceptional in terms of the scale of his professional success, many of these other officers were also national heroes. This book tells their stories, and these stories enrich our understanding of the range of possibilities for people living with a major physical impairment in this period. In addition to Nelson, it focuses on three other amputee officers whose careers are particularly distinguished and particularly well documented: Sir Michael Seymour, Sir Watkin Owen Pell, and Sir James Alexander Gordon. It offers an overview of their active duty service, a look at how the loss of a limb affected their professional and personal lives, and some observations on their changing place in historical memory. This introduction presents a preliminary larger-scale statistical study of the active duty service of disabled officers in the period as context and situates the book within two fields of inquiry: the "new naval history" and disability studies.

Disability and History

In 2001, Douglas C. Baynton wrote, "Disability is everywhere in History, once you begin looking for it, but conspicuously absent from the histories we write."[2] Horatio Nelson is a good example of both this conspicuousness and this absence. The fact that he achieved his greatest victories after losing his right arm has long been central to his popular image, an image initially crafted by the man himself. From the Victorians' high-minded martyr to the twentieth century's effective manager, historians have produced Nelsons that reflect the concerns of their own eras. At the time of writing, a demand for racial reckoning draws new attention to his support for West Indian slavery. Through all these changes, Nelson's empty right sleeve has been a constant presence in his popular image, a feature the man himself did not shy away from displaying. "I am Lord Nelson. See, here's my fin!" he replied when challenged by a ship in the Baltic in 1801, throwing back his boat cloak to reveal his vestigial limb.[3] Nelson's impairment is visible in the monuments, museum exhibits, portraits, anecdotes, and commemorative goods that reflect his celebrity. Despite often being unwell or at sea, and dying at Trafalgar at the age of forty-seven, Nelson is the subject of more formal portraits than any British military hero except the Duke of Wellington.[4] And these portraits confront viewers with the full-frontal view of a military amputee. The image of a conspicuously impaired military hero remained constant in the commemorative goods whose sales boomed after Nelson's death; in popular engravings, mugs, decanters, fans, and fabrics; and in the iconic statue that still looms over Trafalgar Square. To the general public in the years leading up to and following Trafalgar, even a rough sketch of Nelson was recognizable by his empty right sleeve. Although the damage to his right eye did not figure widely in visual representations of him during his lifetime, it was also public knowledge. A late Victorian commemorative display of ceremonial sword hilts and medals given to Nelson to honor his victories includes as its centerpiece one of the combined knife and forks he used after losing his arm, a remarkable example of an assistive device claiming pride of place in a monument to military heroism.[5] A more recent monument is the flagship of the Jubilee Sailing Trust, a three-masted barque that sailed around the world from 2012 to 2014, manned by a mixed crew of sailors with and without physical impairment, dedicated to breaking down barriers that create disability. This flagship's name is the Lord Nelson.[6]

Nelson's long-running public presence as an officer with a prominent physical impairment is particularly valuable because this kind of visibility is quite rare. As Katherine Ott notes, whatever else they intend to show about the past, statues and exhibitions usually feature one sort of body: an idealized one. "The history of public presentations of history goes hand-in-hand with representations of the human body," she points out, but the "healthy, idealized figures in exhibits, films, and re-enactments are as false as the landscaped and manicured grounds of Civil War battlefields."[7] British bodies in Napoleon's day diverged widely and variously from today's ideal. With the exception of installations illustrating progress in conquering disease or poverty, or rare exceptions such as Nelson, such differences have disappeared from view.

In contrast with its prominence in his popular image, Nelson's physical impairment has attracted relatively little attention from naval historians and biographers. John Sugden has shown the most interest in the topic, identifying some of the accommodations Nelson used and remarking on the loss of his right arm as an emotionally significant experience.[8] For decades, the "new naval history" has turned to subjects beyond strategic, operational, and political history.[9] Research on the politics of Revolutionary-era social class, nationalism, and gender has explored the navy's connection to key developments of the time. The institutional culture of the navy itself has attracted particular attention. "We have put Nelson back into the context of the navy," remarks James Davey, the curator of the National Maritime Museum's long-running exhibition, "Nelson, Navy, Nation."[10] R. J. B. (Roger) Knight, author of a magisterial 2005 biography of Nelson, agrees: "it is not possible to understand his brilliant victories without an understanding of the British Navy. . . . Only once these broader and deeper factors are appreciated can one then ask how Nelson reached such extraordinary heights as a leader of men and as a controller of great fleets."[11] The navy's response to physical impairment is one of these "broader and deeper factors" that merits further exploration.

Publicizing these amputee officers' stories is also important because of the navy's sheer cultural significance. As N. A. M. Rodger notes, the navy was a truly "national endeavor, involving many, and in some ways all, aspects of government and society."[12] The navy was deeply woven into national life: at its wartime peak in 1813, there were 142,000 seamen or marines on the books of the active fleet, 3,270 lieutenants, 600 commanders, and 800 captains.[13] The navy was the largest single employer in the nation, and building, repairing, manning, and victualing its ships was the government's most logistically complex project.[14] Voluntarily or involuntarily, sailors commonly moved between the navy and the merchant marine. What this means in human terms was that it was a rare English family that had no connection to the navy. To cite familiar examples from the period's best-known authors, two of Jane Austen's brothers were admirals; William Wordsworth's brother John was a captain who went down with his ship, the East Indiaman *Earl of Abergavenny;* Samuel Taylor Coleridge was Rear-Admiral Alexander Ball's secretary; Lord Byron's grandfather, "Foulweather Jack," was a vice-admiral, and the cousin who succeeded Byron to the title was another admiral; and John Keats had family connections in the Royal Navy and the Royal Marines.[15] And a bright and ambitious young Irish immigrant to England who was called, depending on the source, Patrick Prunty or Patrick Brunty, changed his surname to the much more romantic-sounding title of the great naval hero whom he admired, the title granted to Nelson by the King of Sicily: Duke of Bronte, or Duke of Thunder. Patrick Bronte, of course, became the father of Emily, Charlotte, and Anne.

Moreover, new ways of thinking about disability in the present have opened new lines of inquiry about the past. Since the 1990s, when the Americans with Disabilities Act in the United States and the Disability Discrimination Act in the UK became law, people with disabilities have become increasingly visible in scholarship, as well as in advertising, entertainment, and politics.[16] The Gulf War era increased awareness of military disability: the 2014 U.S. census reported 3.8 million veterans with a service-connected disability. Social historians' interest in the varying effects of impairments on individual experience has risen with the rise of "disability" as a category of identity and a focus of political activism. In works such as David A. Gerber's *Disabled Veterans in History* (2000), historians of the welfare state explored the part that the demands of disabled veterans played in broadening the role of government in the nineteenth and twentieth centuries. Picking up on the visibility of Nelson's physical impairment in his time and our own, cultural historians have examined the role his successive combat injuries played in his public image. Timothy Jenks and Margarette Lincoln, for example, offer insights on how nationalist propaganda used Nelson's battle-scarred body as a "conduit for plebian patriotism," and Kate Williams argues that his injuries encouraged female writers and consumers to frame him as a sympathetic sentimental hero.[17]

Distinguishing between the fact of impairment itself and the experience of disability has been called the "big idea" of the disability rights movement. This distinction identifies disability not as a problem caused by a body alone, but rather as "a complex phenomenon, reflecting the interaction between features of a person's body and features of the society in which he or she lives."[18] To this way of thinking, a physical impairment is only one part of a larger set of circumstances that create "disability." The need to use a wheelchair, for example, disables a person from entering a building only if that building lacks a ramp. Aiming to highlight the distinction between impairment and disability, this study avoids using "able-bodied" or "disabled" in describing the active duty service of amputee officers. There are two more historically specific reasons for this choice. "Able-bodied" sounds too much like a term that had wide currency in Nelson's navy and meant something quite different from "lacking a physical impairment." When a man signed on to a ship's books, he was given a rating based on his experience. Those new to the sea were called Landsmen, those with limited experience were Ordinary Seamen, and those with at least two years at sea and the specialized skills that came with this experience were rated Able Seamen or Able-Bodied Seamen, often abbreviated to A.B. An A.B. was a seaman who possessed a certain set of skills, not a certain kind of body. Similarly, in this period "disabled" most often meant an inability to continue to serve in the military because of injury, not a category of identity. Naval records from the period often use the word "disabled" as a transitive verb, meaning injury or illness has left a man "disabled from service." Indeed, the 1694 charter of the iconic Greenwich Hospital itself uses this term. The charter promises "reliefe and support of seamen serving on board the shipps or vessels belonging to the Navy Royall who by reason of Age, Wounds or other disabilities shall be uncapable of further service at sea and being unable to maintain themselves."[19] By definition, an amputee officer who continued to serve on active duty was not "disabled" in this sense.

After ruling out "able-bodied," we may be likely to think of "normal" as the natural term to use to describe people who experience no impairment in form or function. This word also has a history and a set of connotations, however, that make it a poor choice for this study. Lennard Davis reminds us that, historically, there is nothing normal in using "normal" in this way. This usage dates from the rise of statistics in the mid-nineteenth century:

> The constellation of words describing this concept—"normal," "normalcy," "normality," "norm," "average," "abnormal"—all entered the European languages rather late in human history. The word "normal" as "constituting, conforming to, not deviating or differing from, the common type or standard, regular, usual" only enters the English language around 1840. (Previously, the word had meant "perpendicular"; the carpenter's square,

called a "norm," provided the root meaning.) Likewise, the word "norm," in the modern sense, has only been in use since around 1855, and "normality" and "normalcy" appeared in 1849 and 1857 respectively. If the lexicographical information is relevant, it is possible to date the coming into consciousness in English of an idea of "the norm" over the period 1840–1860.[20]

In addition, although "normal" purports to mean something like "statistically average," it still carries connotations of "natural" in the sense of "ideal." A normal person, body, or event is one that is likely to be taken as being what it ought to be. That is, "normal" usually sounds positive: it contrasts to "abnormal," which usually does not. The problem with "normal," then, is that the term contains a complex range of meanings, some of them highly questionable, but that it is so familiar that we are unlikely to question these meanings. Like many writers influenced by disability studies, I choose instead the term "normative." In its more common contexts in law, philosophy, and the social sciences, "normative" foregrounds the idea of judging an individual instance according to a standard. This idea is also central to "normal," but the greater familiarity of that term tends to obscure the act of judgment that I wish to stress.

Research on the emotional well-being of people now living with disabilities has challenged the once common assumption that a serious physical impairment means a life of misery. Rather, people with impairments report that their quality of life varies according to a number of factors. Tom Shakespeare points out that most people who contract a major physical impairment experience great distress—but with appropriate accommodation, they find that over time their level of happiness "returns to approximately what it was before the trauma struck." Similarly, Alison Kafer stresses that rather than being frozen in a single moment of tragedy, the experience of living with an impairment changes over time through adaptation, accommodation, and changing contexts.[21] Linking disability history with the developing history of emotion, David M. Turner calls for "a more nuanced assessment of the processes by which certain emotional states were associated with disability" in eighteenth- and early nineteenth-century Britain. He argues that many factors shaped impairment's effects on a given individual's emotional condition in the eighteenth century, as they do today: "In practice, experiences of disablement were influenced by a variety of factors, including availability of familial and community support, occupational structures and a person's access to welfare and medical services."²² The personal stories of these amputee officers describe a process of adaptation and eventual emotional well-being. By focusing on amputee officers who continued to serve on active duty, this study considers the effects of physical impairment in the late eighteenth and early nineteenth century as distinct from other "disabling" factors such as poverty.

In his study of twenty-first-century amputees, Steven L. Kurzman, a cultural anthropologist and below-the-knee amputee, stresses that he found very different personal stories: "There was an amazing diversity to how people responded to their loss."²³ One recurring pattern, however, was a process of adaptation following the initial trauma. After amputation, the officers in this study rebuilt an identity that was different in some ways from who they were before, but in others the same. Life in a wooden ship in wartime during the Age of Sail was physically challenging for everyone. Decks lurched and listed to one degree or another depending on the weather and the size of the vessel. People moved about them using ropes and ladders in bad light and wet conditions, often under great pressure to be quick. After losing a limb, these officers still possessed the highly specialized skills they had honed by years of working in these conditions. Some of them made a point of publicly displaying these skills. For example, after losing a leg as a midshipman, Sir Watkin Owen Pell kept his competitive nature and his fondness for "skylarking" in the ship's rigging. He raced other officers up the rigging, including, on one memorable occasion, a visiting one-armed captain, John Strutt Peyton (Pell won).²⁴

In addition, we can glimpse some of the practical accommodations that amputee officers created or found. For example, a Lieutenant Thomas Williams (not the father of Commander Richard Williams, mentioned later) was awarded a pension of 91 *l* (pounds) 5 s (shillings) per annum for "wounds" on July 1, 1816. He also invented a system of oars that could be worked by one hand: for this invention, he won a medal from the Society of Arts. Captain Lord John Hay lost his left arm in a cutting-out expedition as a fourteen-year-old midshipman in 1807. In 1833, he received a silver medal from the Society for the Encouragement of Arts for his invention of a telescope-holder "for one-handed persons."²⁵ Nelson had sets of silverware that combined a fork and knife in one piece to facilitate dining one-handed;

uniform jackets tailored with a black silk loop on the cuff of his empty right sleeve to hook it neatly on a button; and a chair built with an armrest the proper height for his vestigial right arm. James Alexander Gordon and his family took a lively interest in the advantages and disadvantages of the various prosthetic legs that he commissioned and used, and his wide circle of friends made a habit of presenting him with canes as frequently as snuff boxes. When Gordon rode on horseback, a small bucket-shaped device supported the end of his prosthetic leg as a stirrup supports a foot. Everyday equipment could also be used to meet the specific needs of an amputee officer. For example, before the Battle of Copenhagen, Nelson was determined to brave high winds in a small, open boat to attend a strategic meeting in another ship. Believing that clambering into that boat one-handed in the heaving sea from the side of his own ship was an unnecessary risk, Nelson's flag captain, Thomas Masterman Hardy, insisted that he take a seat in the boat and then be hoisted down to the ocean inside it.

More broadly, personal assistance with everyday tasks can be an essential accommodation, but one that is sometimes seen today as prohibitively expensive or stigmatized as childish. These officers were all gentlemen, which meant that on land as well as at sea, they had servants. When Nelson got his feet wet on deck, he took off his shoes and walked around on the carpet in his cabin to dry them rather than trouble his servant to change his tight silk stockings, "which, from his only having one hand, he could not himself conveniently effect."[26] This story is often told to illustrate Nelson's hardiness or his consideration for his subordinates. I would like to call attention to its premise: like other men of his station, Nelson had a servant who helped him put on his stockings every morning and take them off every night. Amputee officers' attitudes toward accepting such personal assistance varied. For example, Admiral Michael Seymour took pride in pulling on his own stockings and tying his own cravat one-handed.[27]

In considering the active duty service of amputee officers, we should perhaps also consider how sharply even imagination is limited by experience. "Do not try to imagine how you would perform a specific job if you had the applicant's disability," the U.S. Department of Labor warns, instructing employers to concentrate on relevant knowledge, skills, and abilities, rather than automatically ruling out whole categories of persons based on a known or suspected disability. "He or she has mastered alternate ways of living and working."²⁸ This book concentrates on the specialized knowledge, skills, and abilities that these officers possessed, as well on as the institutional culture and the built environment that helped make possible the alternate ways of living and working that they mastered. Although they lived and died long before the twentieth-century disability rights movement, this study of their careers is informed by the movement's interest in how social and physical structures of everyday life favor or disfavor full participation.

In thinking about physical impairment as a symbolic marker of difference and inferiority, Tobin Siebers asks a utopian question: "If disability serves as an unacknowledged symbol of otherness rather than as a feature of everyday life, how might an insistence on its presence and reality change our theories about identity?"²⁹ Nelson's navy was, of course, very far indeed from a utopian institution. Nevertheless, these officers' careers offer a valuable glimpse into a professional world that seems, under certain circumstances, to have accepted the loss of an arm or a leg as "a feature of everyday life." Evan Wilson's recent *A Social History of British Naval Officers, 1775–1815* calls attention to "the thousands of forgotten men who orchestrated the everyday work of the navy."³⁰ He hopes his research will encourage future biographers to try the experiment of considering even Nelson as "a mostly ordinary naval officer, rather than a man of destiny."³¹ This study will consider not merely Nelson but also his fellow amputee officers as "mostly ordinary naval officers." Their shared profession both caused their impairment and afforded them opportunities to adapt to it and to get on with their lives.

Amputee officers also belonged to larger society. Scholars of eighteenth-century culture have stressed that this larger society could treat people who had lost a limb with pity or derision. For example, "defect," a negative eighteenth-century term used to describe physical impairment, has attracted a good deal of attention. Helen Deustch and Felicity Nussbaum have shown that familiar eighteenth-century aesthetic theories that posit beauty as a sign of God's design also countenance the energetic derision of impairment seen as "defect," or a departure from this design.³² Similarly, Simon Dickie notes that the military amputee with a prosthetic leg was a popular comic figure in eighteenth-century literary and visual arts. The economic vulnerability of such amputees compounded their physical vulnerability.³³ The amputee officers in this study, however, had a professional status that distinguished them from such figures. They were gentlemen, not beggars. Moreover, these men continued to win command at sea. If in this period one common polite response to a "cripple" was pity and an only slightly less polite response was laughter, then both responses could be baffled by an officer who lacked an arm or a leg, but who still possessed all the attributes of heroic military masculinity, a man who spent his days commanding men, ships, and a great number of large guns.

While standard naval histories of the period mention various individual amputee officers serving on active duty, the field of disability studies now suggests considering these figures as a distinctive group. The story of one successful amputee officer might reveal only his particular talents, but focusing on a group of them draws attention to the institutional culture that allowed their country to take advantage of these talents. Personal bonds shaped their professional world. Many naval officers were the fathers, sons, or brothers of other officers and commonly described their professional experiences in terms of an all-male family. In the present study, this focus on institutional culture dovetails productively with the new naval history's turn toward a fuller examination of naval culture.

The relation between this book and another foundational claim of the disability rights movement is a bit more complex. This is the claim that all disabled people share—or ought to share—a common identity. For example, Rosemarie Garland-Thomson argues for the value of developing what she calls a "sturdy disability identity."³⁴ She claims that knowing there is "a history, culture and politics of disability" is essential to moving beyond an understanding of disability, in oneself or in others, as "a curse, tragedy, misfortune or individual failing." Without a sense of shared identity, people who use a walker or a prosthetic limb, or those who have Down syndrome or impaired vision, are merely "people to whom something unfortunate has happened, for whom something has gone terribly wrong." A likely reaction to this sense of individual misfortune is fear. As Garland-Thomson notes, although such impairments are "fundamental to being human—a part of every life," in the absence of a shared disability identity, they can be a deeply isolating experience. In contrast, the recognition that people living with different impairments share similar personal experiences and political interests can be the first step toward self-acceptance and political advocacy. Disability studies also acknowledges, however, that this sense of a common identity can be difficult to achieve because of the diversity of the disability community, evident in the examples mentioned above, and because of the extraordinary porousness of this community. As Tobin Siebers remarks, "able-bodiedness is a temporary identity at best": most people will eventually experience some form of disability through illness, accident, or the process of aging itself, while others recover from a disability.[35]

Studying the careers of these Napoleonic-era amputee officers suggests the additional complexity of extending the model of a shared identity among impaired people across time. For example, we have no evidence that Nelson felt a sense of solidarity with contemporaries who experienced a wide range of physical and mental impairments, or who belonged to a wide range of social classes. In this regard, the amputee officers this book studies do not appear to have shared the common identity that the modern disability rights movement advocates for people living with impairments. David M. Turner similarly writes of the physically impaired people, working-class or impoverished, who appeared in the eighteenth century in the courtroom of the Old Bailey as defendants, victims, or witnesses, that "there is little evidence that the men and women examined in this brief account shared any common or politicized identity as 'disabled' in a modern sense." However, he also notes the common cultural context in which these individuals operated: "Choosing to identify oneself (or others) as 'lame' or a 'cripple' was not simply a statement of physical fact; it also placed the person described in a mental landscape of shared meanings, attitudes and values."[36] While far from being the basis for a political movement, physical impairment still influenced social expectations and personal identity. Moreover, in their experience of losing a limb in battle, recovering, adapting, and thriving in their careers, these men were linked by their shared profession. Some of the amputee officers that *Lame Captains and Left-Handed Admirals* examines were patrons and protégées, competitive colleagues, or lifelong friends. They fought battles together, traded favors and gossip, feuded with each other, and showed up at the same parties, parades, and funerals. Nelson was an important figure to many of them, as we might expect, given his role in major naval operations as well as his celebrity. Some of these amputee officers were his friends.

Some were his junior officers—or, as he called them, his "children." Six of them served in battle under his command. Contemporaries and historians alike recognize that Nelson enjoyed warm personal relationships with his fellow officers. Described variously as a genius for friendship, brilliant management, or "the Nelson touch," this personal connection between Nelson and his officers was essential to his success. This book suggests that such professional same-sex bonds also framed the kind of disability identity that was available to Nelson and his "brother officers." While it traces personal connections between these figures, as well as considering how physical impairment worked within the navy's larger structures of "brotherhood" and patronage, it does not argue that these amputee officers were part of a disability community.

Within the shared context of their continued professional success, this study highlights some of the ways that their individual differences shaped various choices they made after their loss of a limb. For example, Watkin Owen Pell, a fashion-conscious and wealthy English gentleman who married late in life, invested in a series of expensive prosthetic legs made of cork, minimizing the visibility of his impairment. A conspicuously handsome and considerably less well-capitalized son of minor Scottish gentry, James Alexander Gordon married an English lawyer's dowerless daughter for love and fathered eleven children: he cultivated the persona of a bluff Scotsman and used a series of much cheaper wooden peg legs similar to those issued to common amputee seamen at Greenwich Hospital. After losing his left arm in battle, the Anglo-Irish family man Michael Seymour delighted in showing he could still perform all of the duties expected of the father of a family and master of a household, one-handedly carving roasts at the dinner table and climbing ladders with pruning shears to help his wife garden. And Horatio Nelson, whose hunger for love was exceeded only by his ruthlessness in battle, took pleasure in allowing the people who were dearest to him the public privilege of cutting up his meat for him at table.

Numbers

This study focuses on amputee naval officers who were capable of pursuing their profession after the loss of an arm or a leg, and whose hopes for promotion were rewarded. In the period covering the American Revolutionary War and the Napoleonic Wars, at least twenty-six commissioned officers went on to further active service at sea after surviving amputation due to an injury received in battle (see table). Ten of these officers were lieutenants at the time they received the injury that cost them a limb. Lieutenants were the backbone of the navy's command structure. The fact that so many officers were injured at this rank is consistent with the great number of lieutenants employed at sea and the nature of their duties. Depending on its rating, a ship carried up to six lieutenants. Their responsibilities included especially hazardous initiatives such as leading a party fighting their way on board an enemy ship and "cutting-out" expeditions—attacks by small boats, usually at night, against an anchored and hopefully unsuspecting ship. Midshipmen also commonly participated in boarding and cutting-out expeditions. Unsurprisingly, the second largest group of officers in this study were midshipmen at the time they lost a limb. "Master's mate" was originally the rank of a petty officer not eligible for further promotion, but by this period it was widely used to categorize experienced midshipmen who had yet to pass the lieutenants' exam or to receive a lieutenant's commission. If we combine the master's mates and midshipmen, then they outnumber the lieutenants.

Two of these officers were captains when they were injured. One was a rear admiral: Horatio Nelson, well known for leading from the front, with no regard for his own safety. He had already lost the sight in his right eye by the time he led the disastrous attack that cost him his right arm. In a letter to a friend, Nelson noted with approval that "an old French general when ask'd the difference between a good and bad general . . . replied two words—*Allons—Allez*."[37] After losing an arm or a leg and winning promotion, all of these amputee officers continued to take part in the ordinary hazards of battles at sea. In addition, at least seven of them (Thomas Gill, James Alexander Gordon, Joshua Kneeshaw, Robert Mends, Joseph Packwood, Watkin Owen Pell, William Rivers) continued to say *Allons* instead of *Allez*. They went on leading the particularly dangerous actions often left to lieutenants and midshipmen desperate for a chance to demonstrate their gallantry.

The active duty amputee officers whose family background can be verified came from the range of social positions familiar among Navy officers,

Commissioned officers who returned to active service at sea after surviving amputation due to injury received in battle

NAME	LIMB LOST	AGE AT LOSS, IF KNOWN	RANK AT LOSS	HIGHEST RANK ACHIEVED
Robert Heriot Barclay	Left arm	22	Lieutenant	Captain
John Bedford	Leg		commander	Captain
John Holmes Bond	Leg		Master's mate	Commander
Charles Worsley Boys	Leg	16	Midshipman	Captain
David Colby	Right arm	30	First lieutenant	Captain
William Cuppage	Leg		Signal midshipman	Captain
William Bateman Dashwood	Right arm	21	First lieutenant	Rear admiral
Joseph Ellison	Arm		Lieutenant	Captain
James Henry Garrety	Arm		Lieutenant	Commander
Thomas Gill	Arm	21	Master's mate	Captain
Sir James Alexander Gordon	Leg	29	Captain	Admiral
Alexander Graeme	Arm	40	Captain	Admiral
John Hackett	Left arm		Lieutenant	Vice admiral
Lord John Hay	Arm	14	Midshipman	Rear admiral
Samuel Hood	Arm	43	Commodore	Vice admiral
Joshua Johnson	Arm		First lieutenant	Commander
Joshua Kneeshaw	Right arm		Lieutenant	Commander
Robert Mends	Right arm	13	Midshipman	Captain
Horatio Nelson	Right arm	39	Rear admiral	Vice admiral
Joseph Packwood	Arm		Midshipman	Captain
Sir Watkin Owen Pell	Left leg	12	Midshipman	Rear admiral
John Strutt Peyton	Right arm	21	Lieutenant	Captain
William Rivers	Left leg	17 or 19	Midshipman	First lieutenant, warden of Woolwich Dockyard
Sir Michael Seymour	Left arm	26	Lieutenant	Rear admiral
Edward Stopford	Right arm		Acting captain	Captain
Henry Clements Thompson	Arm		Midshipman	Commander

although clustered more heavily at the wealthy end. Based on a study of 556 officers who passed for lieutenant from 1775 to 1805, Evan Wilson has shown that the fathers of most commissioned officers, although not working class, "were from lower down the social spectrum than we previously thought."[38] The most common professions among naval officers' fathers were shopkeeper, merchant, lawyer, doctor, and—most common of all—naval officer. Only a fifth of all commissioned officers could boast of a titled or landed gentry background.[39] The navy was a relatively affordable profession to enter because navy officers, unlike army officers, did not buy their commissions. In fact, the navy was oversupplied with officers in part because it was one of the best career opportunities that eighteenth- and early nineteenth-century Britain offered to the capable and ambitious sons of such families. Four of the amputee officers in Table 1 came from landed families, three were sons of Anglican ministers, and two were doctors' sons, while seven were sons or close relatives of naval officers. All twenty-six men surveyed in this study first went to sea with all four limbs and very young, often by the age of twelve. Birth dates are not available for all of them, but the time of their first recorded service suggests that they lost a limb as young men: the youngest at the time, Watkin Owen Pell, was twelve years old. Those others for whom birth dates are available were also young when they lost a limb. One was thirteen, one fourteen, and one seventeen; six were in their early twenties, three in their thirties; the oldest was forty. Over half of these amputee officers married and had children. A number of their sons followed them into the navy.

How did the loss of a limb in action affect an officer's prospects for continued employment and promotion? Surviving amputation itself was, of course, the first necessity. After long being suspect, among other reasons, for disfiguring the image of God, elective limb amputation had become more widely accepted by the end of the seventeenth century, largely due to the rise of gunpowder and the particular kinds of damage that gunpowder inflicts on human tissue and bones.[40] Through trauma to human bodies and advances in medical practice, the wars of 1793–1815 greatly increased the number of amputee veterans in England. Relative to civilian practice, the overall mortality rate of amputation in the navy was low, although amputation of the thigh continued to carry a higher risk than amputation of the lower leg and arm.[41] Most naval surgeons carried out amputations very soon after the limb was injured, and those naval surgeons who did so achieved a one-third mortality rate. The more common practice among civilian surgeons was to delay amputation in hopes of allowing the patient time to recover from the initial trauma, which in practice lead to higher mortality.[42] In addition, most patients of naval surgeons enjoyed better overall health and nutrition than the general civilian population. Finally, most naval surgeons recognized the importance of antiseptics and were supported in this goal by naval commanders' characteristic "passion for cleanliness."[43]

The extent of physical recovery after amputation varied, as did career prospects in the navy. As noted above, amputation above the knee was particularly life-threatening, and fewer officers who survived the loss of a leg returned to sea than those who survived the loss of an arm. For example, Lieutenant Frederick Bedford survived the loss of his left leg in battle, but combined with earlier injuries, this loss ended his active career.[44] In 1798, as a midshipman taking part in the capture of a French frigate, Bedford was shot "under the right Eye, [which] fractured the Bone, and so locked his Jaw, that he never since could open his Mouth beyond half an Inch, nor can he distinguish one Letter from another with the injured Eye."[45] Bedford was given leave and could have remained in London for further medical care, but disliking the expense and "finding also that little Advantage was likely to result from it," he accepted his impaired vision, rejoined his ship, the *Jason*, and went back to sea.[46] The following year, still serving as a midshipman, he survived a shipwreck and several months in a French prison. Bedford won promotion to lieutenant in 1799, and in 1801, when his ship ran aground while chasing a French convoy, he volunteered to continue the chase in boats: "In the Attempt his Leg was shot off very high above the Knee, and his Cutter sinking under him he had to swim for his Life."[47] Frederick Bedford became third lieutenant of Greenwich Hospital, an administrative position. He married and had a large family, including two sons who followed him into the navy.[48] Bedford was as tenacious in pursuing what he saw as his pension rights on land as he was in pursuing his career at sea, so we shall hear more from him later.

When histories of the period acknowledge the contributions of amputee officers, later assumptions about able-bodiedness can contribute to errors about them, in even otherwise valuable works. For example, two treatments of Commander Robert Heriot Barclay misdate and misconstrue his loss of an arm. David J. Hepper's exhaustive study, *British Warship Losses in the Age of Sail,* describes the battle on Lake Erie on September 10, 1813. He writes that Commander Robert Heriot Barclay "was wounded early in the action, having his right arm shot off."[49] Hepper is correct that Barclay's arm was shot off in battle, but it was his other arm, and the loss occurred five years earlier. Barclay lost his left arm as a lieutenant in command of a detachment of boats that attacked a French convoy carrying supplies from Nantz to Rochefort.[50] He then served on a number of ships before coming to Lake Erie. In contrast to Hepper, the U.S. National Park Service acknowledges the fact that Barclay was already an amputee at the time he was assigned to command ships in this battle. It implies, however, that an amputee officer on active duty was an expedient the Royal Navy was forced to accept because it was desperately short of officers: "With the nation gripped by the Napoleonic Wars, every trained and experienced officer was needed, even if not able-bodied."[51] But the Park Service draws this conclusion from a false assumption.

Although the Napoleonic-era navy was chronically short of seamen, its oversupply of officers is one of the best-established demographic facts about it. There were far too many talented officers with exemplary service records begging for a ship. As Brian Lavery remarks, "While the seamen were hiding from the press gang in every nook and cranny, the waiting room at the Admiralty was filled with officers soliciting appointments."[52] The stress of managing the backlog of meritorious officers who were stuck on shore and not happy about it echoes through letters by everyone from newly made captains to the First Sea Lord himself. Robert Heriot Barclay's career did not benefit from a shortage of candidates who each had two arms and two legs. Although these amputee officers' memoirs and letters occasionally mention physical difficulties and accommodations, they focus most wholeheartedly on the challenge central to the life of any officer: promotion. They say much more about the difficulty of getting a ship than they do about the difficulty of getting around in one.

According to the findings of recent historians such as Charles Consolvo and Evan Wilson, the amputee officers in this study should be numbered among the period's more successful officers. Because "the number of those it was just to reward bore no relation to the number it was possible to employ," as Rodger pithily states, patronage relationships of one sort or another helped decide who won a chance to serve at sea and who waited on shore.[53] While the patronage system never aimed to offer an equal opportunity to all British subjects, neither did it require a captain to drop a talented and ambitious protégée because he lost limb in battle. There was no legal protection for people with physical impairments as a category of workers, but neither was there any legal requirement that such a person be retired from active service. For better and for worse, "the natural ways in which [the navy's] members dealt with one other were personal rather than institutional or bureaucratic."[54] The careers of these amputee officers were shaped by personal relationships after as well as before they lost a limb. Wilson suggests that one reason for the Royal Navy's remarkable success was its genius for employing as officers men who were relatively diverse in social class: "In an age of social snobbery, it found ways to put talented men from mixed backgrounds in positions to succeed. From a management perspective, the wartime Royal Navy provides a remarkable example of decentralized education and patronage system that was able to identify and develop its most valuable members."[55] In the context of the Great Wars, the ability to do the job could matter more than conformity to social expectations: "The navy could test the boundaries of social acceptability during this period because national survival depended on the competence of its officers."[56] As the wartime Royal Navy was able to benefit from the talents of officers who were relatively diverse in terms of social class, so too was it able to benefit from the talents of officers who were relatively diverse in terms of physical impairment.

Moreover, by taking part in a successful battle against an enemy ship of equal or greater firepower, an officer became a candidate for "hero promotion," promotion in recognition of his role in such a victory. The greatest drawback of hero promotion was that many officers never saw action at all: only 57 percent of the officers in Consolvo's study group of 225 wartime officers were ever in battle.[57] The amputee officers in this study were, then, to many of their brother officers' way of thinking, among the lucky ones. They all experienced combat. Their chance of rising through hero promotion was higher than that of the many officers who had no such experience. That is, while we may assume that an amputee officer would be less likely than one with two arms and two legs to be given command of a ship, the manner in which these men lost a limb puts the weight on the opposite scale. The same battle that cost them an arm or a leg could help win them promotion. Not just in the eyes or hearts of the general public, but in the correspondence of their patrons and the Admiralty itself, the loss of a limb in a successful action could mark them as particularly entitled to the honor of active employment at sea, rather than "disabled" from it.

"Equivalent to the Loss of a Limb"

Far fewer naval men lost a limb to battle injuries than were disabled by accident or illness.[58] Once scurvy was controlled, infectious diseases were by far the greatest danger at sea: a seaman's chance of dying from diseases such as yellow fever, malaria, and typhus was nearly three times that of British civilian of comparable age.[59] In addition to disease, a great variety of occupational hazards threatened life and limb at sea, from the dramatic danger of working aloft in poor light and high winds above a gyrating deck to the more mundane peril of moving by hand awkwardly shaped and heavy items such as casks, boats, and cannons in cramped and hurried conditions. In a naval ship, as Michael Lewis writes, "the ways in which a man might maim himself for life were almost limitless; clearly too numerous even to catalogue."[60] Another occupational hazard may have been mental illness. Awareness of service-related mental illness has increased in recent years. Evidence of mental illness in the Napoleonic-era navy is both incomplete and understudied, but Sir Gilbert Blane, physician to the fleet from 1779 to 1783, estimated that "madness" was seven times more common in the navy than in the civilian population. Interestingly, given the increasing awareness of the long-lasting effects of concussion today, Blane linked mental illness to the high incidence of head injuries in the navy: "The great proportion of maniacs among seamen is chiefly owing to injuries of the head, received in a state of intoxication."[61] That is, drunken men forgot to duck in the low-ceilinged spaces between decks. It also seems that the incidence of mental illness increased from 1809 to 1813, "towards the end of a very long and trying war," and that it was higher among officers than among seamen. This disparity, however, may reflect a greater commitment to treating mental illness in officers on the part of the navy.[62]

Given the fact that amputation was relatively rare among the many impairments caused by naval service, why focus on it now? I have two reasons. The first is practical: amputee officers are clearly identified and well documented. Moreover, the loss of a limb was itself the standard by which the navy judged all other injuries. That is, when determining what kind of claim any service-related injury afforded an officer with regard to a pension or promotion, the criterion that the navy's medical board used was whether that wound was or was not "equivalent to the loss of a limb." Limb amputation could serve as a kind of gold standard of value more generally, a criterion for calculating the cash equivalent of any act of military service. On May 11, 1810, the flamboyant naval hero Lord Cochrane, whose talent for capturing enemy ships at sea was matched only by his talent for making political enemies at home, offered a remarkable extended example of this way of thinking. He used the lost arms and legs of specific amputee naval officers as a kind of currency to attack what he saw as the two most grossly overpaid groups on the Pension List: Admiralty officials and the family of Sir Arthur Wellesley, the future Duke of Wellington: "All that is paid to the all the wounded officers of the British navy . . . is but half as much [as the sinecure of a Commissioner of the Admiralty, 20,358 l.].—Is this justice? . . . I find, upon examination, that the Wellesleys receive from the public 34,129 l., a sum equal to 426 pair of lieutenants' legs, calculated at the rate of allowance for lieutenant Chambers' leg.—Calculating by the pension for Captain Johnson's arm, viz. 45 l., lord Arden's sinecure is equal to the value of 1022 captain's arms."[63] Cochrane's opponent in this debate, himself a Wellesley, insisted that pensions were fairly awarded based on "the rank and suffering of the person who claimed the reward." More broadly, he recoiled with distaste from the rhetorical mountain of severed limbs that Cochrane had conjured up, calling it "one of the most extraordinary speeches, that he believed had ever been delivered in that House . . . a most extraordinary calculation of the number of arms and legs which [the Wellesley's 34,000 L a year] would compensate for."[64]

Military amputation's role as a measure of value suggests my second reason for choosing to focus this study on amputees. Historically, amputation has played an outsize role in the representation of disability in general, and military disability in particular. As noted, in Nelson's navy, not battle but rather disease was by far the greatest danger to both sailors and officers. Even among battle-related injuries, amputation was not a particularly likely outcome. Finally, among sailors in particular, the amputation of fingers or the partial amputation of hands was most likely to be the result of what we would now call an occupational injury, the result of the everyday work of a ship, such as loading casks or hauling on ropes. Nevertheless, the figure of the military amputee remains emblematic, in Nelson's time and our own, of the danger of combat. The emotional and political valence of the military amputee's visual impact varies over time, from the eighteenth-century "mark of honor" or sentimental appeal for pity to, in our own time, futuristic fantasies of a superior human-technological cyborg. *Lame Captains and Left-Handed Admirals* addresses the representational power of the military amputee as displayed in heroic portraits, wartime propaganda, and postwar nationalism. The book concentrates, however, on trying to recover the stories of individual officers' careers and lives and the features of their world that made their successes possible.

Sources

As Baynton's remark about disability's visibility in history suggests, these amputee officers' stories have long been hidden in plain view. Most subjects of this study appear in two nineteenth-century works well known to naval historians: John Marshall's twelve-volume *Royal Naval Biography*, published from 1823 to 1835, and William O'Byrne's *Naval Biographical Dictionary*, published from 1845 to 1849.[65] Both O'Byrne and Marshall see naval history as a series of interrelated personal stories linked by family and patronage relationships. This focus makes them useful in recovering personal stories of amputee officers. The way Marshall and O'Byrne defined their object of study, however, excluded most—but not all—midshipmen, lieutenants, and warrant officers who returned to active duty after surviving amputation but did not achieve further promotion.[66] Marshall includes officers who reached the rank of commander or higher and who happened to be on the Admiralty List from 1823 to 1835. He excludes lieutenants, who outnumbered all other officers put together. O'Byrne goes down in rank to lieutenants but includes only those who happened to be alive in 1849.

In addition, neither one includes all the officers who served in even the categories they aimed to cover.

O'Byrne and Marshall contacted officers for information as they composed their works, as well as consulting Navy Lists of promotions and pensions, official letters printed in newspapers, and private letters. They are a good starting point for major milestones in an officer's career.[67] They are less reliable with regard to officers' self-reported moral character and social status: historians have long noted the tendency in their pages of shopkeepers to blossom into merchants, and merchants into "gentlemen engaged in commerce."[68] We know that Marshall's work met with the approval of at least one of these amputee officers. Admiral Sir Watkin Owen Pell's unpublished diary mentions corresponding with Marshall in April and May 1829 and ordering, paying for, and receiving his work. On February 16, 1832, Pell sent "1 vol. of Marshall's work to Mrs. Vivian," the wife of a fellow captain.[69] O'Byrne was educated at University College School, London (1838–39) and had no personal connection to the Royal Navy.

Of particular interest are the twelve volumes of O'Bryne's unpublished manuscript sources held by the British Library. He sent a printed questionnaire to living naval officers, some of whom responded with detailed remarks about their military service. Since he contacted them nearly half a century after this service ended, their correspondence offers a glimpse of how these men remembered the military experiences of their Napoleonic-era youth as they lived on through Victoria's reign. Not everyone reflected with satisfaction on a long and distinguished career. For example, in 1844, O'Byrne wrote to Lieutenant William Phippard Haydon. Although his time in the navy did not cost Haydon a limb, it left his health "impaired" by disease, a much more common fate. Haydon found the memory of his eleven years of naval service to be unbearably painful. He replied, "I have neither time nor faculty for writing a History of my Services in the navy":

Melbury [Albus?] 18th October 1844

> The thoughts of such and of my experience in those days harrows up my feelings, make my head ach [sic], and disturbs my peace. Tropical climates impaired my health, Shipwreck my pocket, and many things oppressed my spirits. I entered the Service in 1803 passed [the lieutenant's exam] in 1809

and gained the first acting commission and the [?first vacancy?] in the gift of Sir Alex: Cockrane Commander in Chief on the Leaward Station West Indies. In 1814 I applied to be [?suppressed?] and was placed on Halfpay and from that time here have [?resided?]. I am Old and I have a very stubborn condition and I am likely to be off the List ere long therefore hope you will be pleased to omit my name and not think me unkind or disobliging.

> I am, Sir yours
> With the greatest deference
>
> Wm Haydon
> Lieut: R.N.[70]

Whether out of pride or habit, even as he asked to be written out of naval history, Haydon signed himself "Lieut: R.N." His story reminds us of how variable an individual's experience of physical impairment and military service can be.

Although Marshall's work contains no full biographical entries on lieutenants, in another sense one lieutenant is present on every page: Lieutenant John Marshall. Despite a complete lack of formal education and literary experience, and his own ill-health, Marshall managed to publicize a great deal of essential information about a generation of officers in one massive act of memorialization intended to defy the short memories of civilians in peacetime or any other form of oblivion. He hoped his twelve volumes would prevent his fellow officers' "many meritorious actions in the warfare of their country [from being] consigned to an oblivion, which singly they are undeserving of and collectively bid a proud defiance to."[71] Like William Phippard Haydon, Marshall himself had one of the "undistinguished" careers Wilson urges us to remember were essential to the Navy. Marshall was "most ardently attached" to his profession: he went to sea when he was nine years old sometime around 1793, and served on small ships until the massive down-sizing peacetime brought to the Navy. He was commissioned as lieutenant in 1815, seeing no further service. For both Marshall and O'Byrne, the Navy, a far-flung and elaborately bureaucratic institution, was first and foremost a network of personal bonds, the most important of which were variations on father-and-son relationships. Naval historians support this view today. Nicholas Tracy writes that as "often as not, it was a world in which boys grew rapidly to manhood under the guidance of their fathers, or their fathers' friends and relations."[72] A mentoring relationship that began when a boy was accepted into a ship as a captain's servant, volunteer, or midshipman could endure for the length of his entire naval career. During the long wars with France, junior and senior officers' professional success, as well as their lives, were in each other's hands.

Although neither Marshall nor O'Byrne aims to describe warrant officers, a few of these men slip in because of the importance of family and patronage to O'Byrne's and Marshall's vision of the navy. For example, O'Byrne mentions that Mr. Phillip LeVesconte lost a leg in battle on the Glorious First of June, 1794, and died a purser on the *Royal William* 84 at Spithead, May 25, 1807. Phillip LeVesconte had two sons (one also named Philip) who became commanders—which is why he appears in O'Byrne's *Naval Biographical Dictionary*. In his entry on the younger Phillip LeVesconte, O'Byrne briefly summarizes his father's career. Similarly, despite his cutoff for inclusion at the rank of commander, in his entry on Commander Richard Williams, Marshall mentions the commander's father, Lieutenant Thomas Williams, "an old and meritorious officer, who lost his right leg, and was otherwise wounded, while serving aboard the Chatham 50 . . . in action with the French frigate *La Magicienne*, near Boston."[73] On December 19, 1783, Lieutenant Thomas Williams obtained a pension of 200 *l* per annum "in consideration for his service and sufferings." We are told that "on the 8th of November 1781, at which time he was lieutenant of the *Chatham*, at Sandy Hook, [Thomas Williams] had the misfortune to receive a wound . . . which occasioned him to lose his left leg; and that on boarding a prize on the 1st June 1782, he dislocated his shoulder."[74] That is, after Lieutenant Thomas Williams lost his left leg in 1781, he injured his shoulder in another action on June 1, 1782, fighting his way aboard a prize.

This book also draws on personal letters. The National Maritime Museum's Caird Archive holds a collection of Admiral Sir Watkin Owen Pell's papers dating from 1809 to 1863, in the class PLL. Pell's daughter compiled his personal and professional correspondence and transcribed the contents of the forty-one pocket diaries he kept from 1814 to 1860. Her daughter, Pell's granddaughter, took over the project, contacting naval men and representatives of Pell's many clubs to confirm or expand information in his diary. She also wrote to James Alexander Gordon's granddaughter to ask advice on how to write a naval memoir, hoping to draw on her memories of the editorial experience of Gordon's daughters. Pell's granddaughter did not complete the memoir, but instead donated her unpublished materials and drafts of chapters to the National Maritime Museum. They are now included in the Caird Archive's collection of Pell's papers. This collection also includes correspondence from Admiral Sir James Alexander Gordon to Pell. In addition, the Northumberland Records Office holds a trove of letters from the Spencer family relating to Pell, in the class ZB. Much of Horatio Nelson's correspondence is available in print: Marianne Czisnik's *Horatio Nelson: A Controversial Hero* (2005) offers a good overview of the sometimes dramatic choices made by Nelson's various editors, particularly with regard to framing his controversial relationship with Lady Hamilton.[75]

Even aside from editors with agendas, Ellen Gill and Mary Favret remind us that personal letters themselves are complex documents.[76] In wartime, officers knew that letters to friends and family were a source of news that was of general interest, likely to be read out loud, quoted, and passed around. Moreover, Gill argues that even in very personal statements of affection or homesickness, officers constructed an ideal image of themselves as attentive fathers and husbands, an image that was important to them as well as to their families on shore. Because officers could work on a letter for weeks or months before having the opportunity to send it home at a port or through a friendly passing ship, these letters can offer a running commentary on their life at sea similar to a diary, but always with a domestic audience in mind. When the intended audience of such letters home takes on the role of editor, we get a family memoir. Family memoirs of two of these amputee officers further highlight the domestic side of their subjects. In 1878, the Rev. Richard Seymour printed a memoir of his father, Admiral Sir Michael Seymour. In 1890, Admiral James Alexander Gordon's daughters, Elizabeth, Adelaide, and Sophia Gordon, compiled their father's personal letters and records of his career and had them printed in a limited edition for his grandchildren.

All the feats of valor and skill that won promotion for the amputee officers in this book are documented by what were known as "official letters." These documents had a standardized format and function within the navy and appeared regularly, either in full or in extracts, in British newspapers. They are the gold standard for information about what happened at sea.

As soon as physically possible after any significant military action, the most senior officer who survived it was obliged to write a letter about it addressed to the officer in command of that region. That officer would add a brief cover letter and send it to the Lords of the Admiralty back at Greenwich. The format required a brief narrative of the engagement: where and when it took place, key orders received and given, and particularly conspicuous acts of gallantry that an officer's friends could point to in advocating for his promotion. The official letter also offered a precise accounting of gains and losses: the number of enemy ships captured, damaged, or destroyed, the number of the Royal Navy's own ships captured, damaged, or destroyed, the number of captured, dead, and wounded on both sides. These were the statistics the navy needed to carry out its massive, intricate, and never-ending business of building, repairing, supplying, and manning ships. Because captains often acted on their own initiative without contact with their superiors for long periods of time, the official letter also established the difference between roving freebooters and a professional military force under a centralized state authority. When these captains signed themselves "your obedient and humble servant," they affirmed a principle that needed all the affirming it could get, at least from the Admiralty's point of view. Overall, an official letter was a complex document: at once a survivor's tale of bloody heroism and a dry statistical reckoning, a key tool in a venerable system of personal patronage that was also a remarkably modern bureaucracy. In addition, this book draws on visual sources. As did their letters home, amputee officers' formal portraits allowed them to present an ideal image of themselves to showcase their identity as military professionals—in immaculate uniform, medals visible, holding a telescope or casually resting a hand on a cannon, often with a battle or other dramatic sea-scape in the background—for themselves and for a wider audience.

For context on everyday injuries in the navy, I consulted eighteenth- and nineteenth-century "smart-tickets," the Navy's records of injuries incurred by ratings (enlisted men), warrant officers, and dockyard workers in the line of duty that merited financial reward. In this context, "smart" means the pain of a wound, as it does for Alexander Pope when he describes Ulysses writhing on the ground with a javelin in his side, "raging with intolerable smart."[77] The National Archives in Kew (formerly the

Public Records Office) includes an extensive collection of smart-tickets in its ADM holdings (records of the Admiralty, Naval Forces, Royal Marines, and Coast Guard), in the class ADM 82. As the name suggests, "smart-money" was money awarded in recognition of pain. Supported by a six shilling a month deduction from the wages of every officer and rating in the navy, the fund was called the Chatham Chest until 1803, when Greenwich Hospital took over its administration and it became known as the Chest at Greenwich. Smart-money could take the form of a one-time payment or a regular pension. In some cases, smart-money was awarded in compensation for an injury that prevented a man from continuing to serve in the navy or otherwise earn a living. In others, however, smart-money was awarded in simple recognition of the fact that a man had suffered in doing his duty, even though that suffering did not exclude him from continued service or from continuing to draw full pay. In such cases, smart-money resembles the social model of disability in acknowledging pain and physical impairment as significant, but considering these things as distinct from the condition of being disabled from performing a specific task, or "disability" as a general category of identity. Commissioned officers were eligible for Admiralty pensions rather than smart-money. While smart-money was a more standardized bureaucratic system, Admiralty pensions were awarded only to a minority of wounded officers on an individual basis. Admiralty pensions were awarded in recognition of "services and sufferings": they recognized severe injury combined with notable service. Like smart-money, Admiralty pensions were tenable with continued active service rather than being intended to compensate for lost earning power because an officer was disabled from further service. The amputee officers in this book continued to serve on active duty while receiving such pensions. Basic information on amputee officers has been checked against the 1994 edition of the Navy Records Society's useful *The Commissioned Sea Officers of the Royal Navy, 1660–1815*, edited by R. L. DiNardo and David Syrett.

Outline of Chapters

Chapter 1, "Patrons and Followers," analyzes two key moments in the careers of Nelson, Michael Seymour, Watkin Owen Pell, and James Alexander

Gordon: how they lost a limb, and how they used a network of personal patronage relationships to win recognition for this loss in the form of promotion to a higher command at sea. It argues that letters pushing amputee officers' cases for promotion cite their loss as a mark of honor rather than addressing concerns over it as a disability. That is, they treat this loss as a factor for rather than against an officer's right to win command. This chapter also looks at smart-money for further examples of how the navy linked pain, honor, money, and continued service.

Chapter 2, "Looking Like a Hero," examines key issues in representing amputee military heroes. It focuses on the choices that amputee officers made about presenting an impaired body to their "friends," both colleagues and patrons, in the navy, and to family, friends, and strangers in their everyday lives. It places their presentation to a wider public through heroic portraiture in this context. It argues that they not only were "able-bodied" in the sense of fit to move about in a ship and to command it in battle, but also that they strove to ensure that others saw them as able-bodied. It considers the choices amputee officers made about managing the logistics of life, including their attitudes toward assistance and accommodations, as part of their public performance of the role of commanding officer.

Chapter 3, "Love and Friendship," looks at Seymour, Pell, and Gordon's lives as suitors, husbands, and fathers and the conflict between such domestic ideals and passion in Nelson's life. The amputee officers this book studies were conspicuously sexual and conspicuously sociable people. They courted, married, and had families—or, in Nelson's case, had two families, as his wife brought him a stepson and his mistress bore him a daughter. Letters exchanged by James Gordon and his wife Lydia offer a rich record of how his emotional life flourished after the loss of his leg. In addition, all four of these men also lived at the friendly center of a network of same-sex personal and professional bonds, on shore as well as at sea. This chapter charts some of the close and enduring friendships these amputee officers enjoyed with each other, particularly Gordon and Pell, who wound up their careers running Greenwich Hospital together on land after fighting together at sea.

Chapter 4, "Becoming Victorian," turns to how England changed around the amputee officers who lived on through the 1860s. There was a disconnect between their active duty service and some newer medical theories about the relation between the body and the mind. Like so many other Victorian institutions, such theories interpreted bodies through extreme ideas about gender. Symptoms such as phantom pain in a missing limb and spasms in the residual limb had always existed, but in this context they took on new possible meanings. Rather than being an honorable mark of heroic masculinity, amputation could be seen as a sign of hysterical femininity, a remarkable diagnosis that has understandably attracted attention from scholars of cultural history today. However, the diary of the long-lived Watkin Owen Pell and the family memoir of the equally long-lived James Alexander Gordon suggests that they and their circles continued to see their impairment and its effects in terms of the older framework of honorable service rather than in terms of any newer medical models.

In their own time, Nelson's fellow amputee officers were in the news. Their battles appeared in the gazettes, and their bodies appeared in heroic portraits and engravings. Like Nelson himself, they were a public, highly visible combination of gallantry, professional skill, and physical impairment. It is only over time that they have become invisible. This book hopes to counter that process.

A Note on Seamen

Analysis of physical impairment among sailors on active duty at sea, rather than among the officers who commanded them, lies outside of the scope of this study. I would note here, however, that it seems unlikely the Napoleonic-era navy was manned by bodies that were as uniform as we might assume today. The navy had too few trained seamen to overlook any who were able to serve. In his memoir of the postwar period, *Fragments of Voyages and Travels* (1831–40), Captain Basil Hall distinguishes between physical size and specialized skills. He claims that focusing on the first has "more of a military than of a naval cast." In thinking about the men under his command, a good officer will concentrate on skills rather than size or appearance:

> It will seldom happen, indeed, that the biggest and burliest fellows in a ship's company are the leading men. They may chance, indeed, to be poulterers,

cook's mates, or fit only to make sweepers of, personages who after a three years' station barely know the stem from the stern, and could no more steer the ship than they could take a lunar distance. Nothing, therefore, can be more ridiculous than judging of the men by their stature, or putting such lubberly persons as these just alluded to over the heads of thorough-bred able seamen, captains of the tops or forecastle, hardy sailors whose abilities, knowledge, or trustworthy vigilance, and long-tried experience, in spite of diminutive stature, may very deservedly have placed them in the foremost stations amongst the crew.

Hall claims that new officers are likely to bring to their ship prejudices from larger society about physical appearance and abilities, prejudices that mislead them in judging the men under their command: "Officers, however, on first joining a ship, are very apt to be guilty of some injustice towards the people by judging of them too hastily from appearance alone. We are insensibly so much prepossessed in favour of a fine, tall, good-looking sailor lad, and prejudiced against a grizzled, crooked, little wretch, that if both happen to be brought before us for the same offence, we almost instinctively commit the injustice of condemning the ugly fellow, and acquitting the smart-looking one, before a tithe of the evidence has reached our ears."[78] As an experienced officer, Hall himself valued the "grizzled, crooked, little wretch."

While we may assume that a normative body is the most important qualification for working in a fighting ship, an able seaman's skills were so specialized that contrasting them with the incompetence of landsmen, however strapping, formed a common boast. According to the *Edinburgh Advertiser*, May 30, 1780, a seaman who lost an arm on the *Formidable* once made this boast to the Admiralty. A member of a gun crew had his arm shot away and was injured in the abdomen. After being granted an annuity of twenty pounds a year, he "presented a petition to the Admiralty, praying to be rated on board the grand fleet, alleging that though he wanted an arm and part of his belly, he was ten times better, and would be of more use on board, than any fresh water sailor that their Lordships might employ." Although this story may be a patriotic fiction, it suggests a way of thinking that informed the experience of life at sea in the period.

Brian Lavery points to captains' "description books," the notes some captains kept about the appearance of their men to help hunt them down if they deserted. These description books "often depict the seaman as a rather un-military figure": "Captain Rotherham's book for the *Bellerophon*, begun just after the Battle of Trafalgar, shows a great deal of diversity. Some of the men would not have been recruited by any modern navy—John Millikan was an "amaciated thing": Thomas Jewell had lost his right eye, and Henry McGee was blind in one . . . Some were very short . . . John Cook, a watch motion maker from Cripplegate in London, was only 4 feet 11 inches and worked in the cramped conditions of the hold, where small stature might be an advantage."[79] A peculiar body might suit some of the specialized tasks or odd spaces of a working ship. In addition, a physically impaired seaman's friends could see the circumstances of his injury as entitling him a position in a ship. During the Assault on Cádiz in 1797, for example, Nelson's life was saved by his coxswain, John Sykes, who blocked cutlass blows with his own hand during in a boat action against the Spanish. Sykes lost his hand. Nelson wrote to Sykes's mother to reassure her about his future:

> To Mrs. Hannah Huddlestone, 23 September 1797
>
> Mrs Hannah Huddlestone
>
> Your son John Sykes is quite recovered of his wounds, & is now on board Lord St:Vincent's ship the Ville de Paris, by whom he will be made a Gunner—& if he is not before he comes to England I will take care & provide for Him.[80]

Promising to "take care & provide for Him" was a commitment to find Sykes a position. Sykes became a gunner in the *Andromache* and was killed by a bursting cannon sometime before 1799.[81]

The position of ship's cook was considered a particularly appropriate one for an amputee seaman. For example, at the battle of Trafalgar, James Pool, about twenty years old, served in the *Royal Sovereign* as a landsman. The smart-ticket issued to him on November 3, 1805, states that he "received a wound of the left Arm which caused the amputation of it. 21 Oct 1805 at Trafalgar, 3 Nov 1805." A note is written on the back and signed by the *Royal Sovereign*'s captain, Edward Rotherham: "I do hereby recommend this Man as a proper Object for a Cooks Warrant."[82] Captain Hall describes such an amputee cook deftly managing his responsibilities on board: "On arriving at the galley, or kitchen, the captain is received by the cook (or as much as may be left of him, according to the Greenwich Hospital joke,) behind whom stands his mate, generally a tall, glossy, powerful negro, who, unlike his chief, has always a full allowance of limbs. . . . With end of his wooden leg the cook then gives a twist to the cock of the coppers, to let some of the pease-soup in preparation run off and show itself for the noble commander's inspection."[83] Prints and other contemporary sources reflect the presence of amputee cooks at sea, as does the working title of Robert Louis Stevenson's most famous novel. Before his editor suggested the more glamorous *Treasure Island,* Stevenson titled his manuscript "The Ship's Cook," in honor of his favorite character, Long John Silver, a cook as well as a pirate.

Technical Notes on the Napoleonic-Era Royal Navy

Ratings

When a man signed on to a ship's books, he was given a rating based on his experience. Those new to the sea were called "Landsmen," those with limited experience were "Ordinary Seamen," and those with at least two years at sea and the specialized skills that came with this experience were rated "Able Seamen" or "Able-Bodied Seamen," often abbreviated to A.B.

Petty or Warrant Officers

Candidates for promotion to higher duties on board a ship came from the group of able seamen. These men were noncommissioned officers; their rating pertained to the particular ship in which they served. Being rated as a petty or warrant officer in a ship was generally the ceiling for advancement for able seamen—although some of them had sons who rose to the rank of lieutenant or higher. Petty officers and warrant officers included mast captains, gunner's mates, quartermasters, masters-at-arms, carpenters, bosun and cooper, chaplains, surgeons, and the ship's master. Although all officers needed to be competent in navigation to pass the lieutenant's exam, navigating the ship was the particular duty of the ship's master, on the principle that the more people in a ship capable of keeping her afloat and heading in the proper direction, the better. The navy had too few masters during the war years and had too many lieutenants. Nevertheless, few lieutenants were willing to trade their commission's higher social status and hope (however faint) of promotion to the rank of captain for lifelong employment at the rank of master.

Midshipmen

Midshipmen, captain's servants, and first-class volunteers were on the commissioned officer track. Some of these boys were rated as able seamen, but whatever they were called, the key point was that they were all "young gentlemen" who joined a ship in hopes of eventually gaining an officer's commission. They usually joined their first ship before the age of fourteen, generally at the personal invitation of the ship's captain, taking the first step on the ladder of patronage. They helped lieutenants control the crew. They could also command small boats in boarding and cutting-out expeditions, or command prize ships, in the happy event of their capture. Young gentlemen hoped to win promotion to lieutenant. Some, however, were still in this rank in their thirties, forties, or even older.

Lieutenants

Lieutenants were the backbone of a ship's command structure. Depending upon a ship's rating, it could carry up to six lieutenants, ranked in order of authority from first lieutenant downward. Many officers spent their entire career at the rank of lieutenant. They commanded small boats and gun divisions in battle, oversaw watches, and led boarding and cutting-out parties. Like all other commissioned officers, and unlike midshipmen and warrant officers, lieutenants received half-pay when they were not employed in a ship.

Commander

The rank of commander was the next step up from lieutenant. Often assigned on remote duty, a commander was effectively a captain in all but official title—but his rank was temporary. A commander could revert back to the rank of lieutenant when a particular assignment ended if no promotion came his way.

Post-Captain

"Making Post" meant achieving the permanent rank of post-captain. A captain was the ruler of his ship. He was responsible for manning and provisioning it before it went to sea and for the well-being of all aboard until the end of the cruise. A captain had to account to the Admiralty for all provisions and supplies used or bought for his ship, and a captain who lost a ship under any circumstances had to justify his actions to a court martial. Unlike a commander, a post-captain's rank was permanent, and it put him on an often slow but reliable elevator to higher rank as officers senior to him died. Elevation to admiral depended upon seniority based upon a captain's date of commission.

Commodore

Commodores were captains promoted temporarily to take charge of a detached naval squadron.

Admiral

Most admirals lived on shore on half-pay. By the end of the Napoleonic Wars, fewer than a quarter of those available were on active duty. If an admiral did go to sea, his flagship was usually that of the fleet's junior captain.

Ships

Despite their beauty under sail, Napoleonic-era warships are best understood as elaborate machines designed to convey large guns to the most convenient point to destroy other ships, also carrying large guns. The number and weight of a ship's guns determined everything else about it. Different sets of guns required different-sized crews to fight, thus determining the quantity of a ship's people, provisions, and pay. From the seventeenth through to the mid-nineteenth centuries, the most common naval tactic was the line of battle. Two columns of opposing warships maneuvered to bring all the guns along one side of each ship in range of each other, and then opened fire in what was known as a "broadside." Although the Royal Navy prided itself, with reason, on firing faster and more accurately than did the French, the heaviest ships carrying the most powerful guns possessed a distinct advantage in such engagements. Therefore, the natural progression was to build ever-more large and powerful ships. A ship of the line was one that was heavy enough to stand in the line of battle.

In 1677, Samuel Pepys, secretary to the Admiralty, revised the system he had inherited into a "solemn, universal and unalterable" classification of ships of the line based on the number of guns each one carried. Only large guns mounted on wheels were included in a ship's official rating: the actual number of guns it carried, especially smaller ones, could vary widely. A first-rate ship of the line had three decks among which to divide its guns and carried at least 100 of them; a second-rate carried 90–98 guns, and so on down to a frigate, which carried 20 to 24 guns. Frigates were small and fast, more useful for gathering information and independent cruises in search of detached enemy ships than in the line of battle. Sloops, brigs, cutters, and schooners were even smaller. By convention, the number of guns a ship carried is listed after its name. Horatio Nelson's most famous ship, for example, was the first-rate *Victory* 104; his favorite ship was the third-rate *Agamemnon* 64.

1

Patrons and Followers

Printed by his family in 1879, Rear Admiral Sir Michael Seymour's memoir celebrates the fact that he overcame a crippling handicap to achieve professional success. As a twenty-six-year-old lieutenant, Seymour lost his left arm to an injury in battle. The handicap that Seymour's memoir praises him for overcoming, however, is not his lack of an arm, but rather his lack of influential family connections: he won his rank by "hard service, unaided by any favour."[1] Seymour had a distinguished career at a time when many capable officers waited impatiently on shore. By sustaining a major injury while fighting in a successful action, he joined an elite group of officers who were considered eligible for "hero promotion," or promotion in recognition of taking part in a successful action against an enemy ship of the same or superior firepower. In the Royal Navy of Seymour's day, however, even indisputable heroes needed well-placed friends to push their cases. Technical skill, personal initiative, and absolute indifference to bodily harm were not enough. When the amputee officers in this study and their friends wrote to the Admiralty lobbying for promotion, they described their loss of a limb in battle in a particular way: as a mark of honor that increased their moral claim to the privilege of command at sea, not as a disability that diminished their fitness to serve.

This chapter connects pension claims to larger claims about the body, social status, and promotion. It examines two key moments in the careers of Michael Seymour, Watkin Owen Pell, James Alexander Gordon, and Horatio Nelson: the battle in which they lost a limb and the campaign conducted by themselves and their friends to use this loss as a part of their strategy to win further active service. Their success is remarkable. As Evan

Wilson points out, 60 percent of the officers who passed the lieutenants' exam between 1775 and 1805 never rose beyond that rank.[2] In contrast, although most of the amputee officers in this study lost a limb as midshipmen or lieutenants, all but one of them rose further in rank. In *Nelson's Mediterranean Command*, Denis Orde speculates about the effect today that a brilliant officer's loss of his right arm would have his career, on top of the loss of sight in one eye: "In a supposedly more enlightened age such overall disability would have cost him his career in any active role."[3] How valid is this comparison? The presence of officers and seamen who continued to serve at sea with physical impairments suggest that Nelson's navy was indeed not overly influenced by negative stereotypes about such conditions. Seymour and Pell were injured relatively early in their careers. Pell was a midshipman and Seymour a lieutenant, so hero promotion played the most crucial role for these two. They had not yet achieved the rank of post-captain, which promised eventual continued promotion through seniority. As he was the captain of a frigate when he won the battle that cost him his leg, Gordon already had post-rank. Even post-captains, however, competed fiercely for command of a ship and employment at sea, and being wounded in a celebrated victory added urgency to Gordon's claims. Nelson, the greatest hero of them all, was a very different case. He was already a rear admiral when he lost his right arm in battle—and he lost that battle as well.

Smart-Money, Services, and Sufferings

In 1809, Vice Admiral Cuthbert Collingwood was the commander-in-chief of the Mediterranean Fleet, having taken over that command from his good friend Horatio Nelson when Nelson was killed at Trafalgar. Having both been promising young lieutenants under the patronage of Vice Admiral Sir Peter Parker in the 1770s, Collingwood and Nelson had long been close. In 1809, Collingwood complained that something had gone very wrong with the way the navy chose those who commanded its ships. Political influence, he claimed, had undermined the practice of promoting "proper men for the service." In addition to nautical skill, proper men had "gallantry." This quality is best defined as a dashing combination of physical courage and initiative exercised under great pressure in combat. Collingwood implies that a proper man would also have a body marked by battle: "The truth is, that [Lord Mulgrave, First Lord of the Admiralty 1807–10] is so pressed by persons having parliamentary influence, that he cannot find himself at liberty to select those whose nautical skill and gallantry would otherwise present them as proper men for the service. A hole or two in the skin will not weigh against a vote in Parliament."[4] Shot from cannon, bullets, and "splinters," large, jagged fragments of ship's timbers—all could make holes in a man's skin or carry away an arm, a leg, or the sight from his eyes. Collingwood appealed to the principle that such injuries, and the combat experience such injuries represented, should weigh more than political influence toward earning the privilege of command, although he feared they no longer did. Why would an influential senior officer like Collingwood assume that in a well-run navy, the natural reward for injury in battle was the chance to go back to sea and risk further injury, rather than retirement to a more peaceful life on shore with a decoration for gallantry and a pension for disability? The answer to this question is complex. Nelson's navy had no official system of decorations for gallantry under fire, increasing the pressure on using promotion as a way to acknowledge the heroism of junior officers. More broadly, Collingwood alludes here to the practice of "hero promotion., or promotion for "brilliant services against the enemy."[5] Hero promotion sought to recognize officers who displayed merit in battle even if their families lacked political influence.

Hero promotion reflects a way of thinking that recognizes the significance of bodily injury, but that does not necessarily associate such injury with disability. Another example of this way of thinking is the Navy's system of "smart-money." Smart-money suggests an idea of physical pain as a marker of personal duty and honor. It pre-dates the idea of a welfare state, or a system of compensatory benefits based on the rational calculation of future earning power. Dating back to the seventeenth century, smart-money was part of a well-established system of medical relationships. Injured ratings, warrant officers, and dockyard workers acquired a "smart-ticket" by having their injuries examined by a naval surgeon, who filled out the form—the smart-ticket. Each ticket was good for a certain payment from the Chatham Chest—after 1803, the Chest at Greenwich—according to an established scale. The system had far-reaching effects. In 1855, for example, praising the completeness of its records of battle injuries, the

Journal of the Royal Statistical Society reminded readers that "it must be borne in mind that 'in the British service, every wounded man, although merely scratched, reports himself to the surgeon, in order that he may get his smart-money.'"[6]

Each smart-ticket is a full sheet of paper, about 16 x 8 inches, preprinted with spaces to describe the patient, his injury, and the circumstances under which he received it. A smart-ticket certifies that the patient was injured while "being then actually upon His Majesty's service," doing his duty in battle or—much more commonly—in the ordinary work of a ship, loading or unloading casks, for example, or handling sails.[7] When a ship ran out of smart-tickets, they were hand-written following the same format. The ship's surgeon, captain, and officers signed as witness that the injury was received in the course of duty, and not, for example, in a drunken fight. A shorter entry was made later, at Greenwich Hospital, when the ship reached home and smart-money was paid out. On the back of the ticket, a note either records "full satisfaction" if the injured man received one lump sum, or specifies one sum for "present relief" and an additional yearly payment. For example, on May 4, 1761, Jeremiah James, seaman, about thirty-three years old, in HMS *Favorite*, while "heaving Ballast into the Ship" got "some sand into his Right Eye, which caused a great Inflamation with a Swelling, for some weeks, and rendered the Cornea opaque with loss of sight." James's injury was certified on August 1, 1762, and an additional note was made on July 6, 1763, recording that "Jeremiah James lost the sight of his right Eye for which he deserves four pounds a year and four pounds present relief."[8]

How much were smart-money and officers' pensions worth? Variations in the cost of particular commodities as well as regional variation in the cost of living contribute to the difficulty of estimating what a pound was worth during the Napoleonic Wars or their aftermath. For example, Lieutenant Frederick Bedford, third resident lieutenant at Greenwich Hospital, protested to the House of Lords in 1818 that because he was "obliged to reside in the most expensive Spot probably in the Kingdom," his salary for his position at Greenwich, plus his pension of 91 *l* 5 s for the loss of his leg and 5 shillings a day for earlier injuries to his jaw and eye, was inadequate to support "his numerous young Family."[9] Rodger notes that both captains' and ratings' pay "declined in real value by the end of the eighteenth century, and then caught up after the Napoleonic War."[10] For context, we should remember that in the eighteenth century, only about 6 percent of English families had an annual income of 100 *l* or more.[11] Very generally speaking, 100 *l* a year was the lowest income on which a household could make a claim to gentility. At 100 *l* a year, a family could usually afford to hire one very young maidservant at a very low wage: poor curates, government clerks, and well-to-do tradesmen fell into this category. At 300 *l* a year, a bachelor could live in style with two servants; only about 3 percent of households had an income of 300 *l* a year or more. At 700 to 1,000 *l* a year, a family could keep three servants and might aspire to keep a carriage. A house in London and participation in the London social season probably took above 4,000 *l* a year. Broadly speaking, although an officer's commission brought with it the precious right to call himself a gentleman, this title lacked solid financial basis below the rank of captain. Moreover, if they were not lucky enough to be born to property, marry a fortune, or win prize money by capturing enemy ships, even captains had difficulty supporting a family in genteel style. Officers' pay rose according to the rate of the ship in which they served and by seniority, and eventually increased after the mutinies at Spithead and the Nore (1797) brought attention to the issue of naval pay as a whole. In 1806, the pay of a captain of a first-rate ship, before deductions and professional expenses such as keeping good table at sea, was 400 *l* a year—but officers received the full pay amount only when they actually belonged to a ship. In between commissions, officers starting at the rank of Lieutenant received half-pay. Midshipmen and other ratings received no pay when not actually serving in a ship.[12]

While injured ratings, warrant officers, and dockworkers received smart-money, commissioned officers did not. Wounded commissioned officers might receive pensions from the Admiralty, but such pensions were not automatic. As is suggested by a common formulation used in pension awards, "services and sufferings," injury incurred while serving in a victorious battle was better than suffering in and of itself. Payment for the injuries of officers reflected the injured man's rank: the higher the rank, the higher the possible value of the injuries. For example, when Robert Mends lost his right arm at the Battle of Yorktown in 1781 as a midshipman, he was awarded 7 *l* a year as smart-money. Mends returned to sea, continued to perform gallantly in action, received other battle injuries, became a captain, won a knighthood, and by 1816 had a pension for "services and sufferings" of 300 *l* a year. Michael Seymour received a pension of 91 *l* 5 s for the loss of an arm as a lieutenant in 1794; his pension rose to 300 *l* in 1815, when he was a captain who had captured a number of ships.[13]

This process was not invariable. For example, Joseph Ellison is an example of the "competent men of all classes [who] were brought forward by their senior officers who recognized the importance of doing so" in the eighteenth-century Royal Navy.[14] Ellison went to sea at the age of nine with no influential connections and lost his right arm as a lieutenant in 1780, in the *Prudente* 36's capture of the *Capricieuse*. Ellison made post-captain in 1783—but he was then serving in the impress service, not capturing enemy ships at sea. In 1790, he appears as receiving a pension of 91 *l* 15 s, a sum commonly awarded to amputee lieutenants. As noted in the introduction, Lord Cochrane attacked what he saw as the inequities of the Pension List in Parliament on May 11, 1810. He mentioned Joseph Ellison, still giving him the rank of lieutenant and a pension of 91 *l* 5 s.[15]

Both officers' pensions for "services and sufferings" and smart-money differ in significant ways from what may look like their closest twenty-first-century equivalent, the compensatory damages for the loss of earning power due to negligence granted by tort law. First, they carried no necessary connection with a lack of earning power. Smart-money and Admiralty pensions were awarded to injured seamen and officers who continued to serve on active duty, as well as to those seamen and officers who were unable to serve because of their injuries. For example, on May 3, 1814, John Rice suffered contusions and dislocation to the elbow joint "caused by a hurt from the Ship throwing him with great violence." His smart-ticket further notes that he "is found to be recovered and deserves six pounds satisfaction."[16] More remarkable is the smart-ticket recording the "singular accident" of James Fly, an unusually tough seaman, in 1803: "James Fly Seaman Aged about twenty eight years was wounded & bruised on board HMS the Amazon by falling from the Main topsail Yard into a Boat on the booms, passing thro' its bottom, & alighting on the main deck—by which he was wounded in the head and foot; and much contused in different parts of his body; the effects of which singular accident he still seems to feel. On the 13th of November in the year 1803 in service in the Mediterranean.

Certified Nov. 1806." A note added six years later asserts two points: First, Fly recovered from this accident, and second, he had a right to his smart-money: "1812 March 10 James Fly is found to be Recovered and deserves ten pounds satisfaction."[17] As noted above, Mends and Michael Seymour served at sea while receiving pensions: Seymour, for example, captured six French privateers and two transport vessels while receiving his pension.

Although smart-money and Admiralty pensions were different things, positioned on opposite sides of the divide that the social status cut through the navy, a popular mythical Nelson anecdote papers over this difference. Published in 1806 at Lady Hamilton's request, James Harrison's occasionally "fanciful" *The Life of the Right Honorable Horatio Viscount Nelson* tells a "humorous" story of Nelson claiming smart-money for the loss of sight in his right eye.[18] Harrison's joke is that Nelson, offended at the requirement that a surgeon certify that he had lost sight in his right eye, also supplied a surgeon's certificate stating that he had lost his right arm.[19] Robert Southey's best-selling *Life of Nelson* (1813) repeated the anecdote.[20] This joke is an example of what Timothy Jenks identifies as nationalist discourse's tendency to use "Nelson's body as a conduit of plebeian patriotism." It is similar to the *Gentleman's Magazine* story of Nelson shaking hands with, and giving a coin to, a one-armed sailor he saw in a crowd in December 1800, at which point "every circumstance of greatness or distinction vanished for the moment."[21] Both smart-money and an amputee officer's pension link pain and the honorable performance of one's duty, making possible this kind of momentary erasure of social distinction.

The conceptual difference between the honorable recognition of pain and compensatory damages for the loss of earning-power that I stress here was blurred in practice. Some pensions were indeed intended to compensate men for lost earning power, and others, particularly those granted to distinguished senior officers, were clearly intended to confer honor. Nevertheless, they had a necessary connection to pain, honor, and reward, but no necessary connection to disability. This way of thinking about injury and money struck some observers as wrongheaded as early as 1817. A Parliamentary Committee on Half Pay, Military Superannuations, Pensions and Allowances argued that pensions should be awarded only for disability understood as lost earning power; they should not be awarded to honor services and sufferings that did not disable an officer from further active service. This committee found particularly galling the spectacle of pensions for wounds rising with the injured man's rank:

> With regard to the pensions to wounded officers, your Committee have only here to repeat the opinion, which they have before stated, of the inexpediency of continuing the late regulation [of 1815], by which pensions for wounds received in an inferior rank are permitted to increase, as if the wound had been received in every higher rank to which the officer may attain. This is in fact, as they before observed, to give a continually increasing renumeration for wounds, which are not so serious as to prevent an officer's continuing in active service, and attaining higher rank and greater emoluments, and to allot the lowest rate of pension to him whose wounds may have so utterly disabled him, as to oblige him to quit the active line and forego the improving prospects of his profession.[22]

In contrast, amputee officers asserted the principle that their pensions were a reward for their honorable service, not a compensation for lost earning power. For example, in 1819, Lieutenant Frederick Bedford (he who lamented the high cost of living in Greenwich) petitioned the House of Lords that his position as third lieutenant at Greenwich Hospital should not prevent him from receiving his pension for the loss of his leg in battle or prevent that pension from rising as did those of other officers: "Wounded Lords of the Admiralty, Commissioners of the Navy, &c. &c. have not only enjoyed their Pensions (with the recent Augmentations) but their Half Pay also, exclusive of their official Salaries, and for Reasons most just, and equally applicable to the honorable situation of the Petitioner, one Source of Emolument being for past Services or Sufferings, and the other for Duties performed jointly with their Coadjutors in Office."[23] That is, Bedford insisted on the principle that his pension honored his services and sufferings; it did not compensate for being disabled from further service.

In addition, smart-money and Admiralty pensions had no connection whatsoever to negligence. In contrast to the right to a financial award for injury caused by the bad behavior of another party, they were awarded for injury caused by the honorable behavior of the injured person, in the context of his personal relationship with the state. That is, people had a legal right to these awards because they had bled for the king, not because the king was negligent in placing them in the way of loose casks, flying shot, or falling timbers. Because smart-money was a sprawling bureaucratic system, it may today recall workers' compensation—another routinized system of equivalencies between injury and payment. But worker's compensation takes the place of the right to sue one's employer for negligence: it too rests on an idea of fault. It is intended, in some measure, to provide an incentive against unsafe working conditions, as well as to provide compensatory damages for lost earning power. In contrast, smart-money was not intended to promote a safer work environment in the Napoleonic-era Royal Navy, but rather to recognize that injury would routinely occur.

In this sense, smart-money's closest legal equivalent is not compensatory damages but rather the United States military decoration of the Purple Heart or the British military decoration of a "wound stripe," awarded between 1916 and 1946. But smart-money was in fact money, not a medal on a ribbon or a brass pin. Seamen did not hang it around their necks or pin it to their sleeves. They spent it. In this regard, smart-money looks a bit like prize money, the Royal Navy's similarly archaic system of awarding each individual member of a ship's crew a share of the value of any enemy ship that they managed to capture, an unequal share based on their rank. As a legal recognition of pain, smart-money is especially interesting for the contrast it offers to eighteenth-century "Tarism," or the contemporary popular images of the British sailor's superhuman, or subhuman, indifference to pain. That is, even as popular ballads and prints represented common sailors as more or less incapable of feeling pain, the navy routinely paid them a variety of fixed sums in recognition of their experiences of it. Such financial awards acknowledged that an injury incurred in the line of duty could be significant without disabling the injured man from continued service. The place of injury in practice of hero promotion draws on a similar set of assumptions.

Hero Promotion

Collingwood's criticism of the relative values of "a hole or two in the skin" and political influence implies that he witnessed a sudden falling away from the practice of rewarding through hero promotion gallantry certified by injury in battle. The truth is a bit more complicated. The claim that political influence had come to outweigh personal merit marked by such injuries dramatized in its most morally compelling form a set of larger, long-running tensions in the practice of promotion. First of all, as Rodger points out, "the single most important factor governing an officer's prospects in the Navy was his date of birth."[24] When a war began, the navy was short of officers and promoted them rapidly. As the supply of officers increased, promotions slowed; with peacetime demobilization, the promotion prospects of new officers became vanishingly small. Officers commissioned as lieutenants in 1790, for example, were ideally positioned to benefit from the boom in promotion brought by the early years of the wars with France. Even within this group, however, staying employed was a challenge. Both ships and seamen were in short supply, so no one wanted to entrust either to an officer whose incompetence could endanger them. Conducted by a panel of officers, the oral examination to "pass" for a lieutenant weeded out candidates weak in seamanship. The problem the Admiralty faced was the opposite: how to manage an oversupply of capable and deserving officers. Although the navy provided half-pay for officers who were not on active duty, it had no coherent system of retirement: some officers remained on half-pay until they died, while others accepted "superannuation" with a pension. Therefore, not every officer on the "Active List" was in fact actively seeking employment.

Even allowing for those who accepted half-pay as a default retirement, however, there were still too few ships and far too many officers. Charles Consolvo notes that even "at the peak of employment in 1814, only about 50 per cent of the officers on the active list were employed. By 1816, one year after the wars, this had declined to barely 17 per cent employed."[25] In addition, even wartime officers serving at sea often failed to find an enemy ship to engage. Because the chance of battle was not evenly distributed throughout the seas, influential friends could help an officer gain a posting where a confrontation with the enemy was more likely.

Consolvo rightly describes the greatest single factor correlating with promotion in his sample group as "interest, defined as being the protégé of a senior officer, son of a naval officer or son of an influential family."[26]

This broad definition of "interest," however, encompasses two kinds of patronage that were often perceived within the navy as quite different, or even as opposed: interest that rose from naval service itself—either by oneself or one's family—and larger political interest. To Nelson, for example, any junior officer who earned his captain's interest through gallantry, or even the son of a gallant brother officer, clearly had a different and a more legitimate claim to promotion than the son of a politically influential family. The Royal Navy was both a formidable bureaucracy and an informal network of intensely personal relationships. "Friendship," in the eighteenth-century sense of patronage wielded to benefit loyal subordinates, was essential to its functioning. "There is no gratification equal to that derived from pushing the fortunes of deserving men," happily declared Lord St. Vincent, the First Lord of the Admiralty from 1801 to 1804, on promoting William Parker to the rank of captain at the age of nineteen.[27] For an officer such as Nelson, whose commitment to the ideal of the navy as a brotherhood was as strong as his talent for maneuvering within political parties was weak, this sense of "friendship" was even more important. Writing to Admiral Sir Peter Parker eleven days after Trafalgar, Collingwood framed even the strategic value of that victory in these terms: "Had it not been for the fall of our noble friend . . . your pleasure would have been perfect—that two of your own pupils, raised under your eye, and cherished by your kindness, should render such service to their Country as I hope this battle will in its effect be."[28]

Naval historians differ over the extent to which the political influence of great families increased in the navy during the period, often pointing instead to the long-term power of interest or to the Admiralty's gradual centralization of control.[29] Nevertheless, it was a factor that contemporaries feared was on the rise. This context adds significance to Collingwood's complaint about the unjust neglect of officers with "a hole or two in the skin." Evan Wilson stresses the relatively modest family origin of most naval officers up to 1805, in comparison to its handful of prominent aristocrats.[30] Such officers had political influence on a national level, often holding public office, but they were mainly younger sons rather than the heirs to estates. Referring to them collectively as "the Honorables," Nelson neatly captured their distinctive status, using the courtesy title granted to cadet branches of aristocratic families that had used up all of their titles on direct heirs. Comparing 1771 to 1831, S. A. Cavell shows that the greatest boom in officers with connections to the peerage and landed gentry came after the war years. Even earlier, however, she finds among naval officers themselves a rise in "tension . . . over issues of seniority and deservedness."[31] The complaints of career officers such as Collingwood may have reflected "small signs of social change [and fear of] the impact it would have on future generations of command."[32] Nelson also lamented the destructive impact of "the Honorables" on the Navy, fearing political influence was gaining too much power over promotions. Like Collingwood, Nelson holds up as particularly disturbing a vision of political influence sidelining a candidate for hero promotion, writing to the First Lord of the Admiralty: "Your encouragement for these Lieutenants who may conspicuously exert themselves cannot fail to have its good effect in serving our Country, instead of their thinking that if a Vessel is taken, it would make the son of some great man a Captain, in place of the gallant fellow who captured her."[33]

The numbers strained the Admiralty's attempts to follow its own ideals of fairness. "I shall seek merit, and reward it, to the utmost of my power," Lord St. Vincent wrote in 1802, "but at present I am restrained from promoting, by the very great number of meritorious officers on the list of post-Captains and Commanders . . . [who are] unemployed."[34] Defining the most deserving among so many meritorious officers was a complex and contested process, one that reflected different ideals about "family." Having served throughout the long wars, John Marshall assumed that in a well-run Navy, a good officer's son legitimately partook in the merit of his father. He sarcastically refers to the difficulty that the son of Admiral Duncan, a great officer, had in gaining a ship early in his career because his father's services were "not deemed sufficient" to earn him one: "From this period, Captain Duncan used every effort to obtain another appointment; but having at that time no other claim than his father's services, they were not deemed sufficient by the then first Lord of the Admiralty, and he did not succeed until Lord Howick was replaced at that Board by Mr. T. Grenville."[35] As we shall see, Captain Duncan proved an effective officer. Family interest was not always so successfully bestowed. For example, as described in chapter 3, Nelson used his interest to further the career of his stepson,

Josiah Nesbit, a young man who turned out to be entirely unsuited to command at sea.

Like Marshall, Lord St. Vincent also understood merit as accumulating through generations of good naval service, believing a meritorious officer more deserving of promotion if his father had also been a meritorious officer. But other fathers' claims could be more pressing: "A sprinkling of nobility [is] very desirable in the Navy, as it gives some sort of consequence to the service; but at present the Navy is so overrun by the younger branches of nobility, and the sons of Members of Parliament, and they so swallow up all the patronage, and so choke the channel to promotion that the son of an old Officer, however meritorious both their services may have been, has little or no chance of getting on."[36] Those who criticized the effect of a great family's political interest on naval promotion, then, often did not believe merit should be strictly defined as an individual rather than family achievement. Rather, they supported another definition of family, one grounded in the navy itself. Naval historians place different kinds of patronage on a spectrum according to how they affected the navy's functioning, ranging from benign to toxic. Historians today tend to regard positively patronage in the limited sense of a captain's ability to promote his own officers' careers. In keeping with their sense of the navy as an extended family, Nelson and his peers also saw patronage relationships within the service as the natural way to encourage and reward meritorious junior officers. A good captain's own sons and the sons of his friends would have the first claims, but he would, ideally, take a fatherly interest in any outstanding junior officer. He would strive to surround himself with promising young gentlemen and talented lieutenants and strive to deserve their loyalty by furthering their careers.

We can see what it might mean to a captain to see his officers achieve promotion in a letter Michael Seymour received from the Admiralty after he himself had become a captain and fought a successful action. After informing Seymour that two of his lieutenants, a midshipman, his purser, and his master all had been promoted, the Admiralty breaks off, remarking that "no other praise can be at the same moment interesting to you."[37] That is, having just learned of the promotion of so many of his officers, Seymour will be unable to focus his mind on anything else. Advancement of his officers' careers is the most meaningful "praise" of any captain's victory. Likewise, as Nelson blockaded the French fleet in the Mediterranean in the year leading up to Trafalgar, the fate of his worthy young officers seemed to weigh on him as much as the fate of Great Britain. He fretted to Lord Melville that even total victory would not provide for all the deserving men he "ardently" wished to see promoted: "I can only say God send I could take *two* French fleets for one would, with what I have sent me by the late Admiralty and my followers, go but little way towards promoting them, all which I wish ardently to do, for 60 or 70 finer young Men I never saw are in the fleet and who have served their time."[38] In return for such support, junior officers strove to distinguish themselves, and to support their captain in battle and in the less dramatic judgment calls that made up everyday life at sea. Nelson's own career is a good example of this kind of professional patronage working exactly as it was supposed to. He joined his first ship under the patronage of his uncle, Captain Maurice Suckling, who recognized his abilities and watched over the early stages of his career. As he rose, Nelson was proud to use his own influence to advance the careers of his own deserving junior officers. It was in defense of such mentorship at sea that officers such as Nelson and Collingwood criticized promotion in response to a great family's political power in the nation at large. In contrast, a battle injury could be seen as proof of membership in the family of the navy. Promoting officers with battle injuries suggested an ideal navy that identified "deservedness" with heroism, a navy in which careers were built on gallantry, friendship, and brotherhood, rather than on political interest.

As amputee officers maneuvered for command, they pointed to their loss of a limb in battle as proof that they had this kind of right to serve. They and their friends did not try to explain away this loss as a potential disability, but rather called attention to it as proof of gallantry. Margarette Lincoln points to the importance of wounds as "a badge of bravery" in military circles of the time.[39] Battle injury often suggests ideals central to officers' shared professional identity, as Katherine Ott notes: "Generations of soldiers have self-consciously forgone the wearing of prostheses, instead selecting eye patches and empty sleeves and trouser legs as the mark of courage, heroism, and manly sacrifice."[40] Amputee officers and their friends argued that empty sleeves and prosthetic legs should bring not only honor but also the privilege of further active service at sea. For example, in July 1803, the *Racoon*'s Master's Mate Thomas Gill lost his left arm in battle: it was carried off close to the shoulder by shot while he helped capture a French brig. A finger of his left hand had been shot off earlier in this battle. His captain, Austin Bissell, recommended the young amputee officer to the commander-in-chief, Admiral Sir J. T. Duckworth, describing Gill as "a very worthy, promising young man who has served his time in the navy, and will, if he survives, do credit to your patronage."[41]

As an amputee officer, Gill did indeed do credit to Bissell and Duckworth's patronage. On August 17, 1803, off Cuba, *Racoon* defeated the eighteen-gun brig *La Mutine;* on October 14, it captured a French gun-brig, cutter, and schooner. Gill played a valuable part in this second battle, which occurred four months after the loss of his arm, an achievement recognized by a prize from the Patriotic Society: "For his conduct on the latter occasion Mr. Gill, whose wounds were still open, but who did not quit the deck for 27 hours, was presented with 50 guineas by the Patriotic Society." Soon afterward, Bissell was made captain of the *Creole* 38, and Gill followed him as acting third lieutenant. Gill's promotion to lieutenant was confirmed by a commission dated May 8, 1804, and he served in seven different ships in the next ten years. While lieutenant of the *Aurora*, Gill took part in a three-hour battle with several Spanish gunboats near Tarifa, three of which were captured. He also participated in boat operations on the Italian coast and "on every occasion displayed a gallant and characteristic bearing." In particular, in December 1806, Gill commanded two boats belonging to *Kingfisher:* he "chased an armed felucca on shore, then landed at the head of a party of 40 officers, seamen, and marines, secured the prize, plundered a neighbouring village, and ultimately brought off the spoil, although the enemy had rallied, and had brought together a force of 500 men to oppose him." On June 27, 1808, Gill was wounded once again while capturing the letter-of-marque *Le Hercule* 12. After being promoted to commander, Gill commanded the *Sparrowhawk* 19, on the West India station, and was appointed acting captain of the *Magnificent*, a receiving ship at Port Royal, Jamaica, in July 1830. The *Magnificent* was his last command: he invalided home in February 1831 and was promoted to the rank of captain in January 1837. Gill married on August 16, 1816, and eventually had six daughters and three sons, of whom the eldest, Thomas Cadman Roberts, also joined the Royal Navy. Gill received a pension of 200 *l* a year for wounds, dated from May 1816.[42]

An active career did not always bring serious injury such as Thomas Gill's, but being "wounded" could nevertheless serve as shorthand for "gallantry," as in Nelson's note of April 12, 1803, to Vice Admiral Charles Powell Hamilton. Hamilton was pushing him to take his son to the Mediterranean as a lieutenant in the *Victory*. After repeatedly explaining that he had no openings left, Nelson finally sent Hamilton the list of candidates he felt came before his son. This list reflects the interplay of criteria for employment. First appear seven of Nelson's own "followers," whose primary claim he stressed again to Hamilton on May 23, 1804, remarking, "I am as well disposed as you could wish me but I cannot kill folks or remove those who have served with me from the beginning." Then we see a combination of birth and gallantry. After Nelson's followers comes "Bligh Son of the Admiral," then "Williams 1st of the Medusa wounded at Bolonge."[43] In 1801 Nelson had ordered a boat action against the French at Boulogne. It failed at great loss of life, but the *London Gazette* mentions that the *Medusa*'s first lieutenant, "Mr. Williams[,] led his Subdivision up to the Enemy with the most intrepid Gallantry, took One Lugger, and attacked a Brig . . . nearly the Whole of his Boat's Crew were killed or wounded."[44] In contrast to both young Bligh and the gallant Lieutenant Williams, Admiral Hamilton's son combined excellent influence with terrible judgment, soon sabotaging his own career. He never served with Nelson.

To see how family interest and injury in battle could combine to shape a career, consider William Rivers and Edward Stopford. Both were sons of naval families, although at very different levels of society. Edward Stopford was a nephew of Admiral the Honorable Sir Robert Stopford, KCB (Knight Commander), who was himself a younger son of the Earl of Courtown. In August 1811, then acting captain of the *Otter*, Stopford lost his right arm in a successful attack on the island of Java. Because Stopford was knocked unconscious, the seamen who were with him believed him to be dead. However, neither Stopford's life nor his sense of his due as a gentleman had in fact been knocked out of him: "As they were bearing off the field, he recovered his senses and feeling the hot beams of a vertical sun striking directly on his head, his hat having rolled off when he fell, he immediately exclaimed to one of his men, *'Damme, Sir! fetch me my hat.'*"⁴⁵

Stopford arrived at the Admiralty Office in London on December 17, 1811, bearing a dispatch from his uncle, who had commanded the expedition. The dispatch noted that Edward "had his right arm carried off by a cannon-ball, whilst actively employed in the batteries; he is, however, doing well."⁴⁶ In another letter, the admiral explicitly wrote that by losing his arm in battle, his nephew had earned promotion: "Captain Stopford's early misfortune will I hope procure him that next step which he is so anxious to get."⁴⁷ "That next step" was an important one. Once an officer achieved the rank of post-captain, or "made Post," he would automatically rise in rank as death or superannuation opened positions in the Navy List. Longevity alone could make him an admiral. Below the rank of post-captain, however, a lieutenant could serve as the acting captain of a ship and be granted the courtesy title of commander, but he would revert to the rank of lieutenant when that commission ended. He was sure of a lieutenant's half-pay when not employed, but nothing more. Stopford was promoted to post rank on the second day after his arrival in London. He was given command of the *Rosamond* 20 in the spring of 1814 and convoyed three merchantmen to the coast of Labrador, where his missing arm attracted notice: "Captain Stopford's amputated arm arrested the attention of the Esquimaux. They satisfied themselves, by feeling the stump, that the limb was actually deficient, and then appeared to wonder how it could have been lost: but when one of his officers made signs to them that it had been severed with a saw, commiseration was depicted in every countenance."⁴⁸ Stopford lost command of the *Rosamond* in 1814, when it was found to be so damaged by the ice of Hudson's Straits that it was put out of commission. He retained a pension of 300 *l* per year for the loss of his arm.

In contrast to the nearly instantaneous promotion of this admiral's amputee nephew, consider the story of another amputee officer, this one a gunner's son. Gallantry abounds in William Rivers's career; political interest does not. Born between 1786 and 1788, Rivers was the son of the *Victory*'s gunner, a petty officer. Aiming to move up into the ranks of commissioned officers, William Rivers joined the *Victory* as a first-class volunteer. He served from 1795 to 1799 under the command of several different captains. He took part in two battles, Hotham's second partial action on July 13, 1795, and the Battle off Cape St. Vincent on February 14, 1797, and was wounded twice in his right arm. In 1803, Rivers returned to the *Victory*, then Nelson's flagship, and chased the French to the West Indies and back. He remained in the *Victory* at the Battle of Trafalgar: a splinter knocked out three of his teeth and shot so injured his leg that it required amputation. During the procedure, Rivers is reported to have encouraged the wounded men waiting their turn for surgery by claiming, "My men, it is nothing to have a limb off, you will find pleasure when you come here, men to get rid of your shattered limb."[49]

Rivers's gallantry at Trafalgar was recognized: he was promoted to the rank of lieutenant and returned to duty within the year. "As a reward for his valour and his sufferings," on January 8, 1806, he was commissioned as a lieutenant in the *Princess of Orange* 74, under Captain Thomas Rogers. In the next twelve years, Rivers served as a lieutenant on five different ships under eight different captains. In one, the *Cossack*, he was "frequently employed in a boat for the purpose of intercepting any vessels" that might be passing with troops.[50] Rivers married in 1809 and had two sons and six daughters. In April 1816, while serving as a lieutenant on active duty, Rivers was awarded a pension of 91 *l* 5 s per year for the loss of his leg. He served at sea until April 1818. River's last commission was as first lieutenant of a guard ship bearing the flag of Commander-in-Chief Sir Thomas Williams, the only officer in such a position, O'Byrne pointedly notes, "who was not promoted at the conclusion of the war."[51] Rivers makes a brief but memorable appearance in an entry in *Greenwich Hospital: A Series of Naval Sketches, Descriptive of the Life of a Man-of-War's Man* (1826), written by Matthew Henry Barker. Barker was a literary man and master's mate in the navy who lacked influence to rise as high as his abilities might have warranted.[52] His narrator awards Rivers the rank of captain: "I recollects as if it was but yesterday, when Nelson led us at Trafalgar. . . . You remember Mr. Rivers, a smart active midshipman, that lost his leg? I understands he's a captain now; a worthier fellow ne'er wore a head; nay, there wasn't a man aboard (though his precious limb was dock'd) that could beat him in going aloft; and I've seen him lead down a dance with his wooden pin flourishing away as well as the nimblest there."[53] A footnote by "Printer's Devil" corrects the error about Rivers's rank, but not the sense of its injustice:

"The Old Sailor is mistaken, he is still a lieutenant."[54] In 1824, Rivers was appointed warden at Woolwich Dockyard. One of his sons, William Thomas Rivers, also became a lieutenant in the Royal Navy.

"An Honorable Mark Instead of a Misfortune": Sir Michael Seymour

Born in 1768 at Glebe House, Pallas, county Limerick, Michael Seymour was the second son of Reverend John Seymour and went to sea at the age of twelve. His age was typical: boys aiming to be officers usually entered the profession between the ages of ten and fourteen. In addition to the science of navigation, the exclusive purview of officers, this "hardy" profession required such boys to become able seamen. They mastered an enormous body of technical knowledge about handling each rope and sail of a ship and an exhaustive repertoire of demanding and specialized physical skills. Able seamen entered a ship by climbing a rope up its side, for example, and were at home moving through its rigging, high above its decks. As the son of a professional man, though one with good connections, Seymour held a social position that was also typical for a candidate for a navy commission. The Reverend John Seymour was related to the dukes of Somerset who settled in Ireland in the time of Elizabeth I, and his mother, Griselda, was distantly related to the earls of Buckinghamshire.[55] However grand his relations might be, however, Michael Seymour "started in life with nothing but his profession."[56] The bulk of the naval officer corps was born to families that were like Seymour's in this regard: they had no estate to pass on to their sons but aspired to give them a good start in life, one that would allow them to defend—sometimes to the death—their claim to be gentlemen.[57]

We might assume that when Michael Seymour went to sea at the age of twelve in November 1780, he joined the Royal Navy. It is more accurate, however, to say that he joined the *Merlin* 18, a sloop-of-war commanded by Captain the Honorable James Luttrell. It is no accident that at the end of his very long and successful life, Seymour still honored the memory of his first captain, "my very dear lamented patron and friend."[58] From victualing to gunnery, the scale, complexity, and efficiency of Nelson's navy made it a remarkably modern institution. However, its process for recruiting officers did not follow the organizational chart of a twenty-first-century bureaucracy, or even a late nineteenth-century one. The navy vested ultimate authority in the Lords Commissioners of the Admiralty, a board composed of Sea Lords and Civil Lords that resided in London, but most young gentleman who joined a ship were personally invited to do so by the captain. Officially, the Admiralty was not aware of their existence until they appeared as candidates for the lieutenants' exam. A Royal Naval College was founded at Portsmouth in 1729, but only a small minority of future officers (including two of Jane Austen's brothers) entered the profession that way, often because they lacked a patron who could get them aboard a ship. Although the Admiralty tried to exert centralized control over the crucial point of entry to the profession, patronage of young gentlemen was a privilege that captains guarded jealously.

When Michael Seymour went to sea, his name was entered on the *Merlin*'s books, not in a central registry onshore. To say that ships were important to the Royal Navy is to state the obvious, but the ship as an organizational unit shaped the personal, small-scale quality of naval life—including vicissitudes such as injury and its consequences. A captain's "followers," both ratings and officers, literally followed him from ship to ship or found places under his friends through his personal recommendation. They looked to him to protect what they saw as their rights and to advance their ambitions.[59] In many ways, officers belonged to particular ships as much as they belonged to the navy as a whole. A commission was granted for a specific post on a specific ship. A commissioned sea officer's career was a sequence of individual commissions broken up by short or long periods on half-pay, depending on which position became vacant on which ship at a particular time. The practice of half-pay itself was a compromise between the tradition of thinking of commissions as belonging to actual ships and the need for a standing body of professional officers. Half-pay was based on the rate of an officer's last commission.

Boys such as Michael Seymour who started out on a ship were regarded as much better off than students at the Royal Naval College because they experienced work and life at sea—and because they had a chance to earn the goodwill of a captain. As both a successful fighting captain and the son of a powerful family, Captain the Hon. James Luttrell was well placed to exert patronage. He was the younger son of Simon Luttrell, the Earl of Carhampton. Captain Luttrell's sister Anne had made a runaway marriage with George III's younger brother, making herself the Duchess of Cumberland, and Captain Luttrell the king's brother-in-law. Captain Luttrell, his father, and his brothers all served in Parliament. Captain Luttrell held the seat of Stockbridge and in 1775 rose in Parliament to oppose the war with the American colonies.[60] He criticized the British campaign as "unjust, rash and savage."[61] Luttrell became a captain by the age of thirty because he was a talented officer, and because his family had political interest to use on his behalf. He moderated his attacks on Lord North's government, for example, in exchange for promotion.[62] How Seymour's family secured him a place in Luttrell's ship is not known, but both families were Anglo-Irish. Seymour's father was the rector of Abington and the chancellor of Emly in the county of Limerick; his grandfather had been mayor and sheriff of Limerick.[63] Luttrell's family had been great landowners in Ireland ever since the time of King John, who granted them the land known as Luttrellstown sometime around 1210.

Being placed under a captain with interest such as Luttrell's was a promising start for boy from a family with no significant political interest, and the first years of Seymour's career suggest he made good use of it. Naval historians have traced the workings of patronage within the navy by tracking paired assignments of junior and senior officers from one ship to another.[64] Records of the first years of Seymour's life at sea support the idea that he won, as his memoir states, a "permanent place in his captain's esteem and friendship."[65] When Luttrell moved to the *Portland* in March 1781, Seymour moved with him. Luttrell again took Seymour along when he became captain of the *Mediator* 44 in April 1782. On December 12, 1782, Seymour had the good fortune to take part in a battle: Luttrell's *Mediator*, a single ship of 44 guns, attacked a convoy of five armed French frigates bringing supplies to the American rebels. Luttrell captured two of them and forced the others to flee. Ten of the French were killed and 17 wounded, while Luttrell's ship suffered no casualties of any sort. With only 190 men, he carried home 340 prisoners and two prize ships.[66] Thomas Luny and Dominic Serres painted the battle, and George III wrote to the First Lord of the Admiralty that "the skill as well as bravery shown by Captain

Luttrell... deserve much approbation."⁶⁷ Luttrell was given command of a larger ship, the *Ganges* 74, in April 1783, and again took Seymour with him.

Although Seymour won Luttrell's interest, some things were beyond the control of even the eighteenth-century patronage network. One of the most important was disease. In 1784 Luttrell showed symptoms of tuberculosis and gave up his ship, taking up the less taxing position of surveyor general of the ordnance. He procured Seymour a berth on another ship, but Seymour himself was then invalided home from the West Indies. The West Indies station was the most hazardous of them all: tropical fevers killed far more seamen and officers than did battles. When Seymour recovered, after five years of exemplary services as a midshipman that included a brilliant action against the enemy, he had to start up the machinery of patronage once more to regain even a midshipman's berth in a ship. Seymour's biography states that he "had no one to turn to but his kind friend and patron Captain Luttrell."⁶⁸ Luttrell wrote to Seymour on November 30, 1785, "I can do nothing for you until Captain Berkeley gets a ship," and then in April that "Captain Berkeley is to have the Pegase, and will soon have his commission: therefore you had better come over as soon as convenient."⁶⁹

In arranging for Seymour to serve under Berkeley, the fatally ill Luttrell was securing for Seymour not just another captain, but another of Nelson's "Honorables" as his patron. The Hon. George Cranfield Berkeley was the younger son of the Earl of Berkeley and married Emily Charlotte, a sister of the Duke of Richmond. Both William Pitt, the prime minister, and Charles Fox, Pitt's great rival, were his cousins. Within the navy, Berkeley's relatives included Rear Admiral Augustus Keppel, another earl's second son who had been at sea since the age of ten. Berkeley was warmhearted, quick-tempered, and politically reactionary: he supported slavery and the game laws. He called for an inquiry into the Poor Laws, publicly stating that in his neighborhood "the poor were arrogant, and the overseers flagrantly indolent."⁷⁰ Favoring progress in medicine although not in the rights of man, Berkeley was the lifelong friend of William Jenner, chairing the parliamentary committee that rewarded Jenner for his discovery of the smallpox vaccination. His concern with improving the health of seamen was public and longstanding. He was an efficient administrator as well as a successful fighting captain. Appointed commander-in-chief on the coast of Portugal in 1808, Berkeley was responsible for all naval support to the Anglo-Portuguese army during the Peninsular Wars, a post in which he "rendered Britain his most important services."[71]

Berkeley's expected commission for the *Pegase* fell through, and Seymour served under different captains, but these posts were makeshifts until he could join his new patron. When Captain Berkeley was at last given a commission as captain of the *Magnificent* in June 1787, Seymour joined his ship. Seymour stayed in contact with Luttrell, whose last letter to him, written when Seymour was stationed with the Channel fleet, was preserved among his papers until his death. The letter is short and matter-of-fact but manages to cover three subjects of abiding interest to Napoleonic-era Royal Navy officers: health, friendship, and the weather:

> [July 1788]
>
> Dear Seymour,–I am much obliged to you for your enquiries after my health. I have been unwell, but am recovered. I am glad to hear Captain Berkeley was kind to you. I suppose you are tired of your cruise, as most of the time it rained and blew hard, if I may judge by the climate in England.— Yours, very sincerely,
>
> J. Luttrell

Half a year later, in December 1788, James Luttrell died of tuberculosis. Seymour kept his letters to the end of his own life and left to the son who followed him in the navy "a gold Neptune red cornelian seal, given me by my very dear lamented patron and friend, the Hon. James Luttrell, when I was a boy with him in the *Mediator*."[72]

At Luttrell's death, Berkeley declared himself Seymour's patron. Now a twenty-year-old midshipman impatient for promotion, Seymour was Luttrell's "legacy" to his friend. In a letter of December 27, 1788, Berkeley promised that he "had not forgot the legacy my dear, departed friend had left me: I mean by this yourself, who, I trust, will ever look up to me as willing, although perhaps not so able to patronize you as himself." In fact, Berkeley implies that Luttrell's death moved Seymour out of a kind of patronage limbo created by his extended ill-health. Before the "calamity" of Luttrell's death, Michael Seymour had been on loan to Luttrell's intimate friend. Now he belonged to Berkeley: "Before this calamity, which has befallen us, I rather looked upon you as lent to me, and I believe I so expressed myself upon a former occasion; at present I hope I may look upon you as my own, as I think your behavior will entitle me to say, that he would never have patronized you or recommended you to me, had he not thought it perfect."[73] In exchange for continued perfection, Seymour could count on the good will of his new patron.

The step from midshipman to lieutenant was a crucial one: unlike midshipmen, lieutenants were commissioned officers. In the worst of times, they qualified for half-pay while they waited on shore; in the best of times, they had the chance to distinguish themselves in battle and were only a step away from the temporary rank of commander, and then the secure rank of post-captain with its prospect of a secure ladder to further promotion. Because officers were commissioned to serve in a particular ship, a lieutenant's commission was not granted until a suitable vacancy occurred in an appropriate ship. Moving from a "passed" lieutenant to a commissioned lieutenant required friends. No formal system existed by which "passed" lieutenants were ranked by the Admiralty, and there were more lieutenants than there were openings.

At James Luttrell's death, Michael Seymour hoped to secure a lieutenant's commission through the interest of Luttrell's sister Anne, the Duchess of Cumberland. Berkeley discouraged him from pursuing this avenue immediately but promised to do so himself at the "right and proper" moment.[74] Two years later, in November 1790, at the age of twenty-two, Seymour at last received a lieutenant's commission. He wrote jubilantly to his father that he "had health and vigour, and loved his profession."[75] Hopeful of rising further, he declared himself financially independent and urged his father to add his former allowance to the marriage portion of his sister, "then engaged to be married to a gentleman with small fortune."[76] Seymour was commissioned at an auspicious moment. Lieutenants who were commissioned in 1790 had the best possible prospects of promotion, as the early stages of their careers coincided with war with France. Although Michael Seymour received his lieutenant's commission in this fortunate year, his luck may not have been immediately clear to him. In October 1791, the *Magnificent* was paid off, and Seymour spent the next year and a half on a lieutenant's half-pay, living with his family back in Ireland, his career stalled yet again. Berkeley, however, remembered his promise to act "in the light of that friend you have lost."[77] In 1793, Berkeley was made captain of the *Marlborough* and offered a place to Seymour, a place that, Seymour's memoir states, was "promptly and joyfully accepted."[78]

As a lieutenant in the *Marlborough,* Seymour at last won his chance to be considered for hero promotion. In 1794, the *Marlborough* played a distinguished part in the battle known thereafter to the Royal Navy as the Glorious First of June. This was the largest fleet action between Great Britain and the First French Republic fought in the Atlantic Ocean, approximately four hundred nautical miles west of the French island of Ushant. The British hoped to block a much-needed convoy of grain traveling from the United States to France, and even more importantly, they hoped to destroy the French Atlantic fleet. In battles between opposing fleets, the ships of each nation normally sailed past each other in two stately parallel lines, exchanging broadside fire at long range. In this engagement, the British commander, Lord Howe, changed tactics, accepting greater risk in order to inflict greater damage to the French ships. He ordered his ships to turn and break through the French line, each British ship directly attacking French ships. He counted on the superior seamanship and discipline of his captains and their crews to carry out this unusual and complex maneuver. His plan was imperfectly executed by a number of his captains but succeeded in destroying seven of the French ships and damaging the others so severely that they were forced to return to port. The French got their grain, but the British established a blockade that had more long-range significance for the war. Injury and loss of life were great on both sides, although the French suffered the most. The official tally of casualties for the British was 287 killed and 811 wounded; historians today put the final number of British casualties at approximately 1,200. French losses can be estimated only more roughly. N. A. M. Rodger puts the number at 4,200 casualties and 3,300 captured.[79]

The *Marlborough* executed Howe's maneuver perfectly: it broke through the French line only minutes after the first British ship to do so, Captain Gambier's *Defense.* "At a dreadful loss of life," the *Marlborough* dismasted and captured two French ships. It then faced a third, the *Montagne,* of 120 guns, which "came down under her stern, and poured a raking broadside of round, grape, and langrage into the *Marlborough,* which caused a serious destruction."[80] "Round" was solid cast-iron cannonballs, weighing up to forty-two pounds each, intended to break through a ship's hull or masts;

"grapeshot" was a collection of metal slugs or small balls packed tightly into a canvas bag, which then resembled a cluster of grapes. Langrage was a canister filled with scrap metal or metal bars. Grapeshot and langrage were primarily intended to kill and to injure men, although they also damaged the sails and rigging. In the battle, 137 of the *Marlborough's* men were killed or wounded, one of the highest casualty counts of any British ship at that battle.[81] Seymour received shot in his left arm: "While Lieutenant Seymour was rushing up the hatchway with his men [to fight off French boarders], a shot shattered his left arm, and entirely disabled him."[82] The shot struck Seymour's arm between his elbow and his wrist. A few minutes later, Berkeley was wounded in the leg and head by langrage, partially exposing his skull. Berkeley was carried below, and his first lieutenant, John Monkton, took command.[83]

The damage to Seymour's arm and to his general health was made worse by the medical care that he received. He requested immediate amputation, but this request was denied: "His own immediate impression was, from the manner in which it was broken, that he must lose his arm, and he desired that it might be at once taken off; but the surgeon determined, if possible, to save it." Infection spread dangerously. To contain it, the arm was amputated above the elbow joint, rather than below it: "The consequence of this [delay] was much severe pain, which had nearly cost the sufferer his life; for mortification commenced, upon which the arm was instantly amputated, some way above the elbow, instead of below it, as might have been done in the first instance."[84]

Recovering on his ship two days after the action, Berkeley wrote a letter to Seymour's father. Like Admiral Stopford writing about his nephew, Berkeley frames Seymour's loss in terms of professional honor. The opening of Berkeley's letter concentrates on three key facts: Michael Seymour was alive, his behavior deserved commendation, and the *Marlborough* won its fight:

Marlborough at Sea, June 3, 1794

My dear Sir,–By desire of your son Michael, my brave and respectable lieutenant, I write a hasty line to inform you of our glorious victory over the French fleet. The claim of distinction which has been bestowed on the ship I command, I must entirely, after God, attribute to the zeal and fidelity of my officers, amongst whom your son stand conspicuous. He is very well, and I hope will continue so.⁸⁵

Berkeley then breaks the news of Seymour's injury: "He had the misfortune of being wounded a few minutes before his captain, and his arm is so badly broken, that I fear it must suffer amputation." Berkeley is quick to offer consolation: "But as it is his left arm, and likely to do well under the skill of those who attend him, I hope you will think it an honorable mark instead of a misfortune." Telling a young man's family to be grateful that he has lost his left arm, not his right, may or may not be helpful. More pertinent to Seymour's future was Berkeley's claim that the loss was an "honorable mark" of victory, not a misfortune that would disable him from continued active service.

Injury and infection required Seymour to return to England to recuperate. A friend noted in July 1794 that "'Michael Seymour arrived in London *a melancholy object.*'"⁸⁶ He regarded Seymour as an object of pity—a man whose body had been marked by terrible misfortune rather than by honor. However melancholy Seymour may have looked or felt during the summer and autumn of 1794, however, he was also busy lobbying for promotion. His memoir summarizes this campaign. In addition to his generally sterling record, Seymour believed he had two advantages. He had lost an arm, and he had a patron:

> He was aware that his name stood well at the Admiralty, his captains having uniformly given him the most satisfactory certificates of conduct; he knew too that Captain Berkeley had given a good report of his conduct in the late glorious action, and besides this he had lost a limb, by which his health was for the time seriously impaired. All this gave him a solid case to lay before the Admiralty. . . . He knew that Captain Berkeley had considerable influence: he had a seat in Parliament; he had high connections, and he had a high place on the Navy List. Lieutenant Seymour therefore judged, that if he chose to exert himself in his behalf, he could do so successfully. ⁸⁷

Seymour's memoir implies that this twenty-six–year-old combat veteran took an unsentimental view of life, death, and naval politics: "His first friend and patron had been removed by death; Captain Berkeley, who had succeeded to that title, and had so declared himself, might at any time be removed in a similar manner."[88] It is not clear how many of Seymour's thoughts about the mortality of patrons were communicated to Berkeley. In any case, Berkeley wrote back sympathetically: "I cannot blame your anxiety in putting yourself forward. I can assure you that should I hear for a certainty of any promotion, my wish of serving you will prompt me not to relinquish that title which I have taken up, and which I shall ever hope to merit.—Your's very sincerely, G. B."[89] In May, Berkeley sent Seymour to Gloucester to try to raise a crew for the *Formidable* and told him he had brought up his case for promotion to Lord Spencer, who seemed favorably inclined but offered no hope "that it would take place immediately."[90]

If Seymour had remained on shore, Berkeley's description of amputation creating "an honorable mark" would seem nothing more than a platitude. Eight months after he lost his arm, however, Seymour was no longer a melancholy object. He was once again, officially, the brave and respectable lieutenant of Captain the Hon. George Cranfield Berkeley. In February 1795, Berkeley became captain of the *Formidable,* and Seymour was commissioned to that ship. Seymour went again to sea in the *Formidable* still a lieutenant, but Spencer succeeded Lord Chatham as First Lord of the Admiralty in 1794, and in 1796 he gave Seymour his first command: the *Spitfire,* a 16-gun sloop-of-war cruising in the Channel, in which Seymour captured eight prizes. He was made a post-captain on August 11, 1800. Having "made Post," Seymour was at last certain of continued promotion. He served as acting captain of a number of ships and then became captain of the *Amethyst* 43, in which ship he won his greatest engagements. On November 10, 1808, he captured *La Thetis,* a French frigate of superior force. On April 6, 1809, he captured *La Niemen,* another French ship of superior force. Seymour commanded several other ships, won further battles, and was awarded the title of baronet in 1809, then Knight Commander of the Bath in 1816. His pension for the loss of his arm was raised to 300 *l.*[91] He married Jane Hawker, the daughter of another naval captain, and they had a large family. He served as commissioner of Portsmouth Dockyard from 1829 to 1832 and became Rear Admiral of the Blue on June 27, 1832. Seymour died on July 9, 1834, an admiral with a knighthood and a record of highly distinguished service. Born without family interest in the navy, this Irish vicar's son had two sons who became naval officers, founding a naval dynasty.

"So High a Character": Sir James Alexander Gordon

James Alexander Gordon was born October 6, 1782, to a family of Jacobite Highlanders who for generations had been minor gentry in Aberdeenshire, deriving their fortune from the wine and sherry trade in Catholic Spain. His patron was Lady Catherine North, the prime minister's daughter who, for reasons known only to herself, chose to marry Gordon's great-uncle, an obscure but socially ambitious Scottish lawyer who then became Lord Glenbervie.[92] *Letters and Records of Sir Admiral J. A. Gordon, G.C.B., 1782–1869*, a family memoir, notes that Lady Catherine "was a very noble, talented, excellent woman, and Lord Glenbervie's great nephew James owed very much to her constant affection."[93] When James was eleven years old, his great-aunt Catherine began his career at sea. He recalled that at Gordon Hall in 1793, "we heard a coach drive up to the door; we all stared to see who it was, when out came Aunt Peggy [a Gordon relative] . . . she told us she came to take me away, as I was to be sent to sea to fight the French. . . . I was shown a letter . . . saying that Captain Whitshed, a great friend of my aunt [Lady Catherine] had just commissioned the Arrogant, a '74, at Chatham, and would be happy to take with him any young friend of hers."[94] James joined an all-male navy, but it was Great-Aunt Catherine's influence that won him a first-class volunteer's berth in it, and Aunt Peggy's coach that took him to his ship.

Both Lady and Lord Glenbervie took a continuing interest in Gordon's career, whose early stages were shadowed by his vexed history with literacy. *Letters and Records* notes that at eleven years old, James Gordon had not yet learned how to read or write. He left home not only to fight the French, but also to escape his tutor, a Mr. Cruikshank, who once dislocated his jaw while attempting to flog him. As an adult and a father himself, James considered his tutor's violence wrong; as a child, he considered it a secret he had to keep: "Mr. Cruikshank, who always slept in the same room with [my brother and myself], took this opportunity to beg me not to inform my father of his conduct to me. I now know I ought to have made him acquainted with his treatment of us, but I never did." In his first ship, Gordon notes that "I never wrote home, because I could not write, nor do I remember ever receiving a letter from any of my relations."[95] His memoir claims that he was inspired to improve himself when he joined the frigate *Eurydice:* Gordon "was happy to find mids [midshipmen] of my own age on board; they were all fine, smart boys and good sailors. I was soon ashamed of myself, and now began to pay attention to my profession."[96] According to Bryan Perrett in *The Real Hornblower: The Life and Times of Admiral Sir James Gordon* (2014), however, James Gordon's difficulties with literacy persisted through his first three years at sea and were severe enough to nearly end his career. His second captain, Captain Cole, told the fourteen-year-old Gordon that he was unable to recommend him for promotion to the rank of midshipman because he was "semi-literate." Cole granted him leave to discuss with his family the question of whether he had a future in the navy.

It was to the Glenbervies' London house that Gordon went for this family meeting, and the result was Captain Whitshed's agreement to take him back in the *Namur,* still as a first-class volunteer. Gordon apparently made no progress at reading or writing until Whitshed sent him to a friend, Captain Thomas Foley, in the *Goliath.* Foley "took a personal interest" in Gordon and placed him under the instruction of the *Goliath*'s schoolmaster, a Mr. Strachan. "He always behaved so much like a father to us all, that I consider myself to be under great obligations to him," Gordon wrote of Foley.[97] Perrett argues that Gordon's difficulty learning to read and write accounts for a confusion in his service history. Gordon served at Battle of Cape St. Vincent (1797), and the *Oxford Dictionary of National Biography* and other accounts often place him there in Captain Foley's *Goliath,* the ship to which he later moved, rather than Captain Whitshed's *Namur,* the ship to which he returned when his career stalled at the age of fourteen: "It seems that he was understandably sensitive regarding his early lack of literacy, which had . . . resulted in his serving under Whitshed for a second time."[98] The editors of *Letters and Records* seem to have silently corrected any errors in word usage, but James's letters often joke about him having no idea of how to spell words such as "appetite" or elegant French expressions such as "en famille."

With Lord Glenbervie as his patron, James Gordon became first lieutenant in the *Racoon* 18 in 1802, and on March 3, 1804, became the *Racoon*'s captain, in which position he captured a number of prizes. On March 13, 1811, as captain of the *Active* 38, Gordon fought with three other frigates under the command of Captain Hoste, who had started his career as captain's servant to Nelson at the age of twelve. In this battle, off Lissa, outnumbered and outgunned 156 to 284, the squadron of four English ships defeated the French and disrupted their shipping. On November 29, 1811, off Palagruza, Gordon's *Active* captured *La Pomone* 44, in a battle that cost Gordon his leg and cost his first lieutenant, William Bateman Dashwood, his right arm. William James's *Naval History* describes the moment Gordon's injury occurred in the hard-fought battle:

> He was standing on a shot-bag and leaning on the capstan, giving his orders in his usual collected manner, when a 36-pound shot came in through a porthole, grazed the carriage of a carronade, took off a seaman's leg, and struck the captain on the knee joint, carrying all off as if it had been done with a knife, and leaving the leg hanging by the tendons. Although of course, he instantly fell, Captain Gordon did not become insensible, but calmly directed the first lieutenant, Mr. Dashwood to fight the ship; and as he was being carried below, told the second lieutenant, Mr. Hay, who commanded on the main deck, to do his best, should any mischance befall his senior officer. Shortly afterwards Lieutenant Dashwood had his right arm shot away, and Lieutenant Hay, taking the command, fought the Active, although himself wounded, until her opponent's colours came down.[99]

As he recovered, Gordon's friends encouraged him to believe he would continue to advance in his profession as an amputee officer. On December 30, 1811, Captain Rowley wrote to "congratulate you [Gordon] from my soul on your late gallant successes." He saw no reason for Gordon's active service to end: "I feel poignantly that your well and hard fought victories have placed the laurels on your brow with such severe loss; but, I trust in God you will soon recover, and for the sake of my country, I hope you will soon be enabled to aid her with your active service."[100] The more influential Edward Pellew, the commander-in-chief in the Mediterranean, wrote equally hopefully: "It will afford me great pleasure to avail myself of such conspicuous talents and bravery as you have exhibited on all occasions for the good of His Majesty's service."[101] Gordon's immediate commanding officer, Captain Sir William Hoste, was even more to the point: "I hope you are quite recovered, my good fellow.... I hope to see you soon afloat."[102] As he weighed his professional prospects after the loss of a limb, in addition to the inescapable example of Nelson himself, Gordon might have thought of his former lieutenant in *Mercury*, Watkin Owen Pell, who had lost a leg as a midshipman and continued to serve with distinction. We consider Pell's story below. Gordon might also have thought about another former shipmate: Thomas Gill. In 1803, when the *Racoon* master's mate lost his left arm in battle, Gordon was the *Racoon*'s first lieutenant.[103] Gill also had continued to serve at sea, fighting further battles and winning further promotion.

The first letter Gordon's father wrote to him after Palagruza does not mention the loss of his leg at all. Instead, it expands on his pride in James's victory and his gratitude for God's protection, "a sort of inexpressible feeling of pride, joy, and thankfulness . . . in the exultation of my heart I feel a most lively sense of gratitude to Almighty God, who has vouchsafed to shield you in the hour of danger." This father makes no complaints about divine justice. Instead, he prays daily that "the same protecting Arm may go forth with you and shield you in every danger," and eagerly requests "a more particular account" of the battle.[104] Although Gordon's father writes only of his exaltation, his son's suffering was vivid to him. His daughter Frances writes that once he absorbed the news, he nearly passed out. Months later, he still could not speak of the subject without shaking and turning pale: "You would have been quite frightened had you seen the state he was in when James's own letter came. . . . He did not seem so much affected at first, but *then* his agitation had very nearly overcome him, and *now,* even, when he is speaking on the subject, he trembles all over, and gets as pale as ashes."[105] Frances's solution was simple: she forbade any mention of James's loss: "I have prohibited his ever speaking about it at all." This solution left unresolved, of course, the question of how he would react when he met his son again in the flesh: "I am very much afraid for the effects of the first interview that my father has with him," Frances admits.[106]

The Glenbervies were concerned about Gordon's future—not because

Gordon had lost a leg, but because he had engaged himself to marry. He had fallen in love with Lydia Ward six years earlier but had not spoken to her of marriage because both families believed the young people were too poor to marry. As chapter 3 reports, Gordon promised himself after the battle that if he survived his wounds, he would speak. Within weeks of his return to London, walking on crutches, James Gordon spoke, and Lydia Ward answered. Without consulting his patrons, Gordon engaged himself to marry an attorney's daughter who had a cultivated mind, strength of character, elegant manners, and no fortune. He then notified Lord Glenbervie of what he had done. Having risen through his own marriage to Lady Catherine, Glenbervie was no friend to Gordon's imprudent love match. He replied frostily, pointing out that "it would have been to be wished that the one or the other had been more gifted by fortune," and that this was an important moment in Gordon's career. His victories and injury had established his professional character, a fact on which he should capitalize through continued "assiduous applications for immediate employment" rather than being distracted by passionate love for a wife:

Pheasantry, 28 July, 1812

... [Do not] suffer your union with her to interrupt your professional career, in which you have gained so much reputation, and established so high a character, to say nothing of your duty to endeavor by pursuing that career to enable yourself to acquire such an addition to your worldly substance as may secure comfort and independence to you both, and to those who may come after you.

Glenbervie's letter closes more warmly than it began. He refers matter-of-factly to his use of his influence to benefit Gordon's family and assures him of his continued interest: "Tell your father I endeavoured to give his application to the War Office a lift with Lord Palmerston the other day. Let us hear more of your plans, as soon as they are settled, and believe me ever, my dearest nephew, your most affectionate Uncle, Glenbervie."[107]

In July 1812, Gordon was awarded a pension of 300 *l* a year; he married Lydia Ward that August and by September was busy fitting out his next ship, *Seahorse,* then escorting convoys to the West Indies and blockading France. He led a brilliantly successful raid on Alexandria on the Potomac in

August 1814, then took part in the failed bombardment of Fort McHenry, moving the observer Francis Scott Key to compose the poem that eventually became the lyrics of the United States national anthem, "The Star Spangled Banner." Gordon provided vital logistical support during the Battle of New Orleans in 1815 and wound up his career as the last governor of the navy's iconic Royal Hospital at Greenwich. In 1869, he died an admiral, at the age of eighty-six, saying his wife's name.

"An Additional Claim": Sir Watkin Owen Pell

Like Edward Stopford, Watkin Owen Pell combined gallantry in battle with strong interest at home. Unlike Gordon and Seymour, Pell was landed and well connected, with an income separate from his profession. Two senses of "family" combined to promote his career: a fatherly captain known to lobby tirelessly for his junior officers, and aristocratic friends. Pell's family is also a good example of how widely, even in the era of abolition of the slave trade and the emancipation of enslaved people in the British West Indies, "'slave property' had been subsumed into the wider world of landed-property norms" in England itself.[108] As Nick Draper reminds us, slave-owning "lost some of its taint as it was transformed into financial assets, into annuities, marriage settlements and legacies."[109] Pell was born in 1788, the younger son of Samuel Pell of Sywell Hall, Northamptonshire, and Mary Owen, the daughter of Owen Owen Esq., of Llaneyher, Denbighshire. His Northamptonshire neighbors, the Spencers, were his family's patrons. Pell's older brother, Owen Pell, first went to Antigua in 1813 to superintend Royal Navy contracts for victualling ships on the West Indian station. He married an Antiguan heiress and owned substantial estates in Antigua, which he eventually sold for 50,000*l*.[110]

Watkin Owen Pell joined the *Loire* in 1799 under the auspices of Earl Spencer himself, who was then First Lord of the Admiralty and would later stand godfather to his son, Watkin Owen Spencer Pell. Pell's diary notes that his older brother Owen, with whom his relationship was often testy, used a memento of this day as a peace offering half a century later: "March 1, 1852. Received from Owen an old letter of my Mother's to Robert Jones dated the 8th of May, 1799 asking him to take places in Exeter Mail for her and me as she was going to take me to join the Loire Frigate, Captain James Newman Newman."[111]

Pell lost his left leg at the age of twelve on February 6, 1800, when Captain Newman Newman captured the French frigate *Pallas*. In a fragment of an unpublished biography, Pell's daughter draws on his remarks about his early life to describe this event. Pell said that getting carried to the surgeon was worse than getting hit by the shell:

> When the fight was at its height, part of a shell struck my Father's left leg, and threw him from one side of the ship to the other. One of the crew picked him up and carried him head first down to the cockpit where the surgeon put on "the screw" to prevent him bleeding to death, while he attended to the others. When the 38 gun frigate was taken, the surgeon returned to attend to him and decided to take off his leg. . . . [My] Father . . . always said the greatest pain he ever suffered was when the seaman ran down the companion ladder and his wounded leg hit against each step (8).

Pell's daughter describes the twelve-year-old Pell as having an "active, bright, cheery and enthusiastic nature": in the cockpit with the other wounded, Pell asked why the sailors were cheering on deck, and "when told the French frigate was taken, he cried out, 'Hip, hip, hooray' (8)."[112] After two years on shore, Pell returned to active duty. He served on various ships under several captains as a midshipman. On November 11, 1806, Pell achieved a key step in his career: he was made lieutenant into the *Mercury* 28, an event he also commemorated in his diary near the end of his long life: "November 11, 1861. Made Lieutenant & appointed 1806 to the Mercury Capt. G Pelley."

In 1808, while stationed in the Mediterranean, the *Mercury* passed into the command of a new captain: James Alexander Gordon. Pell served as his first lieutenant. On April 4, 1808, Captain Gordon gave Pell command of a boarding party. Pell successfully employed small boats to capture and destroy a Spanish convoy under heavy fire, in cooperation with another ship and its boats. Half a year later, in November 1808, the *Mercury* received a new captain, one who would busy himself with helping First Lieutenant Pell make the crucial step to the rank of captain: the Honorable Henry Duncan, the son of Admiral Viscount Duncan. Duncan was an active captain known for paying great attention to two things: the precision of his gun crews and the careers of his junior officers. "Captain Duncan's great anxiety has always been, to push on the officers serving under his command; and in this respect he has been particularly successful," notes John Marshall.[113] Pell again commanded the *Mercury*'s boats on April 1, 1809, to board a Venetian gunboat, *La Leda*, under "a very heavy fire of Great Guns and Musketry."[114] His daughter describes how Pell endangered his body to protect his men and capture *La Leda*:

> My Father was in command of the Mercury boats on an expedition to cut out 2 Franco Italian gunboats moored close to heavy batteries. . . . They boarded and took the gunboat La Leda, 24 pounder and six large swivels. . . . As the boats were nearing La Leda, my Father in the first boat saw a man raise a large blunderbuss. Realizing that the contents scattered down the length of boats would disable many of his men, he sprang on board and cut the man down, but the contents (7 balls) went through his right hand and arm. The ship was taken and only 3 seamen slightly wounded and one killed.[115]

"I do not think more bravery was ever displayed than by the officers, seamen, and marines employed on this occasion," Duncan wrote in his official letter to William Hoste. He stressed the fact that Pell had been severely injured while doing his duty—both in 1800 and 1809: "They were commanded and led on in the most gallant manner by the 1st Lieutenant, Watkin Owen Pell, who received two severe wounds in boarding, and has before lost a leg in the service of his Country."[116] Duncan's cover letter to the Lords Commissioners of the Admiralty summarizes Pell's case, remarking that his account of the battle "will tend to substantiate the claims of this excellent and meritorious officer and who Lord Collingwod informed me he had recommended very strongly to their Lordships."[117]

When Duncan wrote to Pell's father from the *Mercury* on April 13, 1809, about Pell's "very gallant attack," he stressed the value of Pell's old and new injuries in furthering his career. Duncan wrote that "having before lost a Leg in the service will give him [Pell] an additional claim" for promotion: "When the situation of Rovigno is considered I do not think any exploit ever surpassed this nor can too much credit be given to those employed &

more particularly to him who commanded. His having before lost a Leg in the service will give him an additional claim & I have no doubt the Lords of the Admiralty will take into consideration his sufferings & reward his Gallant services. I am happy to say that he is quite out danger, nor is there any chance of his losing his arm."[118] Duncan's assurance that "the Lords of the Admiralty will take into consideration his sufferings & reward his Gallant services" is a variation on a familiar formulation, one that gave weight to injury incurred in the line of duty. The phrase "services and sufferings" often summed up an officer's claim to a pension in official documents. For example, on December 18, 1781, "Captain Alexander Graeme, late commander of his Majesty's ship Preston, in consideration of his services and sufferings, who, in the action on the 5th August 1781, between the squadron under Vice-Admiral Hyde Parker, and the Dutch fleet, had the misfortune to lose his right arm above the elbow," was awarded, in addition to his half-pay, 300 l.[119]

Hearing of the capture of *La Leda*, Pell's old captain, James Alexander Gordon, wrote from his ship *Active* on August 10, 1809, to Pell's older brother, Owen Pell, congratulating him on Pell's victory and on his improved prospects of promotion:

> Sir,
>
> The time your Brother was Lieutenant of the Mercury under my command, I had every reason to be pleased with this conduct . . . While off Cadiz I had several oportunity's of witnessing his Gallant conduct and tho he had the misfortune of having lost a leg he was always the first who wished to go on Service in the Boats.
>
> I am very sorry he has again felt the sting of War, but trust from the recommendation of Capt Duncan & the severe misfortune he had experienced in the Service of his Country their Lordships will promote him and be assured I shall feel happy when I hear it, as I know how much he deserves it.[120]

Gordon focuses on the likelihood that Pell's gallantry, including the "severe misfortune he had experienced in the Service of his Country" as a twelve-year-old, would soon win him the promotion that he deserved.

Pressing Pell's case in person in London, Duncan hit a setback. He wrote Pell a hasty note to express disappointment and sympathy:

> Monday 1/2 past 4 o'clock
>
> My Dear *Pell*,
>
> I have just on my return to town received your note & an answer from the Admiralty not returning the memorial but saying that as it was asking a Pension it ought to be made to the [?King in committee?] I was afraid that mentioning "no pension had been received" they would take that hole to creep out of & had at one time intended to alter it from what I said ... he well know the intention of the memorial & I fear you must not trust too much to him—indeed they seem a most extraordinary set altogether. I shall be at the Admiralty tomorrow about nine o'clock to give my [?case?]—for Lord Mulgrave & I shall for convenience take breakfast at the [?S.s. Gd..?] Coffee House where if you will meet me I will be most happy to advise you all in my Power
>
> Excuse haste & believe me
Very Sincerely Yours
H Duncan[121]

Duncan's warmth comes through in this invitation to commiserate and strategize over a coffee house breakfast. Also clear is his annoyance at the way the Admiralty treated his reference to Pell's injuries. It seems that by mentioning Pell had received no pension for the injury to his arm, Duncan intended to stress how much Pell deserved promotion. Instead, in Duncan's memorable phrase, the Admiralty "took that hole to creep out of" acknowledging his injury helped establish a moral claim to promotion. A "most extraordinary set altogether," Duncan concludes.

Pell was promoted to the rank of commander on March 29, 1810, almost one year after the capture of *La Leda*. John Marshall gives credit for this to "Captain Duncan, through whose generous and unremitting exertions in his behalf, he obtained the rank of Commander."[122] The two remained lifelong friends. Pell gave a first-class volunteer whom Duncan recommended a place in his ship, and he also tried to transport home a large live turtle from the West Indies as a present for Duncan in 1834 (the turtle died).[123] After Duncan's death in 1835, Pell continued to honor his memory. On October 27, 1840, Captain J. Culp Robertson wrote to Pell to ask him to be kind to a young gentleman who had joined his ship, the *Howe*. Robertson explained that the boy was the presumptive heir to the Earl of Elphinstone and related to Rear-Admiral Sir Thomas Troubridge, a hero of the Napoleonic Wars and former First Naval Lord—and he was also related to Henry Duncan. Robertson assumed that the chance to show his regard for his old captain would mean more to Pell than the boy's other connections: "He is also connected by marriage, to your old captain the Honorable Henry Duncan—This will [count?] more favourable in your attention to the young Gentleman than all I have said [on account?] of his family."[124]

Pell had friends in addition to Duncan who pushed for his advancement, including the rector of his family estate, Sywell Hall. The Rev. Henry Cockayne Cust, the rector of Cockayne Hatley, Bedfordshire, and Sywell from 1806 until his death in 1861, was the second son of the first Lord Brownlow of Belton. Cust wrote to Pell on April 10, 1811 as his "very sincere Friend" to assure him that he would ask his brother, the second Lord Brownlow, to bring Pell's case for promotion to the rank of post-captain to the attention of the First Lord of the Admiralty, the Right Honorable Charles Phillip Yorke. He advised Pell to hope that Yorke's impartiality and "accurate knowledge . . . of your services and severe wounds" would distinguish Pell's application from the multitude of others. He also invited Pell to send a statement of his services and wounds, "as I hope to make it useful in another quarter."[125] In the end, because of the multitude of applications mentioned, Brownlow decided to wait to push Pell's case until 1811.[126] Although Yorke gave "assurances that at the proper opportunity your name shall meet with due consideration & that he will make a particular memorandum of the interest my Brother had expressed in your behalf," Yorke was succeeded as first lord by Lord Melville without doing anything for Pell.[127]

In October 1813, in command of the *Thunder*, a bomb vessel (a small ship armed primarily with mortars to project shells in a high ballistic arc, designed for bombarding fixed positions on land), Pell captured the *Neptune*, a French privateer of superior force. Cust wrote to express his "hearty congratulations on an occurance so well-timed for *jogging their Lordships' memories*."[128] Pell was advanced to post rank on November 1, 1813. His continuing friendly relationship with the Brownlow family, and the ongoing cycle of patronage, are seen in later requests that as a captain in the West Indies, Pell befriend a midshipman who was a protégé of Lady Brownlow, Ronald MacDonald.[129]

As captain of the *Forte* 40, Pell served as senior officer on the Jamaica station in the West Indies from 1833 to 1837, the momentous period between the Slavery Abolition Act of 1833 and termination of the apprenticeship system that kept "emancipated" slaves in a state of servitude. Pell's diary represents the slave owners of Antigua, a group that included his own family, as morally superior to the slave owners of other islands. On February 3, 1833, he writes, "the Slave population of this Island [Antigua] are far superior in intelligence to any other and so well prepared that the Proprietors have determined to emancipate them in August," rather than keep them as indentured apprentices longer. On February 4, Pell points out that "Antigua has more resident proprietors than any other Island and more pains have been taken to educate their slaves, the schools are well attended, the Bishop consecrated a new Chapel in St. Phillips." Visiting Nevis on February 6, he claims that the "Island appeared to be far behind Antigua in the civilization of the Slave population, their appearance and treatment indicate neglect on the part of the proprietors, they grow very little provisions and their slaves look badly fed." On February 7, he finds "the slave population ... neglected and badly fed. A bad feeling between Masters and Slaves."[130] The contrast he drew between Antigua and Nevis suggests Pell's pipe dream: if his class fulfilled the duties of paternalism, a good feeling could exist between masters and slaves, or between the planter class and the nominally free labor force on whose continued exploitation their way of life depended.[131] Pell was knighted in 1837. Through the influence of the Spencers, he was appointed superintendent of Deptford victuling in 1841, and from 1846 to 1863, a commissioner of Greenwich Hospital, serving with his old captain, James Alexander Gordon as governor, a fruitful working relationship examined in chapter 3. In 1847, at the age of sixty, Pell married Sarah Dorothea Owen, who was thirty-four. They had several children, and he died December 19, 1869, at the rank of admiral.

"A Left-Handed Admiral": Horatio Nelson

There is only one Horatio Nelson. The scale of his victories, the power of his charisma, and the circumstances of his death set him apart from other distinguished officers of his time. Nevertheless, Nelson's career resembles those of this study's other officers in one important regard: rather than rendering Nelson unfit for further active service, the loss of his arm helped to make him, in the words of Lord Minto, "the fittest man in the world for the command." In Nelson's case, however, the connection between injury and professional opportunity worked a bit differently. Michael Seymour, James Gordon, and Watkin Owen Pell presented their loss of a limb in a military victory as a mark of honor. In contrast, the loss of Nelson's right arm served to confer honor on a military defeat, the failed amphibious attack on Santa Cruz de Tenerife on July 24, 1797. Nelson and the Admiralty used his personal gallantry, certified by his empty right sleeve, to deflect blame for larger failures of judgment at Tenerife. This loss helped him win the Mediterranean command, charged with the key mission of finding and destroying Napoleon's fleet.

On February 14, 1797, Nelson played an important role in Admiral Sir John Jervis's victory over a larger Spanish fleet near Cape St. Vincent, Portugal. Nelson was knighted and Jervis was made Earl St. Vincent. Five months later, however, St. Vincent and Nelson were less happy. Their attempt to blockade the Spanish port of Cadiz was frustrated, their ships' crews were bored, and the Great Mutinies of 1797 at Spithead and the Nore had alerted every naval officer to the combustible potential of seamen's grievances in the absence of combat's distracting urgency. In this context, Nelson made a hastily conceived proposal to capture the town of Santa Cruz on the island of Tenerife, and St. Vincent agreed to it. They badly underestimated the Spanish defenses. The attack was a debacle that left 30 Spanish dead and 40 wounded, 250 British dead and 128 wounded, and Spain still unquestionably in possession of Tenerife.

Although he was then a rear admiral and had already lost the sight in his right eye invading Corsica in 1794, Nelson still led from the front. His habit of fighting in cutting-out expeditions, amphibious invasions, and boarding parties was unusual for an officer of his rank. During an engagement at sea, quarterdeck officers were visible targets in their own ships, a hazard explored in chapter 2. Officers above the rank of lieutenant usually stayed on the quarterdeck rather than seeking out additional perils by taking part in boat actions. But when Nelson attempted a stealth amphibious attack during the night of July 24, 1797, he personally commanded a division of boats. Nelson's right arm was shattered above the elbow by shot as soon as the boat he commanded landed. His stepson, Lieutenant Josiah Nisbet, saved him from bleeding to death with an improvised tourniquet, and his boat carried him back to his ship, where Nelson endured the amputation of his right arm stoically. After surgery, Nelson continued for months to experience intense pain from a damaged nerve.

The first thing Nelson had to do after losing his right arm and the battle itself was to write his official letter about the disaster. Although they followed a simple format, official letters could set off complicated ripples of responses. In his official letter to St. Vincent, Nelson focused his description of the battle on gallantry under fire, gallantry certified by injury and loss. "I am under the painful necessity of acquainting you that we have not been able to succeed in our attack," he wrote, "yet it is my duty to state, that I believe more daring intrepidity never was shewn than by the Captains, Officers, and men you did me the honour to place under my command." His only reference to his own loss is dramatic in its very understatement. In the usual list of killed and wounded, organized by ship and rank, under "Officers Wounded," the first entry is "Rear-Admiral Nelson, his right arm shot off."[132] Newspapers focused not just on the loss of Nelson's right hand, but on the fact that he had written the official letter with his left. Switching the pen from his lost right hand to his left became another example of gallantry, similar to the popular but mythical anecdote that at Tenerife Nelson switched hands rather than dropping the sword he had inherited from his uncle Captain Suckling.

Like Seymour, Gordon, and Pell after losing a limb, Nelson wrote to his friends about his professional prospects. Unlike these other amputee officers, he did not have the happy task of deciding how to best make use of a victory. Defeat was bad for an officer's career. Nelson feared the loss of his arm in this bungled attack would end his active service. Fortunately, Nelson's friends could not have been better placed. His first letter to St. Vincent after Tenerife expressed professional despair, but also continued attention to the career of his stepson and continued belief in the goodwill of the commander-in-chief of the Mediterranean Fleet:

Theseus, July 27, 1797, to Admiral Sir John Jervis:

I am become a burthen to my friends, and useless to my Country; but by my letter wrote the 24th, you will perceive my anxiety for the promotion of my son-in-law [sic], Josiah Nisbet. When I leave your command I become dead to the world; I go hence, and am no more seen. If from poor Brown's loss, you think it proper to oblige me, I rest confident you will do it; the Boy is under obligations to me, but he repaid me in by bringing me from the Mole of Santa Cruz.

I hope you will be able to give me a frigate, to convey the remains of my carcass to England. God bless you, my dear Sir, and believe me, your most obliged and faithful,

> Horatio Nelson.
>
> You will excuse my scrawl,
> considering it is my first attempt.[133]

Nelson continued to write of both his despair and his faithfulness to St. Vincent in August:

To Admiral Sir John Jervis, Theseus, 16 August, 1797:

A left-handed Admiral will never again be considered as useful, therefore the sooner I get to a very humble cottage the better, and make room for a better man to serve the State; but whatever be my lot, believe me, with the most sincere affection, ever your faithful,

> Horatio Nelson.[134]

However sincere Nelson's bleak fantasy of life on shore in a cottage may have been, he also held fast to St. Vincent's friendship: "I am so confident of your affection, that I feel the pleasure you will receive will be equal, whether my letter is wrote by my right hand or my left."[135] St. Vincent privately pledged he remained Nelson's friend:

Ville de Paris, 16 August 1797

I grieve for the loss of your arm, and for the fate of poor Bowen and Gibson, with the other brave men who fell so gallantly. . . . Give my love to Mrs. Freemantle. I will salute her and bow to your stump to-morrow morning, if you will give me leave. Yours most truly and affectionately, St. Vincent.[136]

A true and affectionate friend in St. Vincent's position was a friend indeed. In addition, Nelson corresponded with his old lieutenant, the future

William IV, who answered "as an old friend" on September 7, 1797: "As an old friend, I cannot but lament the very severe loss you have sustained in losing your right arm. I hope your health is good . . . the re-establishment of a constitution in which I am doubly interested, both as a friend, and as one who is anxious to see the country have restored to her a brave and excellent Officer. Excuse my anxiety, as if proceeds from friendship and admiration of your public character."[137] Nelson was given good reason to believe that recovering his general health would be enough to establish he was physically fit to command.

Nelson was particularly fit to command under these circumstances in other ways as well. Because of the loss of his arm, his body became proof of valor even in defeat. As Colin White points out, when those who gave the orders were being called to account for the debacle at Tenerife, they found it useful to point to a rear admiral who had himself been seriously wounded in the attack. St. Vincent stressed British gallantry under fire, certified by deaths and injuries, Nelson's loss prominent among them. In his August 16, 1797, dispatch to the Admiralty, St. Vincent claims that "although the enterprise has not succeeded, His Majesty's arms have acquired a very great deal of lustre. Nothing from my pen can add to the eulogy the Rear-Admiral gives of the gallantry of the officers and men employed under him." St. Vincent frames the injuries and the deaths caused by this battle as grievous but honorable: "I have greatly to lament the heavy loss the country has sustained in the severe wound of Rear-Admiral Nelson, and the death of Captain Richard Bowen, Lieutenant Gibson, and the other brave officers and men who fell in this vigorous and persevering assault." Although Tenerife was a defeat, St. Vincent's dispatch publicly asserted support for the future careers of the officers who had met with such loss in it: "I hope that both of them [Nelson and Captain Freemantle, also considered likely at that time to lose an arm to wounds] will live to render important services to their King and Country."

White claims that as patriotic discourse and regard for the navy's dead and injured at Tenerife softened criticism of the defeat, Nelson's loss of a limb in that failed attack took on the same connotations of victory that were carried by other officers' injuries in successful actions. By keeping him in London, Nelson's slow and painful recovery contributed to his eventual promotion to the Mediterranean command by foregrounding his empty right sleeve. During those months, his "presence in the capital kept him in the public eye and, most importantly, in the minds of influential men such as Lord Spencer; while his empty sleeve was a visible reminder of his extraordinary deeds."[138] On April 24, 1798, Lord Minto pronounced Nelson, who had lost the sight in one eye, his right arm, and the battle of Tenerife, to be "the fittest man in the world for the command" of the Mediterranean. In a controversial move, St. Vincent ignored the claims of more senior officers and gave Nelson the crucial mission of hunting Napoleon's fleet in the Mediterranean.[139]

Chapter 2 looks more deeply at how amputation worked in terms of visual codes that represented ideals of military masculinity, both in the Royal Navy and in society more generally in the period. This chapter has concentrated on examining how influential friends of amputee officers presented their loss of a limb in battle as a mark of honor rather than a disability. Of course there is only one Horatio Nelson. But although he stands alone as an icon, Nelson also stands with Seymour, Gordon, and Pell as a dedicated navy officer whose loss of a limb in battle promoted rather than ended a distinguished career.

2

Looking Like a Hero

How do we know a hero when we see one? When a physically impaired officer with a record of distinguished service faces the public, in person or in a portrait or monumental statue, this question takes on new urgency. All officers on duty are public figures, performing to an audience. To be in command, they must be seen to be in command. As James Alexander Gordon remarked, "I always put on my quarter-deck face when I put my [uniform] coat on."[1] For amputee officers serving on active duty, such performance became more complex. As they got on with their careers and their lives after losing a limb, these officers entered a state of heightened visibility both inside and outside the navy itself. In their professional and social lives, Horatio Nelson, Michael Seymour, James Gordon, and Watkin Owen Pell became experts at anticipating and shaping other people's reactions to their bodies. As the previous chapter demonstrates, these amputee officers had the service records to support the claim that their visible impairment was a "mark of honor." They also asserted this claim through their self-presentation within the navy and to a wider public. Their skill at managing audiences appears in the choices they made about what prosthetic devices to use; what personal assistance to accept; what to wear; where and how to walk, climb, ride, or dance—and in how they chose to appear in portraits. Their images reveal the complexity of the visual codes through which a body could indicate that a person was a national military hero in eighteenth- and early nineteenth-century England.

"I Have Been Disappointed in the King"

What exactly was an officer like James Alexander Gordon putting on when he donned his uniform coat and "quarter-deck face"? Gordon's uniform was a fairly recent innovation, one that reflected the importance of social status to naval officers' identity. Up to the mid-eighteenth century, neither naval ratings nor officers had a regulation uniform. On land and at sea, they wore clothes that reflected their status rather than any specific military rank: officers dressed like gentlemen, and ratings dressed like sailors. Officers themselves demanded a uniform as a point of pride, asserting they "wished to be recognized as being in the service of the Crown." They also wanted more visibly to mark the differences among officers' ranks.[2] In response, Lord Anson issued uniform regulations for officers in 1748, while custom alone governed what ratings wore until 1857. In *Dressed to Kill: British Naval Uniform, Masculinity, and Contemporary Fashion, 1748–1857*, Amy Miller argues that naval officers' uniforms reveal not only their wearers' devotion to their military duty, but also the assumptions about masculinity they lived within. A uniform was designed to make its wearer look like a certain kind of man: "Male dress, particularly something so heavily regulated as uniform, illustrates the shifting standards of masculinity and provides insight into what British society in the eighteenth and nineteenth centuries valued as the 'ideal man.'"[3] Less gaudy than an army officer's uniform, but still following the unmistakable lines of court dress, the naval uniform invested its wearer with a particular kind of elite masculinity. It announced he was both a gentleman and a professional.

Introduced at a time when the Royal Navy had a problematic image as a "crude and coarse" profession, it is no accident that the 1748 naval uniform was modeled on court dress. Its cut proclaimed the wearer's status as a gentleman. We must not let the glitter of Napoleonic-era officers' coats, heavy with gold lace and braid, distract us from what stood beneath them: tight knee breeches and silk stockings. Beverly Lemire reminds us that "Social standing ... emphatically governed what would be worn on the nether regions of the male body: breeches and hose, or trousers. This was the great divide, a defining mark of status." Long trousers marked their wearer as a commoner, "someone to command, low in status."[4] In contrast, "the legs of elite men symbolized power and sexuality, highlighted in close fitting white hose and skin-tight breeches, showcased in countless paintings of the era, legs upholding the social order."[5] A captain displayed his power through the skin-tight breeches on his legs as well as through the gold lace on his sleeve.

Even after the regulations issued in 1748, officers' uniforms displayed some degree of personal style. The Admiralty issued no actual uniforms: referring to regulation descriptions, officers supplied both a dress and "undress," or work-day version of the uniform, at their own expense, leaving a good deal up to the individual officer's taste, budget, and tailor. Amy Miller notes that a great many memoranda were issued criticizing deviations the Admiralty had spotted.[6] Junior officers were most often reproached for wearing uniforms that flirted with "dandy fashion—with its effeminate, flamboyant, and in some cases, homosexual associations."[7] To some extent, however, such associations were built into the very lines of the 1748 uniform itself, with its wasp-waist coat and closely fitted knee breeches. Captain Whiffle, the notorious dandy of Tobias Smollett's *The Adventures of Roderick Random* (1748), reflects Smollett's experience as a naval surgeon in the *Chichester* in the early 1740s. Predating the regulation uniform, Whiffle's outrageous outfit presents the body-conscious splendor of knee breeches and cutaway coat in its purest form: "His coat, consisting of a pink-coloured silk lined with white, by the elegance of the cut retired backwards, as it were, to discover a white satin waistcoat embroidered with gold, unbuttoned at the upper part to display a brooch set with garnets that glittered in the breast of his shirt, which was of the finest cambric edged with right Mechlin. The knees of his crimson velvet breeches scarcely descended so low as to meet his silk stockings."[8] In Whiffle's getup, gentlemanly elegance clearly collapses into decadent luxury. In practice, the proper degree of elegance could be hard to attain. Not only the coat on an officer's back but even the stockings on his feet mattered. Officers made a point of dressing for battle in entirely clean uniforms. Nelson found he had no clean white silk stockings as he dressed for the amphibious assault on Tenerife and wore instead stockings decorated with vertical blue stripes. When the attack was a disaster, this note of jaunty informality was seen as emblematic of the lack of proper care taken with preparations.[9]

Horatio Nelson and his fellow amputee officers were proud of their visibility as officers. They knew they were being looked at, and they thought about that fact. When James Gordon mentioned putting on his "quarterdeck face" together with his uniform coat, he referred to a kind of performance that was second nature for a successful captain. The quarterdeck was the raised deck running from the stern to roughly the middle of the ship. Only officers had the privilege of walking it. The quarterdeck was a vantage point from which a captain could see his ship, his fleet, his enemy, and—unless smoke blanketed everything—the course of his battles. It was also a stage on which he could be seen. Walking his quarterdeck, a captain demonstrated his command of whatever situation he encountered. In addition to making his authority visible, this elevated position made his body vulnerable. Although the most common cause of death in the navy was disease, the point of cruising the oceans was to find and fight the enemy. When a battle occurred, the quarterdeck was the most dangerous place to be: "It was not unusual in action for casualties to be virtually confined to the quarter deck, or much the heaviest there."[10] As one of the few men in uniform exposed to snipers as well as cannon, a captain was "perhaps the most vulnerable person on ship."[11] Terry Coleman describes the opportunities the quarterdeck created for enemy snipers at Trafalgar: "Most of the *Victory*'s men were on the gundecks below, and with them the lieutenants and midshipmen; on the quarterdeck of each ship, exposed by that position and made conspicuous by their uniforms, stood the captain, first lieutenant, and master. On the quarterdeck of the flagship there was also Nelson, most conspicuous of all, and unmissable."[12] Unlike lieutenants, busy with their gun crews, quarterdeck officers often had little to do during an engagement other than stand upright and conspicuously embody indifference to violent death. Nelson's fearlessness is now so familiar that it is worth noting that more ordinary humans sometimes found they were not eager to position themselves in plain view on an elevated platform and be shot at for hours at a time. "The navy had a real problem with cowardice," Rodger reminds us.[13] Some captains in fact hung back from battle, rendering useless all the skills, courage, and guns in their ship.

In addition to the visibility shared by everyone of their rank, on land and sea, amputee officers also stood out because of their visible impairment. Amputation had a wide range of possible social meanings in the long eighteenth century. Brother officers and civilians could see the loss of a limb quite differently. Within the navy and among naval friends and family, the loss of an arm or a leg in a successful action called attention to amputee officers' status as victors. As chapter 1 argues, such officers could even point to their loss to help make their case for the privilege of further active employment at sea. Nevertheless, citing the example of Nelson, Catriona Kennedy draws attention to the "ambivalent connotations" that such injury could have in both military and civilian circles. Physical injury to a military man threatened the "bodily attributes that underpinned his masculine identity," even as it testified to his courage.[14]

Social status was often what coded a missing limb as either a mark of honor or a mark of ignominy. Low status was linked to amputation's most powerful negative associations: criminality and beggary. A popular image of the military amputee during the Napoleonic era was the disabled, discharged, and impoverished soldier or sailor. These men were most often represented as helpless rather than heroic, an image of physical vulnerability compounded by economic dependence. Prints of caricatures and jestbooks promoted the image of the pathetic or comic military amputee. In his *Cruelty and Laughter,* for example, Simon Dickie claims that amputee military veterans who had a legitimate and potentially guilt-inducing claim to aid from their country were particularly likely to be seen as comical by the public. He paraphrases the point of view suggested by eighteenth-century jestbook humor about such men: "These men had been wounded in the service of their country, but there were just too many of them—and, anyway, who could possibly look at someone with a wooden leg and not burst out laughing?"[15] David Turner makes a similar argument about how the "disabled poor" figured into eighteenth-century trials at the Old Bailey. As defendants, impoverished or working-class people living with impairments were on trial in two senses. They had to contend with the specific charges alleged against them and with more general "stereotypes of the disabled poor as fraudulent and criminal that were fed by satires of 'Wooden leg'd imposters', 'Lymping Dissemblers' and 'sham Disabl'd' beggars."[16] In this context, "lameness," which was broadly understood to refer to restrictions on mobility and diminished strength in hands or arms, carried negative connotations. Turner claims it was associated with "victimhood, weakness, vulnerability, suffering, aggression, deception and fraud," all qualities that "might be drawn upon in various ways to construct culturally resonant stories."[17]

In contrast to this description of working-class impairment on trial, consider another public scene, one at the other end of the social spectrum: a royal levee held three years after the Battle of Waterloo. Linda Colley points to the importance of wounds to the new legitimacy that aristocratic British men had found as a "service elite" through the long wars with France. An American ambassador visited the royal levee at the court of St James in 1818 and, in Colley's words, "saw the upper echelons of the British elite as they themselves liked to be seen." And what affected the ambassador most powerfully and most positively was the sight of how military service had damaged the bodies of elite men. Some of them "had received scars on the deck with Nelson":

> There were from forty to fifty generals; perhaps as many admirals. . . . 'That's General Walker', I was told, 'pierced with bayonets, leading on the assault at Badajos'. And he, close by, tall but limping? 'Colonel Ponsonby, he was left for dead at Waterloo. . . . 'Then came one of like port, but deprived of a leg, slowly moving, and the whisper went, 'That's Lord Anglesea'. A fourth had been wounded at Seringapatam; a fifth at Talavera; some had suffered in Egypt; some in America. There were those who had received scars on the deck with Nelson; others who carried them from the days of Howe. One, yes one, had fought at Saratoga. . . . It was so that my inquiries were answered. All had 'done their duty', this was the favourite praise bestowed.[18]

In this tableau, decades of British military history, from General Howe's defeat by the Americans to Wellington's victory over Napoleon, parade in the laudable form of a "service elite." Whether the fruit of victory or of loss, honor is certified by physical impairment, creating a "splendid tableau of immaculately cut uniforms, glorious wounds, heroic mutilations."[19] Lord Anglesey, known to the history of prosthetics as the user of an innovative and expensive articulated prosthesis, lost his leg to a cannonball at the triumphant finale of the Battle of Waterloo, while Saratoga was a resounding loss for the British. Both this victory and this defeat are occasions for gentlemen to prove their honor by choosing to put themselves in danger, the lasting damage to their bodies the lasting proof of their civic virtue.

Among Dickie's disquieting examples of jestbook humor are anecdotes of well-to-do "bucks" with normative bodies knocking down or otherwise assaulting beggars or working-class people with physical impairments in city streets, to the amusement of onlookers. A story about James Gordon and the streets of London reverses both the social status of those involved in such an encounter and the way it played out. Bryan Perrett relates that after attending William IV's coronation in Westminster Abbey, while walking back to his hotel in full dress uniform, Gordon was "jostled by a crowd of roughs" at the corner of an alley. One shouted, "By God, that's Jem Gordon! He flogged me in the *Active*—now, mates, let's settle him!" Unruffled, Gordon put his back against the wall and replied, "I don't remember you, but if I flogged you in the *Active*, you damned rascal, you deserved it!" Most of the crowd took Gordon's side, cheering him and holding back the others while Gordon went on his way.[20] In a different version of the story told by his daughter Adelaide Gordon, it was some of Gordon's old seamen who sided with him.[21] In both versions, Gordon's status as a gentleman and a military hero, as well as his own unflappability, meant the story played out quite differently than the jestbook accounts of attacks on one-legged street peddlers that Dickie recounts.

Each amputee officer dealt with his visibility in his own way, and the same man could react quite differently in different contexts. Today, some amputees see the process of actively managing other people's perceptions as significant addition to the everyday work of life after their loss of a limb. The perceptions of others may seem a slight or intangible factor, but they can affect something as concrete as the shape of a prosthetic limb. Steven Kurzman, a cultural anthropologist and below-the-knee amputee, describes how one bilateral above-elbow amputee chose two quite different prosthetic arms, one for each of the two main tasks he faced in getting on with his life. These two tasks were manipulating the physical world and manipulating other people's expectations: "James, a bilateral above-elbow amputee, described the different values of his terminal devices to me while getting an adjustment to one of his prosthetic arms. On one side he uses a hook which is more useful than a hand for some tasks, such as picking up grocery bags. He uses a hand on the other side because people expect to see a hand; it causes less surprise and awkwardness when he meets people and shakes hands."²² Although they moved in a very different social world than the one Kurzman studies, the amputee officers in this study were also experts at managing other people's responses to their bodies, responses that included surprise and awkwardness. For example, Elizabeth Freemantle, the wife of one of Nelson's favorite captains, described in her diary the shock she felt on seeing Nelson for the first time after Tenerife: "Nelson came on board at twelve o'clock, he is quite stout but I find it looks shocking to be without one arm."²³

In addition to defusing this kind of initial awkwardness, amputee officers' daily life could become a deliberate refutation of deeply held assumptions about the disabling consequences of physical difference. Kurzman describes this process as "performing able-bodiedness," a performative act designed to assert a measure of control over how others interpret one's body.²⁴ Rosemarie Garland-Thomson similarly distinguishes between "body management" and "social management," identifying the latter as the set of strategies that a person with a visible physical difference develops to navigate social life.²⁵ If amputees' physical impairment remains visible while they accomplish a task, then performing able-bodiedness calls attention to the importance of skills and adaptability rather than a normative body.²⁶ Lennard Davis highlights the idea that disability is in the eye of the beholder, describing it as a "disruption of the observer's sensory field."²⁷ Kurzman offers the opposite point of view: "At one point, my amputation was the obvious disruption to my body and subjectivity, but the physical pain and most of the emotional pain is past me, and I now consider the attitudes of many nondisabled people far more disruptive and actively disabling."²⁸ Horatio Nelson generally countered difficulties created by such attitudes with zest and skill. Significantly, Coleman identifies Nelson's loss at Tenerife as the start of his transformation from charismatic officer to national icon: "The leading of an attack he ought never to have led, and the loss of his right arm, gave him the character and the form which were ever after instantly recognizable. His empty right sleeve was pinned across his coat, his figure was frail, his hair was white, and he was Nelson."²⁹ Nelson pointed out that his ability to command men and ships, not the strength or wholeness of his body, was the source of his military success. When, on first seeing him after Tenerife, King George remarked, "You have lost your right arm," Nelson answered, "But not my right hand," and presented to the king Captain Berry, then his second-in-command.[30] Nelson deliberately incorporated his physical impairments into his role as England's champion. We have already noted his response when challenged by a ship in the Baltic in 1801: "I am Lord Nelson. See, here's my fin!" he declared, throwing back his boat cloak to reveal his vestigial limb.[31] This story circulated. It delighted Captain William Hoste, who had started his career at twelve years old as one of Nelson's midshipmen. The common metaphor of navy officers as family was very close to the truth about their relationship. On August 11, 1798, after the Battle of the Nile, Nelson recommended Hoste to Lady Hamilton as if he were a son: "I also beg your notice of Captain Hoste, who to the gentlest manners joins the most undaunted courage. He was brought up by me, and I love him dearly."[32] Hoste wrote to his biological father about Nelson's dramatic response in the Baltic. He could imagine the scene perfectly: "I think I see him making use of the expression, 'I am Lord Nelson; look at my fin', and exposing his stump to the Danish officer."[33]

Under different circumstances, however, even Nelson could be infuriated by the fact that his body had become a public spectacle. During the invasion scare of 1801, Nelson was given command of the British forces positioned in the Channel. He was stationed there in part to reassure the public, and the public made a point of rowing out to get a look at him. Nelson's biographer Colin White notes that Nelson disliked these crowds disrupting his work. He also disliked their way of seeing his impairment, counting no fewer than fifty boats rowing out "to have a look at the one-armed man."[34] Nelson protested against being "shewn about like a *beast*": "The Countess M., Lady this that and t'other came alongside a Mr Lubbok with them to desire they might come in. I sent word I was so busy that no person could be admitted as my time was employed in the Kings service.... I will not be shewn about like a *beast*."[35] At this moment, the coat on Nelson's back did not protect his pride as an officer or his time, as his service to the king included putting up with being "shewn about." Invited to an official dinner by the mayor of Sandwich, on August 11, 1801, Nelson expressed similar aversion: "I put them off for the moment, but they would not be let off. Therefore, this business, dreadful to me, stands over, and

I shall be attacked again when I get to the Downs.... Oh! How I hate to be stared at."[36]

After losing his left arm, Michael Seymour claimed that human adaptability was part of God's plan: "He used to say that God had given us many of our members in duplicate in order that if we lost one it might suffice to retain the other."[37] Seymour adapted successfully not only to the physical challenges of living as an amputee in a wooden ship in a time of war, but also to the way that formerly mundane aspects of his life now attracted attention as a public performance. When boarding or disembarking from his ship, Seymour climbed up and down its side grasping a rope with his one arm, to the repeated surprise of onlookers: "It was a matter of surprise to many how he was able to climb a ship's side in all weathers, without assistance, by the use of a single rope, and more than once sailors looking on have remarked that he must some day come to an untimely end."[38] Going up a ship's side in foul weather using a single rope was a routine part of the working life of an officer at sea, but for Seymour, it was also a performance of his fitness for his position. As onlookers commented on such feats "more than once," he must have been aware that he had an audience. Confident in his outstanding seamanship, Seymour also took on the work of a pilot as well as a captain: "Captain Seymour was very much on deck, his glass constantly in his hand observing every vessel in sight,... he would frequently take the charge out of the pilot's hands, place his French book of charts (which had been taken in a privateer) upon the capstan, and steer the ship himself, often taking her inside the rocks, and running her close in to the shore, even in the night, with all the skill of the most experienced pilot." He inspired confidence in those he commanded: "Never had offices and men more confidence in a captain than had the Spitfire's in Captain Seymour."[39] In trying to understand how Seymour worked successfully in a wooden ship in the Age of Sail with only one arm, we should remember that he had spent much of his life at sea since the age of twelve. Although he was no longer "able-bodied" in our sense of having a normative body, he still possessed the skills that defined a Napoleonic-era Able-Bodied Seaman.

Like Seymour, Watkin Owen Pell and James Alexander Gordon seized opportunities to display the fact that although each had lost a leg in battle, they remained "able-bodied" in this sense. After Pell's death, his wife fondly recalled the time that he, as a midshipman, raced another amputee officer up the ship's rigging: "Sir Watkin had a race up the rigging with Captain Paton R.N. who had lost an arm. Sir Watkin won the Race."[40] The loser in this anecdote is Captain Sir John Strutt Peyton, who was connected to the navy on both sides of his family. According to John Marshall, Peyton went to sea "under the auspices of the illustrious Nelson . . . his noble patron." He was on Nelson's ship at two of his most important battles: The Nile (1798) and Copenhagen (1801). Peyton's commission as lieutenant is dated October 7, 1805. In July 1807 he was sent to destroy a vessel run ashore near Ortona and was wounded in the right elbow by a musket bullet. A family memoir notes that "the bullet struck a button at his wrist, and ran up his arm splintering the bone. The button saved his life, by diverting the bullet from his heart."[41] His right arm was amputated. Like Pell, Peyton took a conspicuous part in the public activities proper to a country gentleman: "He became marvelously expert in the use of his left hand, and was a good shot, and a good whip. His combined knife and fork is still preserved."[42] Peyton was promoted to commander in December 1807 and commanded ships till near the end of the war, repeatedly engaging with the enemies' batteries and privateers. He married, in 1814, a daughter of Lieutenant Woodyear, R.N., of St. Christopher's Island and had three daughters and two sons.

In addition to racing Peyton up the rigging, Midshipman Pell also displayed his athleticism as a swimmer. "My own dear Sir Watkin," writes his wife, "told me that he swam from the Beach just under Haslar Hospital to his ship the 'Acosta,' Capt. Jas. Athol Wood, lying at Spithead, a distance of about two miles!" Pell "always swam on his side." James Hay, the midshipman with whom Pell attempted this long-distance swim, "became exhausted, & was picked up by the Boat which had taken them from this Ship to the Beach."[43] Another anecdote from Pell's wife suggests that his early shipmates could be even more theatrical: "On Board the "Acosta" . . . the Quarter Master, Cunningham, very good naturedly, used to desire Sir Watkin to go to *bed*, instead of keeping watch, saying *he* would take care the Captain was none the wiser, to insure which, he used to walk on deck with a *broom stick* in his hand, & imitate Sir Watkin walking with his wooden leg!"[44] A quartermaster held a position of responsibility, but he was a warrant officer, not a commissioned one. This story of Cunningham thumping on deck with a broom stick in a very minor plot against their captain suggests a good working relationship between such officers and the young Pell.

Like Pell, who was his former first lieutenant, fellow above-the-knee amputee, and lifelong friend, Gordon apparently enjoyed showing off his physical prowess. His memoir notes that he was "so active, that before he lost his leg he has been known to leap in and out of six empty water hogsheads [water barrels] standing in a line on the deck."[45] Gordon was a remarkably effective officer, in part, perhaps, because he was not touchy about his official dignity. He stopped leaping in and out of barrels after he lost his leg, but he did not stop competing with his own crew in feats of strength and skill: "As a seaman, he excelled in all the nautical exercises; he could heave the lead further than any man in his crew, and was first-rate with the helm."[46] Like Pell, and with similar good humor, Gordon relates that members of a ship's crew recognized him by his prosthetic leg. He writes to his wife on December 4, 1815, that this familiarity increased his hopes of success in the difficult business of manning a new ship: "I hope some of the *Saintsbury*'s men will enter for me, as I know a good number of them. When I went up the side just now I heard the fellows say, 'I am sure it is Captain Gordon, for I know him by his leg!'"[47]

Like Pell, James Gordon could not stay out of the rigging. One point of tension in James and Lydia's letters, most of which were written during his most active years at sea, is his insistence on continuing to perform the functions of an able-bodied seaman. At first James offered Lydia hope that he would refrain from particularly risky actions, remarking that he had "taken so much care of myself" by staying meekly on the deck of his ship. Lydia worried that a gyrating deck was itself a dangerous place for a man with one leg. James replied that he was not the one who was "tumbling about": "I am sure my dear little girl will be happy to hear that I have taken so much care of myself that I have not had a fall yet, nor have I felt inclined to go *to the masthead*. Having so many landsmen on board, poor fellows, they have been tumbling about very much, but I am glad to say without any accident."[48] Like all the other able-bodied seamen on board, James pities the poor landsmen who have no skill at managing a ship's motions. When he does in fact fall, he admits it to Lydia—but, typically, notes that the accident had no lasting ill-effects: "March 10, 1813. I had had a fall just before I went on shore, and when I came back on board, my head ached very much.

The pain went away in the night."[49] Similarly, even when he falls again, he is pleased to note that his balance is better than that of a mere passenger. He cheerfully attributes the fall to his own carelessness and notes that he was unhurt: "I forgot to mention that we were obliged to lash [a passenger] to the table; after she had gone, I was sitting carelessly—the ship gave a roll, and down I went, but I did not hurt myself. We are tumbling about a good deal, with a heavy swell."[50] While Watkin Owen Pell climbed the ropes simply to show all observers how quickly he could do so, James wrote primly to his wife that such frivolous risk-taking would be "improper": "I am much obliged to [a friend] for her kind enquiries for your poor sailor. I perceive, my dear girl, you think I shall run improper risks in going to the masthead. Nothing but necessity will ever oblige me to go above the deck." In February 1813, James admitted that he has in fact climbed above the deck of his ship—and has done so "with great ease": "A strange sail is just seen from the masthead, which we must chase. I went up to the main-top yesterday for the first time and find I can go up so far with great ease, but I do not think I shall ever go up higher."[51] Lydia was left with this half-promise to go no higher than the maintop.

Nelson was the canniest of all amputee naval officers at managing his public image and did so on the grandest scale. Historians have recognized that he created and tended his image with remarkable skill and energy, seeing his public appearances as boosting morale in time of war. He also enjoyed his fame and used it to help win further opportunities to serve with danger and glory. For example, like Michael Seymour, after losing an arm, Nelson demonstrated he was still able-bodied enough to deserve the right to command his ship through the way he boarded it—but unlike Seymour, Nelson did so while drenched in blood. After his right arm was shattered in the failed amphibious attack at Tenerife, sailors rowed Nelson back to his ship with a silk cravat tied around the arm as a makeshift tourniquet, all that kept him from bleeding to death. When they reached his ship, Nelson insisted on boarding it by climbing up the rope on the side, one-handed, instead of being hauled aboard in a chair like a landsman. Coleman, a biographer devoted to debunking the constellation of marvelous stories that have collected around Nelson, admits the truth of this one: "To climb the side of a 74 is no small effort for a fit man with all his limbs, but all witnesses say Nelson did it."[52] As John Sugden notes, this extraordinary detail appeared in newspaper accounts that praised Nelson's gallantry in Tenerif even as they condemned the injudicious planning behind the attack.[53] Once on deck, Nelson continued to display his authority. William Hoste's account reveals the effect he had on his most immediate audience: the men under his command. At the time of disaster at Tenerife, Hoste was a sixteen-year-old midshipman. He wrote his father an anguished account of Nelson's return to his ship. His grief, however, is touched with awe at how Nelson's astonishing "spirit" defined the moment: "Adml. Nelson returned on board being dreadfully wounded in his right arm with a grape shot. I leave you to judge of my situation Sir when I found that the man whom I may say has been a second father to me [sic]. To see his right arm dangling by his side while with his left he jumped up the ship's side and with a spirit that astonished everyone told the Surgeon to get his instruments ready, for that he knew he must lose his arm and that the sooner it was off the better."[54] Nelson's stepson, Lieutenant Josiah Nisbet, who had saved his life with the tourniquet, recalled another key moment: "On getting on the quarter-deck the officers as usual saluted him by taking off their hats, which compliment Nelson returned with his left hand as if nothing had happened."[55] A man with a compound fracture and severed artery "dangling by his side" decorously exchanged salutes with his officers "as if nothing had happened": this scene reads today as surreal. In the moment, however, the spectacular display of command served its purpose. Nelson had lost control of the situation: he had lost the battle at Tenerife. In boarding his ship with this theatrical display of authority, however, he was seen to be still in command. "At no other time in his life," notes Roger Knight, did Nelson "demonstrate more vividly his mental and physical toughness."[56]

Amputee officers could make a point of demonstrating their competence on land as well as at sea. Years later, living on shore, no longer fighting for promotion but rather happily married to a lady who was "devoted to her garden," Michael Seymour still startled onlookers, including his own younger children. As a country gentleman, Seymour climbed ladders instead of ship's rigging and wielded sharp-edged tools one-handed: "Lady Seymour was devoted to her garden . . . she could point to some favourite plants which had accompanied her, like her children, in her change of homes. . . . [Her husband] also might be sometimes seen on the top of a ladder pruning a vine or restraining a vigorous creeper, to the wonder of his younger children, who marveled that one who had but a single arm could attempt such work, and indeed, he surprised many by what that one hand and arm could accomplish."[57] Seymour took charge of what his audience saw. He was still performing in 1831, when he and his wife received Princess Victoria: "The Princess, then in her thirteenth year, showed a lively sympathy with Sir Michael in the loss of his arm, and expressed great surprise and interest in his ability to do so much with the remaining one."[58] Seymour also made it his habit to deal cards one-handed: "He was fond of a game of whist, and always took his own turn at dealing, and in other ways he showed a remarkable independence." Seymour contradicted viewers' assumptions about able-bodiedness by showing, over and over across nearly half a century, "what that one hand and arm could accomplish."[59]

When he was on shore, Watkin Owen Pell engaged in gentlemanly pursuits even more energetically than did Michael Seymour. Born the second son of a landed family, Pell carried on like the country gentleman he was even after losing his leg. His diaries from 1824 to 1860 make for exhausting reading. Pell had an enormous appetite for club dinners and committee meetings. He competed with his brother to get the harvest in, carrying barley and wheat and building haystacks. Most of all, he appears to have loved chasing foxes across the countryside and shooting birds. He fell from his horses repeatedly. Sometimes he hurt his shin; sometimes he broke his prosthetic leg. After a few days or weeks laid up on the sofa, Pell always returned to ride again. His entry for May 16, 1843, reads laconically: "Fine weather. Shooting rooks at Bush, broke my wooden leg, shot 80 rooks."[60] Earlier, on December 18, 1827, he was equally deadpan: "Thrown from my horse in Ecton. Hounds in Gib Close., found at Mauseley Wood, good sport."[61] A sequence of entries from February 1833 tells a similar story of riding, falling, nursing a black eye and broken nose, and riding to hounds again a week later. On March 9, 1836, the forty-eight-year-old Pell was stationed in the West Indies, perched on top of a coach rather than seated safely inside, and clearly pleased with the imposing figure he cut: "Left at 3 a.m. A party of robbers rode up to the coach. I was on the Box, they looked at me and passed on."[62] Like Pell, James Gordon seems to have liked perching on top of a coach better than sitting safely within it: "I daresay you will be angry with me, my dearest Lydia," Gordon wrote to his wife on January 13, 1819, "for coming all the way to Town on the outside of the coach."⁶³

Although James Gordon was able-bodied enough to fight and win battles, when he was presented to the king, the honor had an unusual—and highly visible—disabling consequence. A man with an unbending prosthetic leg cannot kneel. This fact did not prevent James from carrying out his military duty with distinction, but it caused a breakdown in ceremony when he was expected to publicly enact his allegiance to his sovereign by kneeling and kissing his hand. On August 23, 1821, James describes the awkward moment to Lydia: "H.M. asked me how I was, and when I told Lord Graves I could not bend my knee, the King took *me* by the *hand*, and held his and mine so high that I kissed it as I stood."⁶⁴ James was pleased that the king saved the moment by finding a way to confer honor as well as receive it. By mid-September, however, he felt that something was lacking on the king's part. Overall, James Gordon's letters bear out his daughters' description of his "singular unselfishness, and . . . wonderful humility."⁶⁵ He is neither too unselfish nor too humble, however, to feel that King George owed him the chance to explain the meaning of his impairment: "Sept. 13, 1821. I have been disappointed in the King never having asked me where, and how, I was wounded." Losing a limb in battle was a mark of honor. Having spent his life fighting in the king's name, with the king's coat on his back, James Gordon expected the king to ask him to tell the details of his story that his body and his uniform alone could not fully reveal. Face to face with this most important audience, Gordon was disappointed. Typically, in the next sentence, he moves on from his disappointment to hope for pleasure for Lydia: "I hope we shall have some fine weather at Portsmouth, to give you some sailing."⁶⁶

Gordon's letters to his wife give us a running commentary on how he felt about being stared at by other people, people who were full of comments and questions about the fact that he had a wooden "peg-leg" instead of an ordinary left leg. With the support of his very large and very loyal circle of family and friends, and his own outgoing temperament, James Gordon seems to have tirelessly managed other people's reactions to him as an amputee. His letters are unfailingly resilient and occasionally amused. Chapter 3 discusses James and Lydia's marriage in more depth, but there really is no knowing how much Lydia loved James because of his optimism, or how much James remained cheerful because Lydia loved him. When he wrote to her from the Lord High Admiral's yacht at Woolwich, August 13, 1812, for example, he clearly expected her to enjoy the punchline of his story. The Admiral was shamed into rising early because he refused to lie in bed once an amputee officer was up and about: "[The Lord High Admiral] desired us all to sleep till 8. I, however, got up at half past 6, and I was in hopes I had got out of my bed without his observing me, (he would not allow the door to be shut between the place I slept in and his cabin) but at breakfast Sir Edward Owen said he was astonished to find him up at 7. 'Oh, I saw that one-legged fellow slip out of bed, and I thought it wrong to lie in bed after him!'"[67] Similarly, James wrote to Lydia that in Bath he was known as one of the "only two one-legged men in town," as well as an unusually tall man and a war hero:

Bath March 1, 1822

> My modesty would not let me put my name down on the books, but I am well known already. I heard the Chairman saying we have only two one-legged men in town, the big one Sir James Gordon, and I did not hear the other name.[68]

A few days later, on March 13, 1822, James was charmed at the naivety of a friend's children, who assumed that what he would like most in the world was a brand new prosthetic leg: "We dine at the Lawes' to day (March 13th), and I have got the boys a holiday for which the little ones intend to subscribe to buy me *a new wooden leg!*"[69] When he made his way through crowds in London to appear at court on April 27, 1829, James assured Lydia that he met with nothing but friendly questions about his impairment, questions that he apparently was happy to answer. In fact, all the pleasant banter with total strangers about his loss and his heroism had a useful effect: "In coming through the crowd, my loss of leg, their good-natured remarks and my answers cleared the way for me."[70] In James Gordon's generous reading of this crowd, the people who asked how he lost his leg had a perfectly reasonable question. He embraced the opportunity to help them make sense of what they saw when they looked at him.

Although it is less dramatic than climbing up a ship's side with a single arm, one of Michael Seymour's most interesting performances of able-bodiedness is this one: "He never received any assistance in dressing himself." He even tied his own neckcloth.[71] The question of when to accept help in performing everyday tasks sometimes can be loaded for a person living with a physical impairment. Depending on the circumstances, accepting such help may or may not have the effect of lessening one's authority over other aspects of life. Today, help with routine tasks such as getting dressed can carry associations of childish incapacity, associations that I argue were more contested in Nelson's day. The contrasting choices that amputee officers made in this regard show how variable the relationship between assistance and authority can be. Seymour may have simply preferred to dress himself, or his large family may have stretched his household's resources. A very successful officer, but one with thirteen children and no inherited property, he called himself "a poor miserable rascal of a baronet."[72] He might also have been trying to satisfy some version of what Tobin Siebers sees today as a double standard about assistance and accommodation. Today, people with normative bodies are not expected to constantly exert themselves to the farthest reach of their ability, but "the moment individuals are marked as disabled or diseased, . . . the expectation is that they will maintain the maximum standard of physical performance at every minute."[73]

In any case, Seymour held himself to a higher standard of "independence" in this regard than gentlemen of his time often did. Many eighteenth- and early nineteenth-century gentlemen with two fully functional arms did not tie their own neckcloths or manage all their buttons and laces on their own, any more than did their wives or daughters. A determined gentleman might get his own boots on by hauling on the bootstraps, but a crouching servant would yank them off for him. Such personal assistance did not undermine gentlemen's sense of their independence. Indeed, boots were associated with the "military, with violence and with high status," as is still witnessed by the wealth of boot-related metaphors for dominance and aggression: "to boot," "to get the boot," "to be booted out."[74] Unlike Seymour, other amputee officers seemed comfortable accepting such help. For example, with no apparent sense of embarrassment, a letter from James Gordon to his wife mentions a butler who helped him with his single boot when he visited a friend's house:

March 30, 1818

> When Mr. Brodie's butler was helping me off with my boot, he said: "Captain Gordon, I was with you in the Active." "Were you?" said I. "Where did you do your duty—and what is your name?" "I was a boy—officer's servant, and my name, Joseph Hopner." I did not remember him at all; but, from what he told me, I knew he must have been in the ship. He told me I was upon crutches, was very thin, and looked ill. . . . When I was getting up I remembered him. He was a poor little fellow—a dirty little boy—sent on board by the Marine Society—was flogged almost every morning. . . . He is now quite a buck . . . he is an honest, clever servant.[75]

The point of this anecdote is that Joseph Hopner turned out well. Gordon mentions only in passing the fact that he himself looked so much worse soon after losing his leg, and that he accepted help getting his boot off his remaining foot, as would any two-footed gentleman.

Whatever his personal feelings, Seymour lived through a tumultuous time for buttons and neckties. From 1794 to 1834, the years Seymour lived with one arm, what did it mean to let another person dress or undress you? People had complicated attitudes toward assistance with such simple physical tasks, attitudes that reflected ideals about both age and social status. At the same time that it was a fact of life, such help from a manservant or lady's maid was under attack as a sign of decadent luxury. An eighteenth-century household with any pretense to gentility would have at least one to two very hard-worked, female, live-in servants, and charwomen brought in to help out.[76] No one writing for a middle-class audience could imagine doing without such servants, however devoted they may be to ideas of personal independence. In contrast, a manservant was rarely found outside of an aristocratic household, especially in and around London. But although manservants were quite rare, they dominate the eighteenth-century moral debate over "luxury." Seymour's insistence on dressing himself alone might also reflect his personal commitment to a specific and militantly middle-class ideal of independence. He declared, "I am sure the middle line in life is the happiest, and moderate circumstances as to rank and state, *though I love decency and comfort*."[77] Seymour's memoir describes him as a family man, a version of the ideal of middle-class masculinity set out by John Tosh and Ellen Gill. Such men had professional lives centered in all-male institutions such as the navy, but they placed a high value on the time they spent at home and on their responsibility to actively shape their children's characters. His memoir offers as a "specimen of his solicitude for his children, and the spirit in which he exercised it" an extract from a letter he wrote to a son who was embarking on an Italian trip. Seymour urges him to remember the importance of his future career, and the importance of not causing anyone at home to blush: "Most anxiously must I guard and warn you against the seducing climate of Italy, and the insidious demeanour of its natives, which has ruined many of the fairest prospects, and destroyed their peace and happiness forever. You will, I trust, most cautiously guard yourself and your companions from contagion of immoral influences.... I hope and trust you may never give cause to anyone here to blush at the recollection of your trip to Italy; but you cannot be too guarded."[78] As Tosh writes, this highly domestic version of virtuous masculinity was part of the self-image of the insurgent middle class of the eighteenth and early nineteenth centuries. It may seem surprising that Seymour's idea of the "middle line in life" was expansive enough to include himself even after he won the title of baronet. In terms of parenting ideals, however, he was not wrong.

A central goal of this sort of intensive parenting was launching sons who would inherit no income on the path to personal independence through hard-won professional success. Although more distinguished than most, Seymour was indeed a specifically middle-class kind of father: one who had no estate to leave his sons, but who intended these sons to share the personal and financial independence he had achieved through his profession. He proudly declared that "my boys must work their way."[79] He also invested a good deal of money and care in their education and in otherwise trying to smooth that way for them. Seymour sent a son to Winchester, one to Charterhouse, one to the Naval College at Portsmouth, one to the Military College at Woolwich, and engaged a private tutor.

The habit of connecting personal assistance to a loss of moral autonomy and a stigmatized version of childish helplessness, rather than to the glamor of aristocratic power, is related to this way of thinking. Printers such as John Newbery made their fortunes marketing a new kind of children's literature to anxious and ambitious parents such as the Seymours, little books that drew from John Locke's *Some Thoughts Concerning Educa-*

tion (1693) and Jean-Jacques Rousseau's *Emile; or, On Education* (1762). According to Rousseau, the greatest good for a man (although not a woman) is independence: a man's happiness, we are told, depends on his ability to be entirely "self-sufficient" or to "dispense with the help of others."[80] Conflating childhood and disability through shared physical dependence on others, Rousseau attacks the glamour of personal attendance. He criticizes a lazy little boy who "had got it into his head that a man of his rank need . . . do nothing, that his birth would serve as a substitute for arms and legs, as well as for every kind of virtue."[81] In image, Rousseau accuses this lazy little boy of high rank of wanting to be an amputee, with servants as a prosthetic substitute for his arms and legs. Remarkable as this image may seem, Carolyn Steedman suggests the "servant as prosthesis" was an eighteenth-century commonplace.[82] Because the master was thought to own the servant's labor, "jokes were made about the servant as a kind of extra limb, or prosthesis, of the employer. Much painful fun was had."[83] Derision of physical assistance could reflect rivalry between old and newer social elites.

Addressing the everyday experience of social class, the children's books that followed Rousseau urge their readership of "little masters" and "misses" to grow up by achieving physical independence from servants, in contrast to the sickly aristocrat's dependence on them. That is, these books teach that the healthy middle-class adult is independent and proud of it, while sick people and children—and aristocrats, who are both sickly and childish—are dressed and coddled by servants. And such childish and sickly people ought to be ashamed of themselves. For example, Maria and Richard Lovell Edgeworth's progressive child-rearing manual *Practical Education* (1798) tries hard to reframe the traditional prestige of being dressed by servants as shameful dependence. Like many such books, it devotes an entire chapter to "Servants." Citing Rousseau, the Edgeworths write that well brought-up children "should not be waited upon as being masters and misses, they should be assisted as being helpless. They will not feel their vanity flattered by this attendance; . . . they will be ambitious of independence, and they will soon be proud of doing everything for themselves."[84] While Rousseau held that independence defined the happy man, and dependence defined the happy woman, for the Edgeworths, both boys and girls must learn independence. Nobody should enjoy the experience of being helped to get dressed in the morning. The ideal teacher in Mary Wollstonecraft's *Original Stories from Real Life* (1787) hammers home the same message: "Children are helpless. I order my servants to wait on you, because you are so . . . you could not so soon have forgotten that you were a weak, dependent being."[85]

Leonore Davidoff and Catherine Hall describe the ultimate triumph of middle-class ideals such as the stigmatization as childishness of personal assistance: they became the "common-sense" that still shapes us today.[86] This way of thinking may influence how we describe the experience of people who lived with physical impairment in the past. For example, John Sugden devotes more attention than most of Nelson's biographers to the loss of his arm. He helpfully lists the assistive devices that Nelson acquired: a combined knife-and-fork designed to be used one-handedly, armchairs with pads on which to rest his residual limb, and linen shirts with a shortened right sleeve drawn together by a tape.[87] His discussion of Nelson's life after Tenerife, however, focuses on the sense of humiliation he imagines Nelson felt immediately after he lost the arm and found himself fighting a "daily battle to accomplish the most commonplace tasks, familiar since childhood, but now frustrating, time-consuming and sometimes humiliating."[88] Humiliation at needing help with tasks "familiar since childhood" suggests stigmatization of personal assistance as a mark of childishness. Sugden notes a "particularly public embarrassment was the cutting of food at the table" and describes this task as a "burden" on others, particularly on Nelson's wife Frances.[89] Sugden finds little support for this sense of humiliation in Nelson's letters. He interprets this silence as evidence of the depth of his feeling about the issue: "We hear so little of these difficulties that biographers virtually eliminate them from their accounts, yet that silence itself speaks volumes about the spirit of their subject, and his determination to conquer substantial and endless obstacles."[90] Complaining to St. Vincent on August 13, 1801, about his health and spirits, Nelson himself seems less troubled than Sugden by the idea of being "childishly" dependent on others: "I have all night had a fever . . . I have serious doubts whether I shall be able, from my present feelings, to go to the Mediterranean; but I will do what I can—I require nursing like a child."[91] Unlike Michael Seymour, Nelson accepted the help of a manservant to pull on his tight silk stockings in the morning. In the tense weeks he spent chasing the

French across the Atlantic and back, Nelson was on deck in all weather. The *Victory*'s surgeon, James Beatty, noted his consideration for his servants: "He seldom wore boots, and was consequently very liable to have his feet wet. When this occurred he has often been known to go down to his cabin, throw off his shoes, and walk on the carpet in his stockings for the purpose of drying the feet of them. He chose rather to adopt this uncomfortable expedient, than to give his servants the trouble of assisting him to put on fresh stockings, which, from his only having one hand, he could not himself conveniently effect."[92] It was thoughtful of Nelson to refrain from asking for help with his stockings at all hours, but it is also clear that he expected help at the proper time. Nelson was a mercurial man, and his feelings about assistance may well have shifted over time. Nevertheless, stigma about the "childishness" of such help does not appear have weighed as heavily on him as it does on us today.

Nelson seems to have been quite strategic about when he did and did not insist on doing things for himself. For example, as chapter 1 describes, two days after Tenerife, Nelson concluded his official letter about the engagement by referring to the fact that he had managed to write it himself with his left hand. Newspapers picked up on this detail, and Nelson's recounting the loss of his right arm with his left hand became an example of his gallantry. Nelson also chose to use his left hand to write long, passionate love letters to Emma Hamilton. When there was no special occasion for making such an effort, however, Nelson simply dictated letters to his secretary, or wrote them himself but used the loss of his right arm to excuse winding them up as quickly as he pleased. Similarly, Nelson did not always insist on climbing in and out of his ships one-handed. For example, determined to attend a strategic meeting that was to be held in another ship before the Battle of Copenhagen (1801), he was ready to brave high winds and seas that made travel in a small open boat from his ship to the other dangerous. But by 1801, Nelson had also found his perfect second-in-command, one whose calmness balanced his own more highly strung ardor: Thomas Masterman Hardy. Leaping from the side of his ship into that small open boat with only one arm in the midst of the heaving sea was, in the opinion of Hardy, then Nelson's flag captain, a foolish risk: "The captain expressed a doubt of his lordship's being able, with the sea that was running, and having but one arm, to get into the boat. 'But I am determined I will go,' said Nelson. 'Then,' said Hardy, 'I must put you into the boat as she lays on the booms, and hoist you out in her.' This was accordingly done, with every proper and seaman-like precaution."[93] In this context, Nelson's responsibility to get to a key meeting, and Hardy's responsibility to keep him alive, were more important than any conspicuous display of overcoming obstacles.

A key point of modern disability rights activism is the principle that an adult's need for help with a specific life function should not undermine such a person's general right to make autonomous decisions. Needing help getting dressed, for example, should not, in effect, move an adult into the category of "child." Nelson may have had less need to argue this point. In his day, as we have seen, a gentleman with a normative body and a rock-solid right to autonomy might well have demanded a good deal of assistance in dressing himself. He had no need to pull on his own stockings or tie his own neckcloth to prove he was an adult. Moreover, Nelson was a greater celebrity than any other amputee naval officer. For whatever reason, he took a distinctive line on personal attendance. He did not simply accept master/servant relationships as a fact of life for a gentleman, as James Gordon seems to have, or reject them as stigmatized versions of childishness or incapacity, like Michael Seymour. Instead, he positively framed the need for physical assistance as part of an ideal of master/servant relationships. If personal assistance can suggest the neediness of a child, as well as the privilege of a gentleman, then in certain contexts Nelson embraced this need. At sea, not merely his servants, but all of Nelson's devoted male subordinates took care of their one-armed, half-blind, sickly, and victorious admiral as if he were a child. Whatever ship Nelson happened to be in, its officers and any nearby captains coddled him "as if he had been an infant," as Sugden himself writes. They fussed over his wet feet and urged him to wear his greatcoat. They worried about what he ate and how little he slept. "Devoted officers watched him as if he had been an infant. He awoke each morning between four and five to warm milk prescribed by [Captain] Foley. . . . He took lozenges contributed by [Captain] Murray. . . . [Nelson wrote with pleasure that] in the fleet 'everybody [was] devoted and kind to me in the extreme.'"[94]

Anecdotes about Nelson's subordinates ganging up on him out of worry for his health, sometimes enlisting the authority of his servant Tom Allen, have rhetorical power because of the much greater authority Nelson held over them all. "This affectionate domestic watched his lordship with unceasing attention, and many times have I seen him persuade the admiral to retire from a wet deck, or a stormy sea, to his bed."[95] Such anecdotes reflect the gentleman's privilege of being bullied by his valet, the nostalgic dynamic Charles Dickens would exploit so fruitfully with Mr. Pickwick and Sam Weller two decades later. Allen embroidered and trafficked in such anecdotes for decades after Nelson's death. For example, he insisted that he forbade Nelson to wear his many military decorations into battle, thus making him a less conspicuous target: "When he was going into action he used to say, 'Tom, I shall put on that coat,' (meaning the one decorated with his orders,) and I used to answer, 'no, my Lord, you won't,'—and when the battle was over,—'There, now, don't you think this coat looks better than if it was drilled through with bullets?'"[96] This story is unlikely to be true, as silver gilt copies of Nelson's medals of honor were embroidered on his "undress" coats, including the one he wore at Trafalgar. Another story about Allen protecting Nelson in battle, however, is well authenticated. "Under fire from the forts of Valette, which hulled the ship, and knocked away our foretopmast, this faithful servant interposed his bulky form between those forts and his little master . . . this affectionate domestic watched his lordship with unceasing attention."[97] Paternalist rather than anti-aristocratic, these stories are meant to honor both the "little master" and his "affectionate domestic." Unlike the heroes of eighteenth-century children's literature, there is no need for this little master to be ambitious of independence.

Nelson's feelings about accepting help from others seem to have varied depending on who offered the help. As in the examples above, taking care of Nelson could be a privilege rather than a burden. He granted this privilege only to certain people: only those whom he loved, and whose right to love him he accepted. For example, Nelson's estranged wife Frances reacted to reports that his eyesight was deteriorating with an offer of help: "My anxiety, my fondness for him all rushed *forth* . . . and [I] offered to nurse him and that he should find me the same I had ever been to him faithful, affect[tionate] and desirous to do everything I could to please him." As Roger Knight notes, Nelson rejected this offer with "savage finality."[98] He attacked Frances by insisting "I want neither nursing or attention":

To Frances, Lady Nelson, 17 February 1801

> I have received your letter of the 12th. I only wish people would never mention My Name to you, for weither [sic] I am blind or not it is nothing to any person. I want neither nursing or attention. And had you come here I should not have gone on Shore nor would you have come afloat. . . . Whether I live or die am Ill or Well I want from no one the sensation of pain or pleasure. And I expect no comfort till I am removed from this World.[99]

"Indeed, I shall never volunteer my nursing abilities again," Frances wrote to a friend.[100] When Nelson wrote this letter, he had loved Emma Hamilton for many years, and she had given birth to his child a month earlier. Emma often sat beside Nelson at dinner to cut his meat, as Lady Minto's diary records.[101] Lavinia Spencer's diary notes that at a dinner party in 1800, when Frances shelled some walnuts for him, Nelson rejected them so violently that he broke a glass, reducing her to tears.[102] Although he rejected his wife's offer of "nursing or attention," he welcomed both from his lover. Nelson also welcomed help from others he loved. While away from Emma, he wrote to her about who took her place at table: "Parker sits next to me to cut my meat when I want it done."[103] Parker was Captain Edward Thornborough Parker, whom Nelson treated like a son. "He is my child, for I found him in distress," he wrote.[104] Parker also linked personal attendance with love. Nelson sat by Parker's bedside as the younger man died from complications of a thigh shattered in battle. Writing to Emma, Parker called Nelson "my Friend, my Nurse, my Attendant, my Patron, my Protector, nay Him whom the world cannot find words sufficient enough to praise."[105] Nelson asked, "I beg that his hair maybe cut off and given to me; it shall remain and be buried with me."[106] After Parker's funeral, Nelson wrote, "I could not suffer more and be alive. God forbid I should ever be called upon to say or see as much again."[107]

Helping Nelson was also nationally publicized as an honorable act. During the 1801 invasion scare, for example, *The Naval Chronicle* listed the number of aides-du-camp deployed to assist him together with the number of ships deployed to guard the coast. "His active spirit will prove our best guardian . . . whose very name is a tower of strength to his grateful country," the *Chronicle* wrote, assuring the public that their tower of strength had been supplied with ample support:

Government have thought it necessary to adopt every method that prudence could dictate for the defence of the country. To this end, the division of the North Sea Fleet . . . consisting of the following ships, . . . [are] now blockading the Dutch Fleet . . . and twenty additional frigates and sloops of war are stationed along the French coast, from Havre to Dunkirk. . . . The Admiralty have also granted his Lordship three Aides-du-Camp, although unprecedented, in consideration of the inconvenience to which the gallant Admiral is exposed by the loss of his right arm. Every person must rejoice to see Lord Nelson, whose courage, enterprize, and vigilance are so pre-eminent, employed in such service . . . the menaced coasts of England are rendered perfectly secure by the formidable line of shipping under the orders of the distinguished Hero of the Nile.[108]

The Hon. Captain Stewart, son of the Earl of Galloway, and two additional aides-du-camp protected Nelson from any "inconvenience" caused by the loss of his right arm, and Nelson protected Britain.

For amputees who lost an arm, like Nelson and Seymour, self-presentation involved choices about an empty sleeve, choices that are examined below. Those who had lost a leg made choices about what sort of prosthesis to use. Katherine Ott explains that the Napoleonic Wars occasioned the "first large-scale attention" to prosthetic design. The development of prosthetics involves more than technical advances: "If the history of prosthetics is about the history of medicine and technology, it is also about learning strategies to live with one's own body and adapt to circumstances, learning to understand other people's bodies. This is true whether you are a prosthesis maker . . . or you are a fellow human with expectations about health, body appearances, and body functions."[109] Pell and Gordon made different decisions in this regard, decisions in accord with each man's finances and personal style. Pell chose to use expensive prostheses that would decrease the visibility of his impairment. Gordon chose a "Greenwich Pensioner," the nickname for the relatively inexpensive wooden "peg-leg" with which seamen were fitted at Greenwich Hospital, an institution of which he also became the chief administrator.

Looking back on her Victorian childhood, memoirist and daughter of Vice-Admiral Courtney Boyle, Mary Boyle remembers Gordon as "a tall and handsome man, with only one leg, having replaced the other . . . by what was then called the 'Greenwich pensioner'—an ordinary wooden substitute, such as was used by common seamen."[110] She recalls Pell as "being more a dandy in such matters, [who] had provided himself with a shapely cork leg and foot, with its smart silk stocking and jaunty pump."[111] Pell had no reason to deprive himself of expensive stockings and pumps—or expensive prosthetics. Although a second son, he was wealthy and landed; he married late in life and could afford to be particular about his personal appearance if he pleased. And he did please: on April 16, 1825, he rode to Northampton to buy a toupee. That same year, he rode to Chelsea twice on a different errand: "September 27. At Chelsea, buying a new leg. . . . October 28. Went to Chelsea to fit a new leg."[112] December 6, 1828, finds him again at Northampton, where he "paid Mr. Borvil for a new wig."[113] In 1850, Pell was close enough to Gordon as an old friend and brother officer to ask to borrow his sword belt in a pinch, but far enough removed from him in terms of taste and style that he could not endure being seen at court in the much-used sword belt Gordon lent him:

1850 March 20:

Dressed to go to the Levee. Found Mr. Lucas had not sent my sword belt and sword knot home. . . . .borrowed Sir Jas. Gordon's, it was so old and shabby in comparison with my new coat &c., I could not go in it.[114]

The contrast between Pell's new coat and Gordon's old sword belt seems perfectly in character for both men.

Jamie or Jemmy to his friends, Gordon was a member of the minor Scottish gentry and cultivated the persona of a bluff Scotsman. Like Mary Boyle's account, his family memoir notes that he used the cheapest sort of prosthetic leg available, a rigid wooden peg that was fitted to his residual limb by means of a cup-shaped casing padded with cloth or leather. That is, when Gordon wound up his career as the governor of Greenwich Hospital, he made his way around the hospital and its grounds using the same kind of prosthesis as did many of the "sailors disabled by wounds" themselves. Although a Greenwich Pensioner was a relatively simple prosthetic leg, getting one to fit properly and replacing damaged ones took time and care. James wrote to Lydia about the process, admitting to "a little pain": "I have taken to Mr. Drake's leg, and it answers so well that I think, after a little pain, I shall feel as comfortable in it, as I did in the other," he notes early in 1813.[115] April 15 finds him adjusting to another prosthesis: "I have split the upper part of the case for my leg, and I am obliged to take the one I had made at Gloucester, it answers pretty well."[116]

Unlike Pell, James Gordon spent little time or expense on enhancing his appearance. One reason may have been the fact that Gordon did not have Pell's disposable income: he was the devoted, and often indebted, father of a large family. On January 13, 1819, he reminded his wife why he had accepted another command at sea: "I know this letter will give you a great deal of pain, my much beloved, but remember, we have not much to leave our darlings and it is our duty to work for them while we can; do write to me and say I have done right in accepting *Active*."[117] As discussed in chapter 3, although this letter asserts that James is the breadwinner, its mention of "our duty to work for them while we can" is typical of his respect for Lydia's contribution: while he works for their children at sea by managing his ship, Lydia works for them at home by managing their household. Another reason Gordon spent so much less than Pell on enhancing his appearance may have been the fact that his appearance required no enhancement: "In person Sir James was singularly handsome, standing 6 ft. 3 inches, and of great muscular power," notes his family memoir.[118] His family, of course, may have been partial observers, but it seems to have been a truth universally acknowledged that James Gordon was a remarkably good-looking man both before and after he lost his leg. At Gordon's death, Admiral W. A. B. Hamilton found comfort in thinking about the beauty of his old friend's face. "My noble and honored and loved Commander has gone to his *home*," he wrote to James's daughters:

Jan 12, 1869

> I have thought a good deal of his face and features.... It seemed to me to grow handsomer and finer as age and years advanced; there were few faces like it... a benevolence of expression, and of love devoid of all tinge of self or of dross that had a singular meaning, and I was sure, that in the calm sleep of departure and dissolution, that his features and face would be beautiful, more so, probably, that they ever were in life, handsome as he was.[119]

According to Hamilton, Gordon's face was a true portrait of his unselfish soul.

"A Portrait of Our Beloved Hero"

Four months after Nelson's death at Trafalgar, his portrait played a role in the final fleet action of the Napoleonic Wars, the Battle of San Domingo. Richard Godwin Keats, captain of the *Superb,* had chased the French across the Atlantic and back with Nelson and kept a portrait of Nelson in his cabin. As his ship sailed into battle on February 6, 1806, Keats took Nelson's portrait down and hung it above his quarterdeck. His officers responded "with hand and heart": "Captain Keats, before we began, suspended to the mizzen-stay a portrait of our beloved Hero (Nelson). There it remained unhurt, but was completely covered (so was Captain Keats himself) with the blood and brains of poor Brookbank, one of our Boatswain's Mates. Two or three minutes before the work of death began, officers' hats off on the quarter-deck, our band played "God save the King!" then came, "Off she goes!" and next, "Nelson of the Nile!"—Never was enthusiasm greater than ours, and to it we went with heart and hand."[120] The battle left six of *Superb*'s men killed and fifty-six wounded; the British squadron captured or destroyed all five of the French ships they faced and did not lose a single ship.[121]

When they looked at the portrait on the mizzen stay—blood stained or not—Keats and his officers simply saw "our beloved Hero." Nevertheless, the visual codes of heroic portraiture were complex, as was their relation to military ideals and to actual bodies that had been damaged by war. For the general public, to evoke admiration as a hero rather than pity as an object of sensibility or ridicule as an object of contempt, an amputee's well-documented public record of heroic deeds was not enough. He had to look like a hero. Assumptions about beauty, masculinity, social class, humor, pity, nationalism, and dignity affected what an eighteenth-century portraitist did when confronted with an amputee officer with a distinguished service record. All of the amputee officers in this study were well-known figures in their time. Like those of other naval victors, their portraits were painted and engraved as part of their era's production of nationalist heroic images, images that were intended to embody and to inspire the strength of the nation. But these officers confronted Britain's habits of commemorating military victory with this question: how could the bodies of heroic but physically vulnerable men be used to represent the heroic invulnerability of the nation itself? Nelson has by far the richest visual history of commemoration of the four officers who are the focus of this study. Moreover, in foregrounding his empty sleeve, his portraits became a model for representing officers who had lost an arm. In contrast, amputee naval officers who lost a leg appear in their heroic portraits in a "discreet three-quarters view" that obscures the fact of their loss. This choice may reflect the particularly strong visual link, discussed above, of power with "the legs of elite men . . . highlighted in close fitting white hose and skin-tight breeches, showcased in countless paintings from the era."[122] That is, in their portraits, amputee officers who lost a leg look like military heroes with normative bodies. Amputee naval officers who lost an arm made a different choice about how to appear in their portraits: they look like Nelson.

A successful portrait is often described as a collaboration between the sitter and the artist, one that creates insight by merging their different perspectives. Amputee officers made choices about how to present themselves to others' view when they sat for a portraitist, as well as when they took command of a ship or entered a drawing room. Unlike caricatures, which offer an external commentary on their subject in the context of various political issues of the day, a formal portrait generally requires the subject's active participation in sitting for the painter, if not in commissioning and paying him or her. Like James Gordon explaining to the London crowd the significance of his missing leg, portraitists explain the meaning of the particular human body they paint. Marcia R. Pointon explains that portraiture "makes graspable the elusive body" by bringing together "the conscious and the unconscious, the historical and the actual, the real and the imagined."[123] Kurzman claims that something similar can happen in amputees' experience—conscious and unconscious, real and imagined—of their own elusive bodies. "Amputation is a profound loss," he points out. In addition to the shock of change and the practical difficulties of learning to manage day-to-day life in new ways, amputees often experience "disruptions to their body image and self-image." Gaining a new sense of one's body and how this body fits in the world is an active process. It is a bit like making a portrait. Like portraiture, the process involves connecting meaning and appearance and is collaborative: "Partly in collaboration with their prosthetists . . . experienced amputees eventually remake some meaning and understanding of their bodies."[124]

In tension with this focus on collaboration and process is the idea that bodies are—or should be—readable at a glance. As a genre, portraiture makes the remarkable claim that people's insides match their outsides—or, at least, that the gift of a true artist is to make them do so, to reveal essential qualities of individual character through external form. The ability to embody abstract qualities of character is central to the professional status of the portraitist. As Jonathan Richardson insists in his *Essay on the Theory of Painting* (1725), "'Tis not enough to make a Tame, insipid Resemblance of the Features, so that everybody shall know who the Picture was intended for." Catching a mere likeness "is often done by the lowest of Face-Painters, but then 'tis ever with the Air of a Fool, and an Unbred Person."[125] In contrast, the true artist will reveal what the sitter is, not merely what he looks like, proving that the artist himself is an insightful and cultured gentleman rather than an under-bred "face-painter." To this way of thinking, beauty is a sign of God's design, while a physical "defect" is a falling away from divinely ordained order, the order that beauty makes instantly visible.[126]

An eighteenth-century portraitist and sitter worked within the same codes of self-presentation that governed how a gentleman stood, bowed, sat, danced, walked, or rode in his everyday life. Such men were supposed to know what to do with their hands and feet. Lemire reminds us that the "pleasing placement of feet, legs and hands in repeated ceremonial enactments defined the fully civil subject fit for the highest salon and the best company." Overall, gentlemen's "limbs were stylistically deployed through gesture and pose. Politeness as studied by noble, genteel and aspiring men demanded a learned restraint and polished performance, a 'language of the voice and of the body.'"[127] After faces, hands were the trickiest thing to paint, and it was important to get them right: portraitists commonly factored how many hands a portrait contained into the price they charged.

When a public figure sat for a portrait, this project became yet more complex. The portraitist must align a body, an inner truth about character, and a public role. Richard Brilliant points out that portraits of public figures such as politicians, artists, and military heroes use visual cues to demand respect from their viewers. In portraits, such figures "usually bear the gravamen of their 'exemplary' public roles; they offer up images of serious men and women, worthy of respect, persons who should be taken equally seriously by the viewing audience."[128] Eighteenth-century painter Sir Joshua Reynolds's enormously influential *Discourses on Art* (1769–90) popularized what came to be known as "the grand manner," a style that played up the idealizing tendency of this commitment to expressing character. Reynolds explains the need to make a hero look like a hero: "a painter of history shews the man by shewing his action. . . . He cannot make his hero talk like a great man; he must make him look like one." The claim that external form reveals character could be applied in problematic ways to peculiar bodies. For Reynolds, only a certain kind of body can make human greatness visible. A hero must not be "lame or low": "Alexander is said to have been of a low stature: a painter ought not so to represent him. Agesilaus was low, lame, and of a mean appearance. None of these defects ought to appear in a piece of which he is the hero."[129]

In addition to revealing character and making divine order visible, portraits of officers during the long wars of 1793–1815 had a specific political purpose: building morale.[130] As Mary Favret has shown in *War at a Distance* (2009), during the Napoleonic era, Britain learned how to understand a new kind of war, one fought beyond the immediate perception of most of its citizens.[131] Forms as diverse as newspaper stories, landscape painting, meteorology, and popular poetry tried to teach the British not only what was happening on the global military scene, but also how they should respond, personally and politically, to these unseen events. Nationalist images of heroic military masculinity played a part in this education. Not only was the nation literally defended by the physical strength and wholeness of its military men, but the physical strength and wholeness of these men metaphorically represented the strength and wholeness of the nation. Unlike the actual bodies of military men, the heroic ideal was supposed to be invulnerable to injury. As Jenks explains, "The male body . . . was centrally located in contemporary patriotic discourse. Threats to it were, both metaphorically and literally, threats to the stability and permanence of the wider body politic."[132] To this way of thinking, when a true artist painted a naval hero, he also created an image of the strength of the nation as a whole. A military hero's body should represent the invulnerability of the nation. Such assumptions about ideal masculinity could imply that amputees could not be heroes, and heroes could not be amputees. The careers of amputee naval officers contradicted this visual convention.

As a genre, caricature is less wholeheartedly committed than portraiture to heroic ideals, often focusing instead on pathos, satire, or black humor. George Cruikshank's 1825 caricature of a group of military amputees, *The Battle of the Nile*, is an interesting combination of visual codes that call for laughter and pity, but also a measure of respect. This caricature presents pensioners of Greenwich Hospital celebrating the anniversary of the Battle of the Nile at a nearby pub. Founded in 1694, Greenwich Hospital's charter directed it to provide "reliefe and support of seamen serving on board the shipps or vessels belonging to the Navy Royall who by reason of Age, Wounds or other disabilities shall be uncapable of further service at sea and being unable to maintain themselves."[133] This image may offend twenty-first-century eyes. For example, Margarette Lincoln claims that it "is without a trace of respect" for the service of the veterans whom it depicts celebrating the anniversary: "Their mutilated condition—most are missing arms, eyes or legs—is used to make the scene more humourous, since the gestures that accompany their dramatic reconstruction of the battle seem incongruous and extravagant given their obvious incapacity to wield arms."[134]

Lincoln makes a valid point: the image invites the viewer to see the wooden leg of the pensioner on the extreme left as one of a group of wooden legs belonging to a chair, a dehumanizing detail. Moreover, possibly relevant to an image like this one is an eighteenth-century notion that purely mental or emotional pain is of a higher order than suffering caused by visible damage to the body. For example, in *The Theory of Moral Sentiments*, Adam Smith sees amputation as a very "real calamity," but one that lacks the dignity of solely emotional pain: "The loss of a leg may generally be regarded as a more real calamity than the loss of a mistress. It would be a ridiculous tragedy, however, of which the catastrophe was to turn upon a loss of that kind."[135] For Smith, physical loss is incompatible with the high seriousness that establishes suffering as the proper subject of tragic drama.

Nevertheless, this caricature originally appeared in Matthew Henry

The Battle of the Nile, George Cruikshank, 1825. (National Maritime Museum)

Barker's *Greenwich Hospital* (1826), and this context suggests a more sympathetic response. Cruikshank's drawing purports to represent a club of Greenwich Pensioners who gather at a nearby pub for "the purpose of recounting past adventures, and fighting their battles o'er again."[136] Barker himself claims a degree of fellowship with this group. Although he is not a member of the club, he has a "usual seat" among them.[137] He describes these amputees with broad humor, giving them nautical-sounding type names, big noses, "squinting ferret eyes," and the florid skin of heavy drinkers. Similarly, in addition to making fun of the pointy nose and discolored face of "Jem Breeching, gunner's mate of the Ajax when she caught fire and blew up in the Daranelles," Barker notes "Jem has one standing jest—his wooden pin."[138] Ben Marlin is "a short, thick, punchy man, one leg exceeding bandy, the other perfectly straight—but that's his wooden one; a face like a dripping-pan, proving him to be of greasian extraction."[139] Another club member became a sailor when a bullet in his hip forced him to invalid out of the army: "For marching was out of the question, as he bobb'd up and down like a barrow with a broken wheel."[140] Despite the heavy-handed comic descriptions, Barker describes their service with respect. For example, the sailor who walks like a broken wheelbarrow "still would serve his king; so he entered into the navy, and was in the Victory at the battle off Trafalgar, when Nelson fought and Britain triumphed."[141] Bad puns often mingle with admiration in Barker's description of naval amputees: "But who is there, unmoved, can look at the grey-haired veteran—timber to the heel . . . his *left* arm . . . swinging about like the spanker-boom in a calm, a good-humoured smile, and 'What cheer! What cheer!' for every one he meets?"[142] He presents such men as nationalist images of indomitability: "Death and he have been playmates ever since he was a little powder-monkey in the Thunder . . . and though that gentleman has . . . smugg'd (as the boys say) a bit of him now an then, he still lives in spite of his teeth, a French abridgement of an English work."[143] Although he makes fun of their tall stories, he stresses their impressive courage: "Oh if I could persuade you once to pass an hour at the 'Jolly Sailor,' it would leave an impression upon your mind never, never to be erased. There all is honesty and truth."[144] Barker's position of sympathetic observer shapes his reaction to the moment depicted by Cruikshank, the moment when the club president, reliving the Battle of the Nile, called out the order to board the enemy: "He did it so naturally and bellowed so loudly, applying his hand to his mouth by way of speaking-trumpet, 'Boarders on the starboard bow!' that the whole company rose spontaneously, and, with visages 'like the grim ferry-man that poets write of,' seized crutches, sticks, wooden legs, &c. &c. and presented so formidable an appearance, that I began to get alarmed."[145] In this account, the friends' reenactment momentarily transports not just themselves, but also Barker the observer, back to the scene of battle.

Nelson offered a more straightforward vision of the military amputee as hero than does this caricature's mixture of sentiment, humor, and respect. His image had power, within the navy and to the wider public. Like amputee seamen, Nelson was a popular figure in caricatures, but even caricatures of Nelson usually present him as the active champion of his country as well as visibly impaired. They do so through a range of distinctively figurative and fanciful means; for example, "Extirpation of the Plagues of Egypt;—Destruction of Revolutionary Crocodiles;—or, ye British Hero Cleansing ye Mouth of ye Nile," James Gillray's caricature celebrating Nelson's decisive victory over the French fleet at the Battle of the Nile, offers a giant,

Extirpation of the Plagues of Egypt;—Destruction of Revolutionary Crocodiles;—or, ye British Hero Cleansing ye Mouth of ye Nile, James Gillray, 1798. (National Maritime Museum)

stern-faced British hero, striding through the waves and bludgeoning revolutionary crocodiles to death with his left hand, which holds a club labeled "British Oak." Gillray includes the wound that Nelson's forehead received in the battle but takes considerable creative license in representing amputation. He gives Nelson back nearly all of his right arm and adds a hook, tethered to which are the crocodiles that represent captured French ships. The one belching flame behind Nelson's left shoulder is *L'Orient*. Having perished in a spectacular explosion, *L'Orient*'s destruction dominates most visual representations of this battle.

Unlike caricatures, heroic portraits were supposed to be recognizable as a heightened version of reality: no hooks dragging a brace of fire-breathing crocodiles allowed. According to Arline Meyer, the most common strategy that eighteenth-century portraitists followed when creating a heroic portrait of a naval amputee officer was to simply make the fact of loss disappear. Amputation became invisible. Portraits of such officers either angled the figure away from the viewer to hide a missing arm or truncated it to hide a missing leg. A half-length portrait of James Alexander Gordon and

Portrait of Rear Admiral Sir James Alexander Gordon, Andrew Morton, 1839. (National Maritime Museum)

a three-quarters view portrait of Watkin Owen Pell work this way. In neither one is it evident that each man used a prosthetic leg. Instead, as Brilliant suggests, these images foreground "the gravamen of their 'exemplary' public roles." Gordon's portrait was painted in 1839 by Andrew Morton. The son of a master mariner, Morton was the brother of the surgeon Thomas Morton. Although he illustrated five of the books on surgical anatomy written by his surgeon brother, books praised by the Royal College of Surgeons for the remarkable accuracy of their drawing, this portrait shows no interest in Gordon's experience of surgery. In person, the "Greenwich Pensioner" or wooden peg leg that Gordon used was clearly visible, but it does not appear in the portrait. Gordon wears a rear-admiral's full-dress uniform of the 1833–43 pattern, with his collar and star as a Knight Commander of the Bath and the Gold Medal he was awarded for the Battle of Lissa. His hair is cut short. Before making lieutenant, Gordon had worn his hair long and "clubbed," tied at the back of his neck. When Gordon passed the lieutenant's exam as a gangly eighteen-year-old in 1800, his old captain, Sir James Hawkins-Whitshed, advised him to have his hair powdered and curled to add gravitas to his appearance. When this old-fashioned style

Portrait of Admiral Sir Watkin Owen Pell, John Lucas, 1849–1850. (National Maritime Museum)

failed to produce the desired effect, Gordon had his hair cut and brushed forward in a version of the newer Bedford crop or Brutus cut, the style he kept for the rest of his life.[146]

In an 1849–50 portrait by John Lucas, a fashionable portraitist whose father had served as a lieutenant in the navy, Pell wears a rear admiral's full-dress uniform of the 1847–56 pattern and his General Service Medal. In the left background is a frigate, presumably the *Forte*, which Pell commanded on the Jamaica station. Pell prominently holds a telescope, an expensive piece of advanced technology closely associated with naval officers' professional duties and often featured in their portraits. In this oil painting, as in Camille Silvy's 1861 photograph of a seated Pell held by the National Portrait Gallery, the fact that he used a prosthetic leg is not visible.

Portraits of officers who lost an arm tell a more complicated story about the relation of injured bodies and heroic ideals. Meyer points to Sir Peter Lely's portrait of Sir Frescheville Holles as a fine example of "the discreet three-quarters view": Holles brandishes a naked sword at the viewer in

Portrait of Sir Frescheville Holles and Sir Robert Holmes, Sir Peter Lely. (National Maritime Museum)

one hand, standing so as to conceal the fact that his other arm was lost in battle.[147] Charles Jervas's portrait (ca. 1675–1739) of Captain Galfridus Walpole, however, offers another option. Captain Walpole lost his right arm in a naval battle against the French in 1711, then commanded ships for another nine years. His portrait calls the viewer's attention to his empty right sleeve, foregrounding it and contrasting it with the hand and lace cuff that rests on Walpole's left hip. Galfridus Walpole was Horatio Nelson's great-great uncle on his mother's side, the godfather and great-uncle of Nelson's uncle and first patron, Captain Maurice Suckling, the man who took him to sea and who watched over the early stages of his career.

When the time came for Nelson to have his own portrait painted, he made a representational choice similar to that of Galfridus Walpole. After Nelson's victories at the Nile and Copenhagen, the wartime appetite for public images of the victor of England's greatest naval battles was robust. Despite frequently being unwell or at sea and dying at the age of forty-

Portrait of Captain Galfridus Walpole, Charles Jervas. (Bridgeman Images)

seven, Nelson is the subject of more formal portraits than any military hero except the Duke of Wellington. Nelson was also a popular subject for caricatures, in addition to commemorative consumer goods such as mugs and decanters, fans, and fabrics.[148] Portraits painted in Nelson's lifetime do not hide the fact that he lost his right arm. Lemuel Francis Abbott's 1797 portrait is probably the most influential of them all, frequently copied by painters and engravers. It was commissioned by William Locker, Nelson's mentor and the lieutenant governor of Greenwich Hospital, as part of his plan to create a "National Gallery of Marine Paintings, to commemorate the eminent services of the Royal Navy of England" in the Painted Hall at Greenwich Hospital. Locker's hopes were not fully realized until 1824 (seventy-two years before the founding of England's National Portrait Gallery), when the Naval Gallery became England's first "national historical" art museum, dedicated to fostering patriotism and the hospital's charitable purpose. Nevertheless, Locker's intention was clear.[149] This 1797 portrait of Nelson is, then, a very good example of the impulse to enlist portraiture in the creation of naval heroes that Lincoln describes.

LOOKING LIKE A HERO 123

Portrait of Vice Admiral Horatio Nelson, First Viscount Nelson, Lemuel Francis Abbott, 1797. (National Maritime Museum)

Abbott's portrait offers a full-frontal view of an amputee, with the right shoulder and residual arm of the figure angled slightly towards the viewer rather than away. Abbott's portrait also shows the viewer that the right sleeve of Nelson's jacket has been cut open to accommodate the dressing of his still unhealed wound, and is held together by black ribbons.[150] This portrait exploits the visual authority of an element that was not available in Galfridus Walpole's time. In place of the missing arm, Abbot foregrounds signs of Nelson's status as a naval hero: the empty sleeve of a Royal Navy rear admiral's uniform coat is neatly secured across his chest, the cuff angling up toward the gold star of the Order of the Bath. With the exception of death tableaux and allegories, formal portraits of Nelson made during his lifetime consistently foreground this empty right sleeve of his uniform coat. All the portraits of officers in this study who lost an arm follow this precedent: they are pictured in uniform and prominently display the empty sleeve of their uniform coat. James Northcote's portrait of Sir Michael Seymour, here reproduced in an 1809 engraving by Richard Cook, is a good example.

Portrait of Captain Michael Seymour, R.N., James Northcote, engraved by Richard Cook, 1809. (National Maritime Museum)

In John Hoppner's full-length portrait of Rear Admiral Sir Samuel Hood, as in Abbott's portrait of Nelson, the ribbons on the right sleeve of Hood's uniform coat show that the sleeve has been cut open to accommodate the dressing of a recent wound. A portrait by James Lonsdale of Rear Admiral William Bateman Dashwood, James Alexander Gordon's former lieutenant and life-long friend, also uses the empty uniform sleeve in the hand-in-waistcoat pose.

Another convention is evident in these portraits, one that reflects the formal portrait's ability to announce its sitter's elite status. As Meyer points out, the way Nelson wore his empty right sleeve, both in person and in his portraits, conforms to a portrait type that "appeared with relentless frequency in England in the eighteenth century . . . the familiar image of a gentleman poised with one hand inside his partially unbuttoned waistcoat." The "hand-in" pose was a genteel staple, one of the most popular standard poses that portraitists employed.[151] In formal portraits, the hand-in pose alluded to traditions of self-presentation derived from classical oratory. It conventionally represented "manly boldness tempered with modesty," often implying a contrast between the solid reticence of

Portrait of Rear Admiral
Samuel Hood, John Hoppner.
(National Maritime Museum)

the English national character and the unstable volubility of gesticulating Frenchmen. Ironically, as Meyer notes, today the pose is best known as that of a Frenchman's, Napoleon in David's famous 1812 portrait. As they gained additional military decorations and insignia of higher rank in accordance with Nelson's career, copies of Abbott's portrait continued to showcase all the gentlemanly qualities of dignity and restraint that are associated with the hand-in-waistcoat pose.

The visual impact of the naval uniform and the hand-in-waistcoat pose is clarified by the contrast between Abbott's dominant portrayal of Nelson and a less familiar image by Guy Head, painted c. 1800, after Nelson was wounded in the head at the Battle of the Nile. This portrait represents a climactic moment in the battle: the injury to Nelson's head was being dressed when he heard that *L'Orient* was on fire and ran up on deck without his coat. Unpopular as it was with the public, Nelson is believed to have liked this portrait.[152] Sometimes criticized as "effeminate" and never widely reproduced, it departs in a number of ways from the heroic masculine ideal seen in his more popular portraits. Although in this portrait Nelson wears one military decoration (his St. Vincent medal), without his coat he appears to be out of uniform with a concomitant loss of authority. Here, the soft flesh of his throat is exposed rather than being encased in the usual stiff collar and stock. The parted lips, upturned gaze, and soft facial contours of this figure differ from the composed expression more generally seen. The fresh blood on the bandage and shirt also suggest the immediacy of crisis rather than the settled composure of a formal portrait. This image's overall air of intimacy has promoted speculation that it was intended less for a general public eager for patriotic images of invulnerable masculinity than for one particular viewer, Emma Hamilton, whom Nelson was eager to supply with an image of himself looking vulnerable. Whether or not it played a role in that personal story, for a general viewer, this portrait calls attention to hands and arms. Instead of being covered by a uniform sleeve in the familiar and gentlemanly hand-in-waistcoat pose, here Nelson's amputated right arm simply ends; directly above him is the most dramatic spectacle of the battle: the explosion of *L'Orient*. Although the blood sprayed over his right shoulder comes from his recent head wound, it is difficult not to visually associate this blood with the violence of amputation. And nearly as conspicuous as his missing hand is his remaining hand, for Nelson's left hand is central to this image, resting prominently over his heart. Echoing the conventions of a love portrait in the midst of a scene of battle, as the National Portrait Gallery notes, this "curious gesture" is striking.

The question of the proper way to make Nelson's body express the truth of his life was discussed most fully when this life ended at the Battle of Trafalgar. Strong opinions were expressed about how to represent the moment of Nelson's death. Like an amputated body, a dead or dying body differs from the ideal figure most commonly used to suggest the invulnerability of the nation. Representing Nelson's last moments at Trafalgar meant confronting all of these issues: "The dilemma over truth versus epic imagination pervades all the 'death tableaux' pictures of the Georgian era, none more so than the many pictures of the death of Nelson," as Peter

Portrait of Rear Admiral Horatio Nelson, First Viscount Nelson, Guy Head, c. 1800. (National Maritime Museum)

Harrington notes.¹⁵³ A deluxe set of prints sold after Trafalgar tried to satisfy the demands of both verisimilitude and the masculine heroic ideal by representing Nelson in one print "in the full vigor of manhood, with both his arms; [in] the other after he had lost one arm."¹⁵⁴ Like many allegorical representations, Benjamin West's 1807 painting *The Immortality of Lord Nelson* avoids the question by placing a cherub immediately below Nelson's bare chest and right shoulder.

Those building monuments to Nelson could also face the question of how to incorporate amputation into a visual code that relied on the physical strength and wholeness of the male body to stand for the strength and wholeness of the nation. Some simply exclude the human form entirely. For example, Edinburgh's Nelson Monument includes no likeness of Nelson. Financed by public subscription and constructed from 1807 to 1816, this monument's dedicatory plaque explains that the citizens of Edinburgh erected it "to teach their sons to emulate what they admire, and, like him, when duty requires it, to die for their country." Rather than representing the damaged, dead, or dying human body, however, this monument takes the form of a gigantic upside-down telescope. Resting on a large pentagonal stone building that looks much like the crenelated battlements of a medieval castle, the monument represents the idea of military defense rather than any one military defender. During Nelson's lifetime, relatively cheap commemorative goods such as pottery and glass paintings commodified a simple, easily reproduced and easily recognized image of Nelson as the one-armed admiral. By the time monumental statues such as the Trafalgar Square memorial began to appear, Czisnik asserts, this "image . . . seems to have been too settled to allow for a right arm to be added."[155] That is, no statue representing Nelson "in his perfect figure" would actually look like Nelson to a wide popular audience. Given the political function of heroic military portraits, the image popularized by commemorative goods may have influenced these portraits in the same way that it influenced Nelson's later monumental statues, as is considered in chapter 4, "Becoming Victorian."

The portraits considered above try to incorporate Nelson's slight, short body as well as his empty right sleeve into an ideal of heroic masculinity, and they were generally well received. However, in 1807, a *Times* review of Samuel Drummond's death tableaux, *The Death of Nelson*, suggests the enduring power of the association of masculinity, military might, physical strength, and physical wholeness. The reviewer praises the painting by praising the impressive manliness of the large, brawny, and unmutilated figures who surround their dying, drooping admiral: "each of them is a true soldier or sailor . . . none are maimed or halt, but the wounded or the dying, all else are men and heroes!"[156] Here, a Christ-like Nelson is bathed in the white light appropriate to the savior of Britain, and the loss of his right arm is strategically concealed by the white-shirted sailor who helps to carry him below deck, performing the same function as the cherub in Benjamin West's allegory. According to the *Times*, this Nelson is, nevertheless, not quite a man and not quite a hero. The very familiarity of the earlier heroic images of Nelson that we have considered here, their very success in manipulating eighteenth-century visual codes, may obscure for us the extent to which they depart from convention. The casualness with which this reviewer excludes the maimed and halt from the ranks of men and heroes reminds us that is a remarkable achievement.

The Death of Nelson at the Battle of Trafalgar, 21 October 1805, Samuel Drummond, 1807. (National Maritime Museum)

Visual images such as Drummond's responded to a clear political agenda, but we should remember that heroic portraits had a more private life as well. Early in his career, James Gordon had himself painted in his captain's uniform and the Gold Medal he was awarded for the battle of Lissa. The 1814 engraving of the portrait by William Greatbatch crops it to an oval; the original portrait was a three-quarters view. It did not impress Lydia Ward Gordon. She did not comment on whether this portrait reveals or conceals Gordon's missing leg. She was bothered, instead, by something else that was missing: her husband's smile. Discussing the expression on his face and the coat on his back in this portrait, James and Lydia also discussed how James's authority as an officer related to his life at home as a husband. On July 19, 1812, Lydia praised the portrait for its technical

Portrait of Captain James Alexander Gordon, R.N., engraved by William Greatbatch, 1814. (National Maritime Museum)

skill, but claimed that it does not capture the truth of her husband's character. The painted face lacked James's usual "smile which gives such a benevolent expression to the countenance." While others might think the portrait "a very capital likeness," Lydia was displeased by its look of command: "Mrs. T. Ward thinks your picture a very capital likeness, so it is to those who only look at the features, and I am unreasonable to require anything more, but it certainly would be much more valuable to me, if it were not so wanting in expression. My Mother supposes that with your coat you put on your quarter-deck expression."[157] On December 8, 1812, James replied that when he put on his captain's coat, he put on, not simply a different "expression," but a different face than the one that was his at home: "I hope you told your dear Mother that I always put on my quarter-deck face when I put my coat on."[158] Two years later, however, he promised to take off that face when he took off his uniform coat and left his quarterdeck behind. On April 15, 1814, he wrote "If I am put on half pay I think London would be as good a place as any to take up our quarters in till we can look about us a little; but I leave all that to you, my dear, as you must be commanding officer when I strike my pennant. God bless you."[159] James tended to call on God to bless Lydia in moments of strong emotion, when he felt more than he could find words to say: "May God ever preserve you, my dear, dear wife. I have not words to express how much I love you," he wrote during their first separation.[160] The next chapter explores their relationship more fully and, through it, some of the ways that the loss of a limb affected the personal as well as the professional lives of amputee officers.

3

Love and Friendship

"THE GREAT HORATIO," Thomas Dixon remarks, was "the ultimate military man of feeling: a romantic warrior-hero, a creature of tears and kisses."[1] Not all amputee officers were as free as Nelson with their tears, kisses, or other expressions of emotion, but some were—including freely expressing their feelings about life and love after the loss of a limb. Michael Seymour, James Gordon, and Watkin Owen Pell were friends, suitors, husbands, and fathers. Horatio Nelson was all of those things, plus the leading man in one of the most famous sex scandals of his time. Gordon's letters to his wife explore how his loss of a limb affected his relationship with her, and how the richness of this relationship helped him come to terms with his loss. On shore as well as at sea, these amputee officers also had a second family in the Royal Navy. Seymour, Gordon, Pell, and Nelson were sociable people, and they were at home in a professional world that was held together by emotionally charged bonds among men. Some of these amputee officers enjoyed enduring friendships with each other. Moreover, both before and after Trafalgar, they all lived in the glorious shadow of Horatio Nelson. Although they did not share a common political identity based on physical difference itself, none of them stood alone as officers who served with a physical impairment.

To their naval friends as well as to their wives and lovers, Nelson and Gordon wrote proudly as men of sensibility. As Mark S. Micale notes, the tasteful display of deep feeling was a "sign of good breeding, refined manners, and elevated morality" in the long eighteenth century.[2] Nelson and Gordon framed positively much of their experience of physical vulnerability, nursing, and personal assistance by describing it in terms of emotions privileged by sensibility: tenderness, sympathy, and affection. When Gordon's third daughter, Maria, decided to marry the son of physician and brother officer Sir William Burnett, Gordon rejoiced. He did not mention Burnett's distinguished record of service, including the battles of Cape St. Vincent and the Nile, bloody victories in which Gordon himself also fought, or the fact that Burnett was a fellow of the Royal Society and the reform-minded physician general of the Royal Navy. Instead, Gordon recalled tenderness over a sickbed: Burnett was "one of the very oldest naval friends I have—who brought me through a dangerous illness [in the West Indies, in 1806], when I could not go to rest without his hand being in mine."[3]

Friendship: "I Found Lots of Friends at the Navy Club"

Among the motley collection of "ideas, narratives, myths, and stereotypes" that Tobin Siebers calls the modern "ideology of ability," he includes a claim about loneliness: "Loss of ability translates into loss of sociability."[4] James Gordon had a gift for friendship that stands in strong contrast to such stereotypes. He and his wife threw a large party every year on the day his leg was shot off, celebrating November 29 with his wide circle of naval friends as a day of national triumph rather than personal loss: "The anniversaries of Lissa, 13th March and the 29th of November, 1811, were always kept after his marriage by Sir James; he gave a dinner party to as many of his officers, and to those of the other ships engaged, as was possible, supplemented in after days by any other naval friends, young and old, who thought it a privilege to be invited."[5] As this annual party suggests, Gordon's naval friendships helped him live out his long and eventful life, including the loss of his leg, with good cheer. Taking Gordon as its center, this section outlines the network of friendships among several amputee officers and highlights moments that offer insight into how their loss of a limb figured in their personal lives. Gordon's wide circle of brother officers included at least three other amputees who were lifelong friends: Michael Seymour, and two of Gordon's old lieutenants, Watkin Owen Pell and William Bateman Dashwood. As capable and ambitious officers thrown together at important moments in their careers, these men might well have been friends even if none of them had lost a limb. The fact that they were amputee officers, however, afforded them occasions to collaborate on "performing able-bodiedness," or publicly confounding negative expectations of what an officer with such an impairment could do.

During most of the careers of Gordon, Seymour, and Pell, Horatio Nelson was not their personal friend but rather a standard for professional excellence and sacrifice. Even before Trafalgar, the scale of Nelson's success raised him above other naval heroes. After his death in that victory, he became the navy's Christ. A letter from Sir Fleetwood Pellew congratulating Gordon on his appointment as superintendent of the Naval Hospital at Plymouth in 1828 reminds us of Nelson's status as an exemplar of services and sufferings:

Worthing, Dec. 11

My Dear Sir Jemmy,
 I have just seen, with great delight, your appointment to Plymouth. . . . You must not leave it—*except* for your flag [reaching the rank of admiral carried the privilege of flying a personal flag]. You have done enough, and may fairly say to any of us, as poor Lord Nelson did, *"Go thou and do likewise."*[6]

In Luke 10:37, Christ tells his disciples to imitate the example of the Good Samaritan and show compassion to strangers. Nelson borrowed the words to frame the "Sketch of My Life" he wrote in 1799 as an exhortation to young men, not to be charitable, but rather to be ambitious: "Thus may be exemplified by my Life, that perserverance in any profession will most probably meet its reward. Without having any inheritance, or having been fortunate in prize-money, I have received all the Honours of my Profession, been created a Peer of Great Britain, and I may say to the Reader, 'GO THOU, AND DO LIKEWISE.'"[7] In using these words after Nelson's apotheosis at Trafalgar, Pellew invokes Christ's own death on the cross. What is most striking about this allusion is its economy. As chapter 2 notes, after Trafalgar, heroic paintings such as Arthur William Devis's *The Death of Nelson* represented Nelson's Christ-like status to the public. For brother officers in 1828, no monumental portraiture was needed to invoke this idea.

Nelson was proud of his sensibility. "I am all soul and sensibility," he wrote to Emma Hamilton, and went on to say he wanted even the Admiralty to respect his feelings: "A fine thread will lead me, but with my life I would resist a cable dragging me."[8] This looks perhaps more like stubbornness than sensitivity, but Nelson's comfort in representing himself as a man of feeling is clear. Biographers trying to capture his leadership style find themselves talking about feelings as well as tactics and strategy. Admiral Edward Codrington, one of Nelson's captains at Trafalgar, tried to describe Nelson's leadership by describing how he made his officers feel, commenting that "the predominant feeling [Nelson inspired] was not fear of censure, but apprehension of not gaining his approbation."[9] This description of officers' eagerness for Nelson's approval does not capture the warmth of the relationships that bound them. Emotion charges Nelson's own letters, including sympathy for the feelings of his officers at a delay in seeing action: "Yet, if I know my own thoughts, it is not for myself, or on my own account chiefly, that I feel the sting and the disappointment! No! it is for my brave officers; for my noble-minded friends and comrades. Such a gallant set of fellows! Such a band of brothers! My heart swells at the thought of them!"[10] When Nelson explained his battle plan before Trafalgar, he claimed some officers wept with joy at the prospect of the imminent pell-mell fight: "Some shed tears, all approved, it was new, it was singular, it must succeed."[11]

After these swelling hearts and falling tears, it seems deflating to explain that Nelson fostered such relationships by hosting dinner parties. However, the level of sociable exchange he cultivated at his table was unusual at the time for a superior officer. Nelson also tended a sprawling network of professional contacts through tireless and very personal letter writing. He showed himself to be a sympathetic friend to Captain Sir Thomas B. Thompson, for example, when Thompson lost a leg at the Battle of Copenhagen. He wrote, "Patience My Dear fellow is a Virtue (I know it) but I never profest it in my life yet I can admire it in others. I will assuredly see you before we part and I beg you will believe me as ever your affectionate friend."[12] He consistently set an example of professional ardor, in battle and outside of it. In the Baltic, during a freezing five-hour row in an open boat into wind and tide, fearing he would be too late to join the fleet before a battle, he refused the offer of a boat cloak by referring to the warmth of his feelings: "No, I am not cold; my anxiety for my country will keep me warm. Do you think the fleet has sailed?"[13] Despite his sociable nature,

Nelson was not clubbable. As Marianne Czisnik points out, he showed an unusual lack of interest in the "near-ubiquitous" club life of eighteenth-century men, responding with "polite disinterest to approaches from institutions or invitations to events that might have offered such opportunities."[14] Nelson made occasional contributions to the charitable Marine Society and the Patriotic Fund at Lloyd's Coffee-house but did not attend their meetings or dinners. Friendly and comfortably stocked though it was, Nelson's own dinner table had a singleness of purpose incompatible with the more diffuse sociability of club life.

Before exploring their network of friendships, we should note that not all relations between brother amputee officers were in fact friendly. Michael Seymour and another amputee captain, Robert Mends, were involved in the capture of the same French ship and feuded furiously about the prize money for the rest of their professional lives. Mends lost his right arm at the Siege of Yorktown (1781) as a fourteen-year-old midshipman, in the frigate *Guadeloupe* with Captain Hugh Robinson. Because of difficulties with his recovery, he endured two separate amputation procedures. John Marshall reports Mends's description of the experience: "Mr. Mends, on being asked after his recovery how he felt whilst the surgeon was performing the painful operation of removing his shattered limb, replied, 'Very well until I saw my arm lying on a table beside me I then became sick.'"[15] He was awarded a pension of 7 *l* a year. In 1786, Mends was back at sea, serving in the *Grampus* 50 on the coast of Africa, under Commodore Edward Thompson. On August 26, 1789, he was commissioned as a lieutenant to the *Childers* sloop of war, under the command of Sir Robert Barlow. On March 3, 1797, Mends commanded the *Diligence* 16 and captured *La Nativetas*. He was made post-captain on May 2, 1800, and continued to serve at sea. As captain of the *Arethusa* frigate, on April 6, 1809, he joined *Amethyst*, commanded by Seymour, very late in action in which *Le Neimen* was captured. *Le Neimen* fired one shot at *Arethusa*, and Mends was struck on the back of the head by a splinter that knocked him unconscious, the only man in his ship to be injured. In contrast, both the *Amethyst* and *Le Nieman* were badly damaged. Out of the *Amethyst*'s 222-man crew, 8 were killed and 37 were wounded, while the French crew of 339 had 47 killed and 73 wounded. Although they initially exchanged cordial letters, Seymour and Mends eventually went to court over Mends's claim that he was entitled to half of the captain's share of prize money. The two officers remained enemies to the death. Mends commanded a squadron stationed on the north coast of Spain, cooperating with Spanish patriots in a number of actions. He was knighted by Spain on May 25, 1815, and made a Knight of the Bath, also on May 25, 1815. In April 1816, his pension for the loss of his arm was 300 *l*. In June 1821, Mends was given the chief command on the coast of Africa and died of cholera on board the *Owen Glendower* frigate at Cape Coast, September 4, 1823.

James Gordon seems to have been a man difficult to dislike. Early in his career, Gordon moved in Horatio Nelson's orbit: Gordon served at the Battle of Cape St. Vincent, where Nelson earned himself a knighthood, and at the Battle of the Nile, where Nelson commanded the British forces in a decisive victory. Michael Seymour became a friend of Gordon's, although the first mention of Seymour in Gordon's papers is not especially propitious. Two years after Gordon lost his leg, a young officer liked Gordon better than Seymour and wished to transfer from Seymour's ship to Gordon's. A mutual friend, Captain Griffiths, wrote to Gordon about the etiquette of this move:

May 27, 1813

Captain Griffiths, Arundel, Sussex

By a letter from Dawson's father, William wishes to go with you . . . he venerates you much. So he ought. Ever speaking of you in terms of highest gratitude. I often abused you on purpose to make him savage. I understand you were disposed to take him. I have already said to Mr. Dawson, "Gordon will not, I am sure, receive him unless with the approbation of Captain Seymour (of Leonidas) as it is the universal custom among brother officers." Tell me, dear fellow, how you get on. Does your leg annoy you?[16]

When Gordon found himself under Seymour's command in 1821, his first opinion was neutral at best. In an era of fine seamanship, Seymour took legitimate pride in being an exceptionally good seaman. His memoir notes that as captain of *Spitfire*, Seymour would often take "the charge out of the pilot's hands, place his French book of charts (which had been taken in a privateer) upon the capstan, and steer the ship himself, often taking her inside the rocks, and running her close in to the shore, even in the night, with all the skill of the most experience pilot."[17] When a Falmouth pilot once refused to take his ship out to sea against a foul wind, Seymour simply took over as pilot.[18] Similarly, when a captain under orders to sail replied that he was "waiting for a fair wind," Seymour replied, "Oh! Is that all? Then I recommend you to get out to sea as fast as possible, and look for a fair wind there."[19] Gordon was not impressed by this way of doing things. He wrote to his wife on meeting Seymour in 1821 that he had "not seen enough of Sir M. Seymour to form an opinion of him," but he was skeptical: "He is determined to keep the sea with all winds; but I am certain when the novelty of the command wears off, he will be like the rest of us, and see there is no use in doing more than is necessary, and I should not be surprised to hear before the night is over, of his having anchored close to us; for winter nights are not to be played with in the narrow seas."[20] Later, Gordon's account of sociable comings and goings among ships in the squadron strikes a friendlier note toward Seymour. When winds made it risky for Gordon to return to his own ship after a dinner out, he seems to have felt as welcome to spend the night in Seymour's ship as he would have in a friend's house on dry land. He writes on September 4, 1821, "I went on board Pelham's yacht to dine, but I ordered that my boat should not be sent if it blew very hard. And as it did not come, I went to Sir M. Seymour's as he had plenty of room, but I could not sleep, it blew so hard."[21] April 27, 1829, brings a matter-of-fact reference to Seymour among Gordon's friends in the service: "I found lots of friends at the Navy Club who appeared glad to see me, Sir Michael Seymour, Sir R. Williams . . ."[22]

Eventually, as amputee officers, Gordon and Seymour seem to have enjoyed teasing each other—and onlookers—in a kind of public performance of mock-pity: "Amongst [Seymour's] contemporaries of a similar character with himself was the late Admiral Sir James Gordon, and a friend has been known to express his amusement at hearing a humourous dispute between those two, as to which was the better off, he who had lost an arm or he who had lost a leg, each maintaining his own loss to be the lightest."[23] There is a well-rehearsed quality to this anecdote. According to Seymour's son and biographer, either the friend "has been known to" express amusement while telling the story, performing a repeated action in the telling, or these two amputee officer friends repeatedly played to their audience. In any case, the humor of this "humorous dispute" depends on a shared understanding and solidarity between the two men. By professing to turn the other into an object of pity, Gordon and Seymour used black comedy to highlight the self-serving quality that pity for another's loss may hold.

William Bateman Dashwood lost an arm in the same battle that took Gordon's leg and remained Gordon's lifelong friend. Dashwood was born September 1, 1790, and joined his first ship, the *Defiance* 74, in 1799. As an eleven-year-old first-class volunteer, he served at the Battle of Copenhagen in the *Defiance,* then the flagship of Rear Admiral Thomas Graves. He was commissioned as first lieutenant into Gordon's *Active* 46, in October 1811. On November 29, 1811, Dashwood lost his right arm a few minutes after Gordon's leg was shot off. Dashwood was promoted to commander on May 19, 1812, and by 1813 he was awarded a pension of 200 *l* a year for the loss of his arm. He gained command of the *Snap* 16 on July 23, 1813, and captured a French privateer, *Le Lion* 16, off the coast of France on November 1, 1813. On January 13, 1814, Gordon's wife wrote of Dashwood's helpfulness in transporting her and their children: "Captain Dashwood succeeded in getting the Admiral's tender for us, which would take us and all our traps admirably."[24] In August 1816, Dashwood took part in the bombardment of Algiers. Before the battle started, he carried away the wife and daughter of the British consul of Algiers disguised as midshipmen, a romantic exploit that landed him in the news.[25] Dashwood was promoted to post-captain of the *Amphion* 32 on October 21, 1818. From 1819, he remained on shore on half-pay, marrying Louisa Henrietta Bode on April 17, 1820. He retired with the rank of rear admiral in 1857 and died in 1869. At the end of James Alexander Gordon's long life, his brother officers wrote of him with love. Admiral Dashwood described his "most heartfelt sorrow" at his old captain's death, noting that this sense of loss was one of the most profound emotions of his life: "I know not what I have more sincerely felt, for I loved, honoured and esteemed him."[26]

James Gordon and Watkin Owen Pell were woven into each other's lives for decades, on land as well as at sea. Pell's letters reveal him to be an affectionate husband, but his diaries reveal his daily routine in England to have been an energetic and exclusively male round of hunting, committee meetings, and club dinners. He was an active member of the United Services Club, the Thatched House Royal Naval Club, the Royal Naval Benevolent Society (of which he was chair), the Association for Relief of Seamen and Marines, and the Council New Cross School. He attended frequent board meetings for the Unity Fire and Life Insurance Association, as well as board meetings with his "brother Commissioners" for Greenwich Hospital. Even his briefest diary entries include an honorific title for Gordon. "Sir James Gordon," "Sir J. A. Gordon," or "The Governor" often appears in friendly contexts other than the management of Greenwich: visits, dinners, concern over ill-health, and satisfaction when Gordon gets better. In 1856, when Pell made his last major decision about his career, he made it with Gordon. Because the Royal Navy had no standardized system of retirement, moving from the "Active List" to the "Retired List" was a personal choice, a choice with emotional as well as financial significance. Taking Gordon's lead in these negotiations, Pell followed Gordon into retirement as he had followed him at sea. During January 1856, his diary entries work through the process of "placing me with Sir Jas. Gordon the Governor on a reserved list." Pell's move to the Retired List was not the only change he faced in January 1856. January 9, a snowy day, also mentions a personal loss: "Captain Cuppage buried."[27]

Cuppage was another longtime friend—one who, like Pell, lost a leg as a midshipman and went on to have an active career at sea. William Cuppage was the son of Lieutenant General William Cuppage of the Royal Artillery and a cousin of two Royal Navy officers: Commander Adam Cuppage and Lieutenant James Heyland. Cuppage lost a leg in a skirmish with the French near Toulon, on November 5, 1813, while serving as signal midshipman in the *San Josef* 120, the flagship of Rear Admiral Sir Richard King. He was awarded a pension of 91 *l* 5 s per year on April 4, 1815, and a lieutenant's commission on April 6, 1815. Between 1815 and 1827, Cuppage served on eight different ships and sailed to the East Indies, the West Indies, and South America. He was promoted to commander of the *Java* on December 24, 1827, and to post-captain on July 22, 1830; then he did not go to sea again. In the 1850s, Pell's diary mentions numerous dinners and social calls with Cuppage and his wife, a consultation with him about a nephew's prospects, and a final visit to London on hearing he was dangerously ill. Cuppage is one of the few men Pell refers to simply by his last name, but the entry for January 3, 1856, grants his full rank: "Captain Cuppage departed this life at 2 p.m. at No. 13, Waterloo Place."[28]

If Gordon and Seymour's "humourous dispute" over which of them should be pitied the most played on one polite response to amputees, then a different performance by Gordon and Pell took on another response: ridicule. The "cripple race" is one of the best-known examples of cruel eighteenth-century humor. Two or more impoverished and physically impaired people were paid to race each other in what was seen as a parody of able-bodied athleticism. As Simon Dickie explains in *Cruelty and Laughter,* the crowd was expected to laugh at the racers' expense. Frances Burney's *Evelina* (1779) made a point of telling readers that people of sensibility really should not enjoy cripple races. When some of the novel's most unpleasant men organize a race between two elderly and infirm women, most people laugh, but the hero looks grave and the heroine is distressed. Evelina explains that pity, not laughter, is the appropriate response to a cripple race for people of sensibility: "I could feel no sensation but that of pity at the sight . . . the poor creatures, feeble and frightened, ran against each other: and, neither of them able to support the shock, they both fell on the ground."[29]

When Gordon and Pell were living on under Queen Victoria, middle-aged, loaded with honors, and attending a party held by a third naval friend, Gordon challenged Pell to a cripple race: he proposed a "race between the two one-leggers." Mary Boyle describes the event in her memoir, calling Gordon a "tall and handsome" family friend of her childhood. Boyle was born in 1810 into a naval family and died in 1890. As she was sitting on Gordon's knee when he proposed the race, it seems likely it occurred before the mid-1820s: "Sir James Gordon, on whose knee I was sitting at the moment, asked if the children would like to see a race between the two one-leggers. The dining-room was divided from the drawing-room by a long and somewhat spacious hall. This he proposed as their race course, and amid the clapping of hands large and small and cheering on, and the backing of Sir James Gordon (who was an idol) by the younger ones, the two admirals started, and the Scotchman won in a canter to our infinite delight."[30] In this account of two old friends galloping down a hall together, we can recognize the midshipman Pell, who raced a visiting one-armed captain up the rigging of his ship, and the equally exuberant young Gordon. This "race between two one-leggers" proudly foregrounds physical difference. Because of Gordon and Pell's secure social status, it plays as a kind of parody of a cripple race. If there was laughter mixed in with the clapping, cheering, and "infinite delight" of this scene, then the laugh was not at the expense of the two admirals.

These amputee officers were drawn together by many other circumstances than their loss of a limb. However, in moments like Gordon and Pell's "race between two one-leggers" and Gordon and Seymour's "humourous dispute," they asserted a solidarity grounded in their shared experience of living as members of distinctive group within the larger community of naval officers. They called attention to their visible difference and helped each other frame this difference for observers as a mark of honor rather than stigma.

Money: "My Expenses Are Enormous"

Admiralty pensions link professional honor and financial reward through recognizing exemplary service. For an individual officer, however, either the honor or the money could be of greater interest. The desire to support a family was the central motive for many—although not all—officers' careers. Ellen Gill reminds us of the significance of money and social status in officers' careers in her study of their private letters. "Few naval and military officers aspired to the heights of fame achieved by Nelson and Wellington," she writes. Rather, "for the majority of officers, advancement in their careers was primarily a means to support their family financially and secure (or improve) their standing socially."[31] Gill argues that in their letters home, these officers built an image of themselves as devoted fathers and as loving husbands, an image that gratified them as well as to their audience. Similarly, Evan Wilson notes that most officers did not aim to become a "god of war," as Lord Byron described Nelson, but rather a successful professional who could live as a gentleman and support a family: "Most had far more pedestrian concerns, about their professional future, about their incomes, and about their families."[32] The sense of familial obligation among "brother" officers could help them meet their responsibilities as actual fathers. Nelson had a particularly strong sense of the duty to look after the careers of the sons of brother officers: "If we did not take particular care of the children of our Brethren we should assume to be reprobated," he wrote.[33]

Although more successful than most, Michael Seymour and James Gordon fit Gill's and Wilson's profiles of the naval warrior as a conscientious professional, a dutiful patriarch who worried about paying the governess while he took, burned, or destroyed enemy ships. In contrast, Watkin Owen Pell was a landed gentleman. As the son of Samuel Pell of Sywell Hall, Northamptonshire, and the grandson of Owen Owen of Llanrhaeadr, Denbighshire, Pell had a more secure social and financial position. His diaries follow the rhythms of a comfortably propertied life: getting in the harvest and hunting figure prominently. Nevertheless, he too was concerned with fiscal probity. Pell lost his limb at a younger age than the other officers, and he waited longer to marry. In October 1825, he traveled to Wales and visited Maesmynan, the "kind and hospitable house" of Mr. Edward Owen, Esq., where he spent time with his grandparents on his mother's side, Mr. and Mrs. Owen Owen of Llanrhaeadr, Denbighshire.[34] Edward Owen's daughter, Sarah Dorothea Owen, was then thirteen years old. At the age of sixty, Pell married Sarah Dorothea, who was then thirty-four. Pell's career at sea was over; the year before, he had been appointed a commissioner of the Royal Naval Hospital at Greenwich. Before he bought the wedding rings, Pell visited Althorpe to declare his intentions to his patron, Lord Spencer—who would eventually stand godfather to his son, Watkin Owen Spencer Pell. On March 8, Pell "rode to Althorpe to inform Lord Spencer of my intended marriage," and on April 9, rode to London to get "my Licence at Doctor's Commons. Bought a tea kettle, wedding rings, &c. of Messrs. Turner, Bond Street."[35] Sarah Dorothea and Watkin Owen married on April 21, 1847, at Sywell Church. While visiting the Lake District one October, sometime after the birth of their daughter and son, Pell wrote a ponderously flirtatious note to "My Dearest Sarah," which she preserved to her death:

> Yesterday I went round the Lake of Windemere in a Pleasure Boat the weather every thing you could wish a few light passing clouds which displayed the various tints and shades of the Mountains Glens and Woods to great effect the Waters very dark but clear and deep the whole combined was delightful but alas one thing was wanting to complete the enjoyment can you guess that one thing not you you are so dull I will therefore inform you it was the presence of my dear Wife that was wanting to make my enjoyment

complete I shall leave this Tuesday . . . Kiss the dear children and believe me your affectionate Husband

WO Pell[36]

Pell valued professional success in part for the honor it brought his family. When he reached the long-awaited rank of admiral, his private papers record his promotion through its significance to his most important family members, both living and dead: "my dear Wife"; his brother Edwin, who was dying at the time; and his mother, who had passed away years ago. Pell notes that September 6, 1848, is "Sarah's Birthday, born 1812. Left Sywell at 11 a.m. arrived at Greenwich 4 p.m. Sarah gave me the first information that I was an Admiral."[37] He writes to Sarah three days later from Edwin's deathbed at Sywell Hall, expressing his grief at his brother's mortal illness, his pleasure that "you had written to your Mother announcing yourself the Wife of an Admiral," and his anxious solicitude for Sarah's health:

> 9th Sept. 1848
>
> My Dear Sarah
>
> I found my dear Brother very very weak but perfectly sensible and delighted to see me. He said it is now upwards of thirty years since our dear Mother said to me, You my dear Edwin may live to see your brother Watkin an Admiral but I cannot expect it. He then said I have lived to see you an Admiral, may the Almighty God in Heaven bless and protect you for many years. . . . Be careful of yourself the changeable cold weather not to take cold, do not sit down on any benches after walking if it is dangerously cold [?heavy?] weather. . . . Edwin has had a quiet night, but alas it is as he says only waiting for a few more hours. . . . Kiss Sarah Maria for me.
>
> Yours most affectionately WO Pell.[38]

After his death, Sarah wrote up a summary of Pell's naval service, labeling it "dearest Sir Watkin's Commissions, and the time he served in each Rank."[39] She noted that "had it pleased God to have spared his life for five weeks longer he would have lost his leg 70 years!!"[40]

The diaries Pell kept from 1824 to 1863 feature social engagements and business appointments rather than emotional introspection, although they do contain a few vivid observations. For example, Pell clearly was not pleased with the Duke of Somerset's visit to the Greenwich Hospital Schools on June 29, 1860: "The Duke slow, mean looking and cold as ice, did not address the boys."[41] Pell's long-standing affection for one brother and annoyance with the other come through in his terse entry on January 1, 1840: "Edwin in bed very ill. Owen and his wife at Northampton with Dr. Robertson [the husband of Pell's sister Lucy], but never came to see his brother Edwin."[42] Although Pell does not directly discuss how he felt about his role as husband and father in these diaries, his financial transactions suggest the seriousness with which he regarded it. After his death, the brother Pell loved best is "poor Edwin," as in the February 17, 1851, entry on winding up debts: "I rode to London, paid one pound poor Edwin's arrear of subscription to the Royal Agricultural Society."[43] Similarly, one of Pell's most open expressions of affection to his wife appears in a business transaction, a provision for her future financial welfare. Twelve years into his marriage, he made a note on a bill of exchange in a shaky hand:

Queen House
6 October 1860

My dearest Beloved Wife
 This Bill on Coutts & Co is the most immediate necessary payment when required by [???]. My Executors will get it cashed for Lady Pell.

WO Pell

On the back of the bill Lady Pell wrote in pencil:

To Mr Coutts & Co
 It was not Legal to cash it after my [?darling's?] death 1870[44]

Although Pell's papers do not reflect the ever-present concern most officers felt about supporting their family in an appropriate style, he too saw fiscal probity as his first duty as a husband and father. In the first year of his marriage, he wrote in his diary on January 8, 1848, "all demands by Bill or wages discharged. Commence this year perfectly clear of debt."[45]

 Michael Seymour and James Gordon were both the fathers of eight children who survived infancy. Davidoff and Hall remind us of the difficulty that such family size can raise for the historical imagination today: "After several generations of the one or two child family, how can we come to terms with the permutations of families of an average of six or seven, often up to a dozen or more offspring?"[46] Such large families changed the experience of family life itself, creating a "dense network of relationships, unheard of today."[47] They also created financial challenges, especially for a father who had "nothing but his profession" and who feared the prospect of his children falling below the social status to which they had been born. Gordon and Seymour never claimed, as did Pell, that they were free of all debts. They mention their obligation to support their families as a motive for their careers. After capturing the *Neiman*, Seymour, the son of an Anglican minister, wrote to his brother-in-law about what his new title and his prize money would mean for his family. "I hope to get 4,000 L or more . . . but my expenses are enormous, and I shall be a poor miserable rascal of a Baronet."[48] Nevertheless, he hoped to be "able to afford the woman I most love on earth a carriage which she ought to have, for she deserves every comfort I can afford her; and I do not want the cash to hoard it, for my boys must work their way."[49]

Written by his son the Reverend Richard Seymour, Seymour's memoir claimed he united "to a remarkable degree, so many of the great qualities of a commander with so much of the gentleness and affection that endears a man to his family."[50] Allowances must be made for the elegiac in any family memoir, but Seymour's final command demonstrates that he took his responsibility to his family seriously. His early involvement in his sons' education and careers is noted in chapter 2. His commitment to their success did not lessen with age. In 1829, Seymour became commissioner at Portsmouth, a "form of semi-active retirement" for distinguished but relatively poor flag officers, a position in which he enjoyed a pleasant life on shore.[51] He read extensively and gardened with his wife. When reform slated this position for abolition, Seymour refused the option of holding it for two more years and then retiring fully. Instead, at the age of sixty-four, in questionable health, he returned to sea, accepting the post of commander-in-chief of the South American station in 1832.[52] He hoped to advance the careers of two sons by returning to active duty. He took his eldest son, Lieutenant Edward Seymour, with him as his flag lieutenant. The Admiralty refused his request to take another son, Captain Michael Seymour, as his flag captain but gave the younger Michael Seymour a ship on the South American station a year later. Seymour died of a fever in Rio de Janiero in 1834.[53] His son Michael rose to the rank of admiral. Edward died young and was posthumously promoted to the rank of commander.

James Alexander Gordon's letters also show him to be the kind of financially concerned patriarch that Gill describes. On November 11, 1813, soon after his marriage, Gordon wrote to his wife, "Depend upon it, I often think of you, and I must tell you what I am afraid you will hardly believe, I would give up my ship in 10 days if I thought we had enough to live upon on shore."[54] In October 1825, Gordon admitted to telling his father that he and his family were unable to live within their income, although "we did our best."[55] On April 27, 1829, on visiting the same waiting room where he had so often lingered in hopes of active employment, he thanked God for the career that had allowed him to provide for his children: "Here I am in the Captains' room at the Admiralty where many a time I have been before looking out for something, but now, thank God, all those feelings are gone, and I am content, because, with what I have been able to do for the good of our darlings, I am happy."[56]

In addition to the sheer scale of Nelson's ambition, his charisma, and his victories, the open scandal of his affair with Emma Hamilton sets him apart from conscientious family men such as Seymour, Gordon, and Pell. In abandoning his wife, Nelson chose the opposite of the respectable domesticity that they embraced. Like Seymour, Nelson started life as the son of an Anglican minister. Like so many other naval officers, he had useful family connections but no independent fortune. Sexual infidelity was common among husbands of the time, but the public nature of Nelson's relationship with Emma Hamilton was not. Moreover, he failed to fulfill the patriarch's first duty to provide financially for his female dependents and to launch his male dependents in successful careers. Nevertheless, elements of the domestic values Gill describes are still visible in how Nelson dealt with love and money. In fact, his greatest departure in this regard was his habit of acting as though the moral claim of dependents to financial support did not depend on a legal claim created by marriage.

During Nelson's lifetime, his status as England's defender enabled him to force polite society to extend a measure of acceptance to his lover. At the same time, remarks by contemporaries suggest that his loss of a limb in that defense reduced sympathy for his passion. "I have no patience with [Nelson]," wrote Elizabeth Wynne Fremantle, the wife of Vice Admiral

Thomas Freemantle, one of Nelson's close friends, "at his age and such a cripple to play the fool with Lady Hamilton."[57] As Marianne Czisnik notes, another contemporary observer, the upper-class Whig Pryse Lockhart Gordon, took a similar tone. Gordon seemed to assume that Lady Hamilton could not in fact have felt desire for a body like Nelson's. He claimed that while valuing only Nelson's military reputation, she was wily enough to trick him into believing she liked his unattractive body: "There can be no doubt but she persuaded poor Nelson that she was actually in love with him, not as a Mars but as an Adonis!"[58] Of course, there is no reason to assume Lady Hamilton pretended to find Nelson attractive.

Pryse Lockhart Gordon's snobbish ire against Lady Hamilton as a blacksmith's daughter who had soared above her proper station in life is obvious, but what he finds more alarming still is the way she and Nelson appear to have reversed gender roles of sexual aggressor and passive object of desire. Others saw this role reversal in positive terms. Nelson "blushed like a fair maiden" when Lady Hamilton sang his praises, claimed Lieutenant Parsons in his 1840 *Nelsonian Reminiscences: Leaves from Memory's Log*.[59] Parsons had been one of Nelson's midshipmen and felt he owed his promotion to Emma Hamilton's support of his case with Nelson: he saw nothing wrong in Nelson's blushes and considered Emma Hamilton an "unjustly treated and wonderful woman."[60] As Czisnik observes, however, Gordon is horrified by this inversion. His horror is richly expressed in his writing: Nelson's "heart was corrupted, and his mind paralyzed by a female fiend. . . . How lamentable to see the greatest sea captain submit to and glory in being made such a puppet!"[61] Similarly, the anonymously published *Memoirs of Lady Hamilton* (1815) describes Emma Hamilton as mastering Nelson through a combination of "brute force" and delusion.[62] To naval historians throughout the nineteenth century, Emma Hamilton was not a woman who desired a man and who was desired in return, but rather a cold schemer as well as a hypersexual witch, both an ambitious puppet master and a "female fiend." William James's *The Naval History of Great Britain* (1826) simply claims Nelson was "possessed by a demon."[63]

Some of this extraordinary language can be explained by the impossibility of reconciling the well-known fact that Nelson abandoned his blameless wife for a mistress with the writers' goal of presenting him as the exemplar of British virtues, domestic as well as martial. Some of it stems from dislike of the reversal of conventional gender roles, as Czisnik argues. Some of it also reflects a desire to find a scapegoat for the least credible period in Nelson's career, his involvement with the Neapolitan counterrevolution of 1799. Another factor, however, may be the fact that, as Betsey Wynne wrote, the hero of this grand passion was not a strapping young man but rather "too old" and "such a cripple." A short, thin, herniated, scarred, concussed, malarial, half-blind amputee in his forties, Nelson may have had the wrong kind of body to suit these writers. Perhaps they had difficulty imagining that such a body could be desirable.

On this point, it is best to give Nelson the last word. On August 11, 1798, after the Battle of the Nile but before they had become lovers, he wrote to Emma about his body as stiffly as he wrote about it to the Admiralty. As does his note to St. Vincent after the disaster at Tenerife, this note refers to his own body as a mutilated corpse: "My dear Madam, I may now be able to shew your ladyship the remains of Horatio Nelson, and I trust my mutilations will not cause me to be less welcome. They are the marks of honour."[64] In claiming that his injuries are "marks of honour," Nelson resorts to the language of patronage and promotion considered in chapter 1, but "my mutilations" echoes the pain of his first letter to St. Vincent after Tenerife, with its description of "the remains of my carcasse." By August 11, 1801, although he still calls his body "my own carcase," the term seems to have lost some of its negative force. Now he speculates about his title evading his grasping male relatives to go instead to his and Emma's possible future son: "it may never get to any of them; for the old patent may extend by issue male of my own carcase; I am not so very old; and may marry again, a wife more suitable to my genius. . . . Ever, for ever, your's, only your, Nelson & Bronte."[65] Although the wound Nelson received at the Nile scarred his forehead permanently, by October 6, 1803, all trace of defensiveness about his body is gone, together with any mention of "my mutilations": "I am for ever, with all my might, with all my strength, yours, only yours. My soul is God's, let him dispose of it as it seemeth fit to his infinite wisdom, my body is Emma's."[66] "My body is Emma's": Emma Hamilton was open to the point of extravagance about the fact that she liked Nelson's body as it was. Perhaps her passion helped him like it as well.

Even while bent on death, glory, and passion, Nelson thought about providing financially for his dependents. Despite the scandal of his love life, Colin White stresses Nelson's ongoing connection to his family of origin, pointing out that his letters show him "always centred in his family, remaining concerned with the minutiae of their lives even when he was at the height of his fame."[67] Although, judging by the outcome, Nelson was a disaster as a stepfather as well as a husband, we should note that he fulfilled a naval father's first duty. He took his stepson Josiah Nisbet to sea with him and used the full extent of his influence to push his career. His very public infidelity to Josiah's mother strained their relationship, and Josiah proved to be a terrible officer and left the Navy in disgrace, eventually finding success in a career as distant as possible from his stepfather's sphere: as a stockbroker in Paris. Still, Nelson had done his best to make Josiah Nisbet a successful officer.

Nelson's sense of "family" extended beyond relationships within the navy. He seems to have felt that a long-standing sexual relationship created a moral obligation for financial support without the legal obligations of marriage. His brother Maurice had such a relationship with a woman who lived with him for years but did not marry him; at some point, she lost her sight. Nelson's letters refer to her as "poor blind Mrs Nelson" or "poor blindy." Acting as if she had a claim on him similar to that of a sister-in-law, at Maurice's death, Nelson paid her debts and settled a 100 *l* annuity on her. Sometime around September 6, 1803, he wrote to amend his will in her favor: "sooner than this legacy, or any other, should go unpaid, I would saddle Bronté, or any other estate with the legacies ... I want to give several other small legacies, and continue the annuity of L100 a year to poor blind Mrs. Nelson."[68] When Nelson left his wife, Frances, he divided his income between her household and the one he created with Emma Hamilton. His failure to make adequate provision to support Emma and their daughter Horatia after his death suggests a mistaken confidence that the British government shared his sense of family obligations unsupported by the legal claims of marriage. Nelson thought the money he would win through the honor of victory at Trafalgar would include Emma and Horatia as well the members of his legally recognized family. In a famous codicil to his will written immediately before the battle, he left Emma and Horatia "as a charge to the Nation." Unsurprisingly, the Nation loaded his brother and his widow with titles and pensions and did nothing for Emma and Horatia.

Nelson died as a military man of feeling, and one who was concerned to the last to provide for his dependents. His back broken by a sniper's bullet, he spent three hours dying in *Victory*'s cockpit, his sight failing, surrounded by friends as the greatest battle of his career raged above. In the most widely accepted account of this death, that published by his surgeon, William Beatty, Nelson asks three things of his close friend Captain Thomas Masterman Hardy. First, a plea to convey his body back to England instead of throwing it overboard. Second, the most direct and most famous request: "Kiss me, Hardy." Finally, "take care of my dear Lady Hamilton, Hardy; take care of poor Lady Hamilton": "The Captain now knelt down, and kissed his cheek; when his lordship said, 'Now I am satisfied. Thank God, I have done my duty.' Captain Hardy stood for a minute or two in silent contemplation: he then knelt down again, and kissed his lordship's forehead. His lordship said: 'Who is that?' The Captain answered: 'It is Hardy'; to which his lordship replied, 'God bless you, Hardy!'"[69] Laurence Brockliss, John Cardwell, and Michael Moss trace the process through which Beatty crafted and polished this account, which was embraced by the public. Although it may not be a word-perfect transcript, in its lucent fusion of pain, honor, and love, this death is entirely consistent with the life that came before it.

Marriage: "What Do You Think of That?"

In 1806, a gallant young naval officer and an elegant young lady "whose strength of character [was] perhaps unsuspected by those who did not know her well" met, fell deeply in love, but did not marry because of lack of fortune.[70] They did not speak or write a word to each other through the next five years, which the officer spent at sea fighting the French and the lady spent waiting at home. When he returned to England in June 1812, they found themselves together at a series of formal social events at which, through tortured gazes and indirect statements, they at last managed to reveal the fact that they remained passionately devoted to each other. In August 1812 they married. The perfect confidence in each other they then enjoyed made remembering their courtship, with all its delays and uncertainties, a source of acute pleasure to them both. This story will sound familiar to readers of Jane Austen's *Persuasion* (1817). The lady, however, is not Anne Elliot but Lydia Ward, and the officer, not Captain Frederick Wentworth but Captain James Alexander Gordon. Their courtship and married life feature prominently in a memoir produced by their daughters in 1890: *Letters and Records of Admiral Sir J. A. Gordon, G.C.B.* In this quick summary, I have not altered any facts—but I have left some out. I have omitted the vulnerability of men's bodies to illness and violent trauma, and the role that this vulnerability played in Gordon's courtship and marriage. James and Lydia met when he was home recovering from yellow fever, and they married six years later because his right leg had been shot off while capturing a French ship. Their letters offer an intimate look at how physical impairment could be experienced in the early nineteenth century in the context of love and family.

James Gordon and Lydia Ward's courtship was occasioned by one of the leading causes of death in the navy. Yellow fever sent James home from the West Indies to his father's house in Marlborough in 1805, which meant that he missed the Battle of Trafalgar but met Lydia. After going to sea at the age of twelve, James now took to domestic life with a vengeance. When Lydia first encountered Captain Gordon, the six-foot-three-inch-tall veteran of the Glorious First of June, the Battle of Cape St. Vincent, and the Battle of the Nile was devoting himself to the archetypically feminine pastime of needlework. James's sister, Lydia, and a friend were working on the friend's wedding trousseau. Remarkably enough, James helped sew the bride-to-be's undergarments: "In his weariness and weakness James begged to be taught to work, and there still exists a *chemise* which he made for the bride elect, and which she left to her only daughter, who still possesses it and keeps it as a valued relic."[71] James spent his convalescence sewing with these women and falling in love with Lydia. If this image of a battle-hardened officer with a needle and batiste in his hands seems surprisingly free from stereotypes about masculinity, James's letters show a similar freedom with regard to emotions.

When he met Lydia, James was a twenty-three-year-old Scottish officer, "singularly handsome," with two arms, two legs, and good family connections, but no income beyond the uncertain fortunes of a young captain very far down on the list for promotion. When not prostrated by yellow

Lydia Gordon. (National Maritime Museum)

fever, he was exuberantly energetic: "He was withal so active, that before he lost his leg he has been known to leap in and out of six empty water hogsheads [water barrels] standing in a line on the deck."[72] Cultivated and elegant, Lydia Ward was the nineteen-year-old daughter of an English solicitor, "a man of property who was the principal person in the town [of Marlborough], and universally esteemed and respected."[73] Her portrait shows a young lady with dark hair pulled back in the classical style, curls framing her fine eyes. Years later, secure in his marriage with Lydia, James would look back fondly on this time of unspoken feeling. He wrote to her from Marlborough on March 6, 1822: "I am now sitting writing in the room and at the table, where many and many a time I have looked at you and tried to look forward to the time that was to come, but I never could bring myself to think that I ever should have you for my wife, while [I] felt a pleasure in your company that I never felt in that of any other person."[74] In 1807 James and Lydia parted without speaking of marriage, in deference to their parents' feeling that a long engagement would cause Lydia "peculiar anxiety and trial."[75] Although they did not correspond during the next five years, Lydia remained excellent friends with James's sisters, hearing all the news he wrote to them—and she sent him a lock of her hair in one of his sister's letters.

In 1812, James and Lydia met again because something else was wrong with his body: his right leg had been shot off above the knee. When James arrived in London walking on crutches, half a year after losing his right leg, Lydia was no longer at home in Marlborough. She and her parents were waiting in London. As *Letters and Records* tells it, the fact that James had lost a leg did not matter to the whirlwind courtship that ensued. What mattered was the fact that James had gained the income required to support a family—or rather, that he had gained enough glory to convince Lydia's family and his own that he had good prospects of securing such an income. Perhaps even more importantly, James's near-death experience seems to have emboldened him. His sister Frances makes this point to Lydia, who seems to have been taken aback by an abrupt and less than completely coherent offer of his hand and heart: "James suffered so much unhappiness, since he last left England, that he was determined that nothing should prevent his declaring his sentiments to you, if he lived to come home."[76] James and Lydia had always had a wartime romance, but the battle that took James's leg is what pushed him to move from silent yearning to open courtship.

James "declared his sentiments" to Lydia at some point during a celebrated performance of *Coriolanus* by Philip Kemble at Covent Garden that they attended on June 22, 1812, with a large family party. This play, which opens with a warrior's noble reluctance to display his wounds for popular praise, seems an appropriate choice for James, who was at that point moving through London's public spaces for the first time after losing his leg. Kemble was a star of the London stage and Coriolanus a particularly successful role. On June 22, however, there were at least two people in Kemble's audience who were not paying attention to him. During the performance, James blurted out some version of his passion to Lydia; she offered a polite but guarded reply. Letters then flew from family to family among siblings eager to promote the match. Lydia's brother Rawdon and James's sister Frances helped explain James and Lydia's feelings to each other:

30 June 1812, Miss Gordon to Lydia:

> I hasten to thank you for the happiness you have conferred upon [James] by permitting him to hope [through a letter by Rawdon to Miss Gordon] that the attachment which he had so long felt for you, is reciprocal. You have relieved his mind from a world of care, my dear girl. You know "that he who greatly loves, must greatly fear," which was exactly dear James's case. . . . He returned from Town as miserable as possible, because he had not been able to open his heart to you as he wished, and he feared you were offended with him for saying what he did at the play. Charles and I both assured him he had no great cause to be so miserable, as you could not have said more than you did in such a place, and if you had been very angry you would have told him![77]

James's father wrote to Lydia more formally on August 20, 1812: "His attachment to you has been long known to me, and I believe I had some suspicion you was not altogether indifferent about him—the time has, thank God, at last arrived when both have been able to with propriety to avow their mutual inclinations."[78] James's father here thanks God for the battle that cost his son's leg but prompted his marriage. Gordon's family insisted loudly that he was a hero to be admired rather than a cripple to be pitied: they refer to him as their "timber-toed hero." His sister wrote to Lydia that their brother Charles, an army officer, boasted to his fellow officers about his gallant navy brother: "Charles is very envious of his brother's wooden leg, and he says that all his brother officers are very envious of *him*, they would all wish to have such *a brother.*"[79] Charles was the one who met James when he returned to England on crutches. Charles traveled with him to London and walked by his side as he made the rounds to see family and friends for the first time after his loss. In a letter to Lydia, James's aunt starts the practice James himself will follow of using "lame" as a term of endearment within the context of his relationship with Lydia. She calls him "this lame man of yours," adding, "I trust that you and our beloved James will be one of the happiest couples in the three kingdoms."[80]

James's wealthiest and most influential relative, Lord Glenbervie, is a partial exception to the happy chorus of letter writers. He accepted the fact that James and Lydia were determined to marry but feared they were still too poor to do so prudently:

Pheasantary, 28 July, 1812

> It would have been to be wished that the one or the other had been more gifted by fortune. . . . I should have agreed fully with your father in his advice that you should wait till you got a little richer, if I had not perceived that your own heart is so much on the other side of the question.

This problem could be solved only by James's resolving to energetically pursue his profession at sea. Glenbervie urges him not to "relax in your assiduous applications for immediate employment." He stresses that James, like the officers Gill studies, should see his career as a means to provide for his family, reminding him of "your duty to endeavor by pursuing that career to enable yourself to acquire such an addition to your worldly substance as may secure comfort and independence to you both, and to those who may come after you."[81]

Lydia's reply to James's account of all this shows that she fully expected her husband to go back to active duty at sea:

1st August, 1812

> You did perfectly right in assuring Lord Glenbervie that it would not be my wish to prevent your fulfilling the duties of your profession, and however deeply I may, and most assuredly shall feel our frequent separations, it would in my opinion be so entirely wrong, that I trust nothing will ever tempt me to influence you to give it up contrary to your better reason and judgment, but I shall look forward with hope to happier times, when you may be allowed to retire with honour to a situation of less peril.[82]

James and Lydia married at St. Mary's church, Marlborough, on August 28, 1812. They lived together in lodgings in London, then together in the *Seahorse* at Portsmouth while James was fitting it up for sea. He sailed in November and was soon escorting convoys to the West Indies and blockading France.

Letters from the two decades of their marriage offer an open and vivid commentary on what the loss of his leg entailed for James Gordon, physically and emotionally. As Gill suggests, writing letters home connected him not only to his family on shore, but also to his own identity as husband and father during long and repeated separations. James's letters home often summarize the key aspects of his identity in a sentence or two: he mentions that he belongs to Lydia and to their children, that he is physically impaired, and that he is successful in his profession. "The Royal Oak's Admiral [a fellow Scot, Sir Pulteney Malcolm] has been particularly kind to me, and I do think that your poor, lame sailor is a bit of a favourite," he writes on March 10, 1813.[83] In the same year, "Frigates, my dearest girl, in a general action, cannot do more than look on, so your poor lame sailor will have only the honour of saying he commanded a frigate in the action off Cherbourg."[84] Later, when his victories had brought a knighthood, James seems to enjoy combining that new title with his other titles of "wooden-legged Papa" and "much-attached Husband": "I am now writing this in the post-office, and an old fellow will not leave off calling Sir James, Sir James, so you must not expect a very fine letter, my Lady.... Kiss our darling for her poor, wooden-legged Papa, and believe me, I am most anxious to assure you in person I shall ever remain your affectionate and much-attached Husband."[85]

In her account of officers' letters to their families from this period, Gill sums up the marriages they describe as "a combination of patriarchal domination and companionship." She points out that even the most private letters build a "personal identity in line with social and personal expectations."[86] James and Lydia's letters reflect a deep affection and commitment to companionship within the structure of patriarchal domination they inhabited. Especially in the early years of their marriage, their letters show lively interest in how their attempts to construct their personal identities as husband and wife lined up—and did not line up—with social expectations for men, women, and marriage in their class and time. These letters reach us within a printed compilation of correspondence and official papers framed by biographical notes that Lydia began and their daughters completed in 1890. Its very title, *Letters and Records of Admiral Sir J. A. Gordon, G.C.B*, proclaims the value of James's public achievements rather than his wife's more private accomplishments. The book itself, however, foregrounds the importance of Lydia. James Gordon lived a long, rich, and complex life, one that can be interpreted through various frames. Bryan Perrett, for example, suggests that C. S. Forester found the model for his swashbuckling Horatio Hornblower in Gordon's action-filled career at sea.[87] *Letters and Records* chooses instead to present Gordon's life as a love story.

The weight this collection gives to his role as a husband suggests that Elizabeth, Adelaide, and Sophia may have been as devoted to their mother's memory as they were to that of their more famous father.

Chapter 1 discussed James's early difficulties with literacy. His letters read today as engagingly informal: his sentences run together, particularly when he is suggesting something that he hopes Lydia will like, and the words he chooses are vivid but short. "I am very happy to find you have at last trusted yourself on the outside of a horse, I am sure that sort of exercise will do you a great deal of good," he writes on June 25, 1813: "Why don't you buy a nice little horse, you know you must ride when I get on shore on halfpay, for I cannot walk. I wish you had one of my horses which would just do for you, though we fire the large guns close to him, he does not start, and Christie rode him in action, he also goes well in a gig."[88] Escorting the king on a ceremonial visit to Ireland on August 26, 1821, James is even more direct: "I do not find myself as happy away from you as I did when I had a chance of having my head shot off," he writes.[89] In contrast, Lydia's letters favor stately formality and an abstract vocabulary. She likes personification. For example, of the portrait discussed in chapter 1 that captured only the authority of James's "quarter-deck face," not the warmth of his smile, she remarks that she "shall now and then contemplate the inanimate Ivory, and memory aided by affection will enable me to fill up the painter's deficiencies."[90] James admired Lydia's elegant reflections so much that he sometimes copied them out and repeated them to her. On March 21, 1813, he wrote of the suicide of an acquaintance: "Your reflections, my dearest Lydia, on this melancholy event are admirably expressed, but be assured, my beloved girl, that our attachment '*does* rest upon a firmer basis, and that whatever afflictions we may have, we shall ever retain that regard and esteem for each other which will render all lesser evils light.'"[91] James apparently dictated to Lydia the recollections of his childhood that are placed at the opening of *Letters and Records*, but the style of that section of the book is far more hers than his.

Letters and Records includes far fewer of Lydia's letters than those of James: much of her writing seems to have been destroyed at her own wish. Concerned for propriety, Lydia requested that James burn her letters. He refused but acknowledged her freedom to do as she liked with them herself: "What put it into your head, my dearest Lydia, that I should be so careless as to have your letters lying about my cabin. No, no. I take more care of them, and I have too great a regard for the dear person who writes them to burn one of them. I will promise when we have the happiness to meet again to allow you to do so, for *I* cannot."[92] Expectations about propriety in the physical expression of emotion seem to have weighed more strongly on Lydia than they did on James. Her letters are as stoical as they are abstract. In contrast, seven years into their marriage, in a letter dated May 28, 1819, James mentions choking up and longing for "a good cry" upon leaving her to return to his command: "When I left you I was almost choked, and I would have given anything to have had a good cry. God bless you, my dearest."[93] James mentions nearly crying again in January 1820, when he was treated with leeches for pain in the head. Lydia's latest letter did him "more good than all the physic the Dr. gave me. . . . If the letter had not arrived, I know I should have sat down and cried. Fancy my having been so long without a letter from my dearest wife! . . . The swelling caused by the leeches is going down, and I expect to-morrow to have a head and face of the proper size."[94] James often describes himself as on the edge of bursting into tears in response to their trials and separations.

In letters from the first years of their marriage, James and Lydia consider who they are to each other, and who they want to be, within the social framework of patriarchal expectations that Gill describes. James's early letters invoke these expectations playfully, with a measure of ironic distance. He jokes about the idea of himself as Lydia's lord and master on June 17, 1813: "I am made happy by a letter from my dear wife, though made a little uncomfortable by her saying she was much fatigued by her journey. If she writes so kindly always, *I shall begin to think she has some regard for her lord and master!*"[95] On December 21, 1813, James again invokes their hierarchical roles as husband and wife, apparently replying to a letter from Lydia that refused to "stomach" these roles: "My Very Dear and Dutiful Wife,— Though you do not stomach my styling myself your lord and master, you know I am, and must tremble in my presence," he begins. Then, as usual, he assumes that Lydia will do whatever she thinks best. If he must sail before they can both look at a house they are thinking of leasing, she can view it herself and "then decide if you will have plenty of room, if not, there is a house next door."[96] He signs off with a question: "Believe me, your much attached husband, and lord and master—what do you think of that?"[97]

This kind of self-conscious joking about his role as lord and master drops away after the early years of their marriage, as James settled into the more congenial role of much attached husband.

When he was away at sea during Lydia's first pregnancy, James wrote to offer her his patriarchal authority as a tool she could use to strengthen her position in any disagreement she might have with her parents, in whose house she then lived. He urges her to use his name as she thinks best to achieve what she herself wants: "Don't you think it would be best to ask your mother to look out for a servant for you? and then you will be able to mention as *my* wish to your mother what *you* think proper on the subject we are so anxious about. For God's sake keep up your spirits."[98] Chapter 1 discusses James Gordon's awareness of the role he played as captain, putting on his "quarter-deck face" when he assumed command of a ship. Writing to Lydia, he introduced the image of her as the "commanding officer" of their home. As it was James's role to command at sea, so it was Lydia's role to command in "our quarters" on land. The image is playful, but James's confidence in Lydia's judgment is genuine: "April 15, 1814. If I am put on half pay I think London would be as good a place as any to take up our quarters in till we can look about us a little; but I leave all that to you, my dear, as you must be commanding officer when I strike my pennant. God bless you."[99] This declaration that Lydia must be his commanding officer when he returns to the home that she has managed alone in his absence suggests awareness of the complexities of authority that can arise when an active service member, however beloved, rejoins a household that has learned to function without him or her.

A year into their marriage, James states his "great opinion of [Lydia's] abilities," affirming his respect for her intelligence and good sense. She is not merely James's "dearest," but also his most able adviser. He asks Lydia to read and approve a draft of a letter before he sends it:

Dec. 5 1813

I have just finished a letter to my Aunt West [Aunt Peggy] if you do not approve of it, return it to me, I have so great an opinion of your abilities that if I had to perform any difficult piece of service, I should desire no abler advisor than my dearest Lydia.[100]

James may have asked Lydia to "approve" the draft of his letter to Aunt Peggy because of his respect for her as a writer. His own insecurity in this regard was lifelong: "My almost total lack of education prevents my *expressing* half of what I feel for you in a proper way," he wrote to Lydia on November 21, 1815.[101] However, the general principle that a wife is her husband's chief "adviser" was central to James Gordon's idea of marriage. He objected to a friend's belief that a wife should be kept ignorant of her husband's financial affairs:

July 17 1822

I find Jane knows nothing of MacDonell's affairs, I don't like that, as a wife ought to know everything. What *should* I do if my dear girl was not my confidant? I do feel such a comfort in uncharging my mind to my beloved.[102]

James serenely informed his family that he relied on Lydia for advice on "public" matters as well as private concerns:

Gordon Hall, August 3

My father was much astonished when I told him I never had a secret from you. "What! do you tell her all your public secrets?" "Yes to be sure, when I can without putting it on paper." "Ah! Well, I believe you may do so, my dear boy, for she is a woman of sense." What do you think of that, my love? *Fanny* [James's sister] said *she* should have been surprised, if I did not trust you with everything.[103]

The "public secrets" that James did not risk trusting to paper are confidential naval matters. But he entrusted them to Lydia. Despite his father's initial astonishment, Lydia's in-laws accepted the fact that James would trust her good sense with "everything." The letters that the memoir includes from this twenty-three-year marriage brim with mutual regard. The sight of Gibraltar on September 25, 1820, reminds James of his voyage home to propose marriage to Lydia: "The last time I was here I thought almost as much of you as I do now, as I was then afraid you would have nothing to say to a wounded sailor." Two months later, on November 20, Lydia also writes of how her feelings have grown: "After more than eight years' marriage, I may acknowledge without a blush that you were very *very* dear to me, even long before, though my attachment was not then to be compared with that which now engrosses nearly my whole heart."[104] James sails into one battle after another with no apparent concern for his own safety, but a heart that overflows with concern for Lydia: "May God ever preserve you, my dear, dear wife. I have not words to express how much I love you."[105]

It seems no coincidence that Lydia was a military wife. On the one hand, this role accords with an ideal of public men and private women: the husband fought abroad while the wife waited safe at home. On the other hand, during the years when James was often away at sea, Lydia was responsible for a good deal of "masculine" public business. Their family depended on her ability to manage financial affairs such as leasing properties, investing and drawing on funds, moving herself and their children about the country from one house to the other, and engaging and dismissing servants. Given the time lag involved in communicating by letter, James could do little but affirm his confidence in her judgment. He did so, cheerfully and with no qualification whatsoever:

1823 Nov 2

> If you should be obliged to decide whether you take Miss Bedingfield [a possible governess for their daughters] or not before my return, do, my dearest Lydia, that which you think best. You are the best judge, and you are certain that which you do I shall think right.[106]

"That which you do I shall think right": This remark sums up James and Lydia's usual mode of doing business. James's letters are full of instructions for Lydia, but even more full of his confidence that whatever she chooses to do will be right. "Do, my love, take a comfortable lodging near the Admiral," he advises on March 21, 1812, but adds "without you like another part of the town better."[107] On December 18, 1813, he remarks to Lydia, "If you do not think you will be as comfortable at St. Helens, just say so, my dear girl, and we will think of something else." Their daughters summarize the remainder of the letter, which follows the familiar pattern: "Here follows the account of the lodgings and terms as in previous letter, most anxious his dearest Lydia should do what she liked best."[108]

James and Lydia both had physical courage, remaining self-possessed when their lives were in danger. In December 1815, they and their young children set out on what should have been a short and pleasant trip in the *Meander* from Sheerness for Leith Roads. The weather changed, however, and the *Meander* struck a shoal. An officer describes "the dangerous and awful situation" for the *Naval Chronicle:*

> The wind blowing a gale, with a tremendous sea, the ship making upwards of 20 feet water an hour, and nearly 12 hours' darkness before them; not a moment was to be lost, for not a hope of safety was entertained, save in the mercy of the Almighty, and the united exertions of every soul on board. By the zeal and energy of the captain and his officers, and the almost unparalleled exertions of the men, the ship was kept free until morning [when] the Great Dispenser of All Events . . . lulled the storm and hushed the raging sea.[109]

With sails fixed over the damaged hull to slow the leak, the *Meander* reached Shearness on December 22. James Gordon won praise for the remarkable fact that he had managed to keep his ship's company from despair and drunkenness. His courage inspired the seamen who worked the pumps for over twenty hours straight while the officers handled the sails. James and Lydia's children, however, grew up believing that during "those terrible hours" the bravest person in the *Meander* was their mother: "His wife's calmness and self-command were of infinite comfort and support to [James] in those terrible hours. Often did he speak to his children of her wonderful fortitude and quiet courage, holding her up as an example to them."[110]

Lydia's courage in the face of physical danger is also evident in another set of letters from 1813. On March 21, 1813, it appears that Lydia told James that she was pregnant with their first child, news that brought fear as well as happiness: "Your information most certainly gave me the greatest pleasure, at the same time that it has given me cause to be more anxious about you," James wrote.[111] They had good reason to be anxious. At that time, after tuberculosis, childbirth was the greatest cause of death among English women.

On top of the already dangerous proposition of bearing a child in 1813, Lydia faced another risk: she wanted to be with her husband. James's ship was headed home, and he was eager to see his pregnant wife. His favorite trope of inexpressibility is all over this series of letters, gesturing at feelings that soar beyond his powers of description: "I feel so happy at the prospect of seeing you so soon, my much beloved, that I can hardly write a word," he wrote on March 21, 1813.[112] On May 5, James wrote from Plymouth, still hoping to see Lydia at Portsmouth: "I have only time to say I am off this port—Plymouth—on my way to Portsmouth. . . . I am now so happy in the prospect of seeing my much beloved wife so soon that I can hardly write."[113] James did not, however, reach Portsmouth until June 30, by which point Lydia's pregnancy had advanced past its eighth month. Portsmouth is sixty-eight miles from Marlborough, where Lydia lived with her parents while James was away at sea. Now an hour and a half by car, it was then a two-day journey by coach. The idea of Lydia making the journey nine months pregnant terrified James: "As for your coming to Portsmouth now, for God's sake, do not think of it," he wrote. He proposed an alternative plan for meeting once the danger of childbirth had passed: "If I should be ordered on foreign service, I shall do all I can to see you before I go, if only for a few hours. If I can keep off Cherbourg until after your confinement, I am determined to ask for 10 days' leave, and if you wish then to return with me there can be no objection."[114] This letter attempts a reassuring assessment of Lydia's situation, then trails off into inexpressibility: "Indeed, indeed, I wish much to hear of the safety of my dear affectionate little wife, but as you are now with your dear mother, who, with the love she bears her dear Lydia, added to her knowledge, I think you are quite safe, and look forward with pleasure to the day when I shall see you and our dear little one in your arms. I cannot, my love, express what I feel just now."[115] James rallies his powers of expression, however, to discuss "what money will be at your disposal." He offers Lydia advice on how to invest the funds he has sent, but he resorts to a metaphor drawn from his profession to urge her, above all, to buy herself anything she wants. Childbirth is a battle, and the funds James has sent Lydia are ammunition: "Do not, my dear, dear girl, deprive yourself of one comfort, while there is a shot in the locker."[116] Shot is of no use if the battle is lost, and their income would be of no use if Lydia were dead.

Ignoring James's exhortation to remain at Marlborough, the heavily pregnant Lydia traveled to Portsmouth by coach, accompanied by her family, to see James. She reflects on this meeting in a letter written in

July 1813. Elegant and correct as ever, she states that she has given birth to their daughter: "Our late meeting my dearest James was even shorter than a dream, but like a delightful one on which we reflect with pleasure while we cannot help being angry at being awakened so unseasonably ... I am much pleased with having seen my beloved husband so well. ... Thank God with me for all His mercies, my dearest husband, here I am safe in bed with a dear little girl by my side. Ever thine most truly, L.G."[117] This first daughter, Hannah, was born on July 25. James did not, however, learn of this event and Lydia's safety until October. He was on a cruise near Iceland, where Lydia's letters did not reach him in a timely way:

July 1813

I have now left my dearest Lydia with as sore a heart as a poor man ever had. I feel glad that I had the pleasure of seeing her, though it was for so very short a time, and I look forward to the time when she will be if possible dearer to me than ever. May I hope that the prayers of a sincerely attached husband may be heard for her safety in bringing into this world a being that will be a comfort to her when the father is away, and be assured my dearest Lydia, whether boy or girl, I shall feel a something when I see you both, that is impossible to express.[118]

Lydia continued to write him reassuring letters about her own and the baby's good health, and the importance of family over fame:

26 August 1813

Rawdon ... wants me to put off the christening, till you have achieved some great thing, in order that I may call my little girl by some grand and glorious name, but I shall be perfectly contented to see my beloved husband safely returned, and should you fall in with an enemy, may God in his goodness preserve you, and grant you to be successful.[119]

James continued to cruise the North Atlantic with no word, reading any English newspaper he could find in search of news of his wife. On September 15, he tried to imagine how much better he would manage during a future pregnancy: "I have got some English papers from August 27th to September 6th, but not a word about my dear wife. I wonder I did not think of naming a paper for you to have your safety mentioned in, I should then have known what papers to have asked for, on my arrival at any place, I shall be sure to do so when I have again the same cause of anxiety."[120] On September 19, James was simply "most anxious." Bargaining with his worst fear, he vowed to be "very, very happy" with any news at all—as long as that news was conveyed in Lydia's handwriting. Even if their baby were dead, James would thank God that his wife was alive to write to him of the loss: "How very, very happy I shall be when I see your hand-writing, I shall then be thankful to God for having preserved you though our dear babe may not have been spared to be a comfort to us both. . . . I am most anxious about my dearest wife."[121] On October 6, Lydia's good news has reached him at last: "Your letters have given me the greatest pleasure, I cannot express half what I feel," he writes to her.[122]

James's letters are full of concern for Lydia's health. He likes thinking of things that might benefit it. For instance, in his letter of June 25, 1813, mentioned above, he uses the fact that he has only one leg as an excuse to urge Lydia to buy herself a "nice little horse" and ride for exercise. She might as well buy the horse now, he argues, because she will need it when he gets home. When they are together, Lydia will ride because James cannot walk: "You know you must ride when I get on shore on halfpay, for I cannot walk."[123] Elizabeth, Adelaide, and Sophia Gordon inform us that their father, however, "walked rapidly and easily" using a cane.[124] He enjoyed long walks, with great benefit to his own health, until a bad fall late in life. Given this ongoing concern with Lydia's health, to a twenty-first-century reader, the letters' silence about reproductive choice is striking. Although these letters question other social expectations about gender and married life, they do not discuss whether a woman should be able to control her own fertility. In England, it was only in 1918 that Marie Stopes's best-selling *Married Love* brought contraception into wide public discussion. In Lydia Gordon's lifetime, abortion was illegal, dangerous, and common, particularly among married women who already had a number of children: "It was not mostly unmarried girls in trouble who resorted to abortion, but the 30–40-year-old married women."[125] In the space of twenty years, Lydia bore eleven children, eight of whom survived infancy. Although less dramatic than battles at sea, her repeated pregnancies were hazardous. In nineteenth-century Britain, Geoffrey Chamberlain writes, "the Four Horsemen of Death in maternal mortality were puerpal pyrexia, haemorrhage, convulsions and illegal abortion."[126] The maternal mortality rate between 1800 and 1850 is estimated at five deaths per every thousand live births.[127] After a live birth, the World Health Organization now recommends waiting at least two years before attempting to begin another pregnancy to reduce the health risks to mother as well as child. Lydia and James's eleventh baby was born in March 1833 and died at the age of ten months. Lydia's "health began to fail" soon after this event, and "although she had the advice of London physicians, the serious symptoms were never removed."[128] She died in 1835 at the age of forty-seven, of an unidentified illness. James never remarried. He died at the age of eighty-three, and he died saying Lydia's name.

When he told his wife that I "trust you with everything," James Gordon included his body. He trusted Lydia with his pain and his weakness. James seems to have been a remarkably cheerful person, one who was eager to make the best of things. He tended to downplay his own pain. "Our father always declared that he never felt much pain from this severe wound," his daughters write. "Our father also consoled himself for the loss of his limb, with the reflection, that as he had had to lose a leg, the left one was that he could spare the best, as he had had several accidents to it and had suffered very much in consequence of his having accidently stepped upon a quantity of broken glass, some of which had entered his foot."[129] He managed to make his wide circle of friends as comfortable with the fact that he walked with a wooden leg and a stick as they were with his lifelong fondness for snuff. Both facts were seen as opportunities for showering him with well-chosen presents: "He never wore any other than a wooden leg, and he walked rapidly and easily; when walking out of doors he always used a stick, and the presents of sticks which he received in later life were as numerous as his snuff-boxes."[130] His optimistic tone matches that of his family. From the beginning, family letters focus on recovery and rehabilitation: "I trust by this time he is almost well again, and his wound perfectly whole," wrote his sister Frances. "Indeed, it was only two inches open when he wrote, and that is now six weeks ago. I should think he would be very soon able to bear the pressure of a wooden leg."[131]

Nevertheless, when writing to Lydia, James was candid about the difficulties he faced in living with his impairment. The first time he left after they married, he mingled declarations of love for her with remarks about his trouble getting used to various prosthetic legs (favoring one made by a Mr. Drake) and favorite canes. He acknowledges both emotional and physical pain, although with characteristic optimism, he looks forward to an end for both:

> Nov. 27, 1812
>
> My Dear Dear Wife,
>   Nothing but our meeting again can, I am sure, repay us for the pain we have felt this day. . . . I hope, my dearest Lydia, you have got the gold head for the cane our dear Father gave me the day he gave me *you*, my dear, dear wife, for I cannot find it. . . . I have taken to Mr. Drake's leg, and it answers so well that I think, after a little pain, I shall feel as comfortable in it, as I did in the other.[132]

He tells her about everything from the awkwardness of being unable to kneel when kissing the king's hand at court, to his pride in keeping his balance on the deck of his ship while landsmen with two legs apiece were "tumbling about very much . . . poor fellows," to becoming mired in the Louisiana mud during the Battle of New Orleans. "I have been lying here several days and have been on shore, trying to get a shot," he wrote, "but I am a bad shot, my love, and the ground is too soft for my wooden leg."[133]

The first time James goes to sea after their marriage, he writes on the anniversary of Lissa to complain that nothing seems right:

> November 28th
>
>   I feel more and more uneasy every mile we go. To be sure, I always felt a little queer when I had sailed from home before, but the moment I went on deck I found something to amuse me. Now it is not so. I cannot walk about. Everything seems to go wrong . . . This night a year ago (November 28th, 1811) we were looking for the French Squadron in much better spirits than I am now.[134]

It is not clear whether James "cannot walk about" because of the difficulty of navigating a moving deck on new wooden leg, or because of the depression his spirits have suffered at being separated from Lydia—or both. He even mentions a nearly unthinkable wish: giving up the hard-won privilege of command: "In short, I wish I could give my ship up." When he has better news to share about his health and mobility, he fits in the announcement that he is walking without a cane between expressions of love: "May God ever preserve you, my dear, dear wife. I have not words to express how much I love you. I forgot to mention that I have, for several days, laid aside my stick."

James dwells on the support that the very thought of Lydia gives him, waking and sleeping. He acknowledges having "melancholy fits," but thanks God that these fits "but seldom" attack him, and he thanks Lydia for making him feel better, even in his dreams:

December 23rd 1814

> I have had a pain in my stump all day, and have been particularly low-spirited. You, I believe, my much beloved wife, never saw me in one of my melancholy fits, thank God I am but seldom attacked by them. . . . A good night's rest and dreaming of you, my love, all night, has quite recovered me.[135]

Two months later, he imagines more comfort from Lydia: "I hope you will take care of yourself for my sake. I have got some flannel for my stump, but if the coverings had been made by your dear hands they would have been more comfortable."[136]

Although James was open about the difficulties he experienced, he generally described pain or illness as something that has passed, or that he expected to pass soon. Even when the ill effects of Jamaica's climate on his stump made him consider giving up his command, he still stressed his overall good health and the primacy of his connection to Lydia and their family. He writes on January 3, 1813, "I hope to be ordered home with a convoy from Jamaica, if not, I am determined to give up my ship, as the warm weather does not do for my stump. I know my much beloved wife will be happy to hear that I am quite well, and as happy as a man can be, who has left everything he holds dear in the world so far from him."[137] By March 16, his condition was improving, as well as his state of mind: "My stump is not quite well yet, but it gives me no trouble; thank God, I am well and in good spirits."[138] By March 24, the news was even better. No longer in pain, James cheerfully anticipates a long stretch of continued good health: "I am sure my dear girl will not be sorry to hear that the doctor has quite cured my stump, and as the pain, which I mentioned to you I once felt, has not returned, I suppose I shall not be ill again for some time."[139] He continues to be matter-of-fact yet hopeful about difficulties on April 15: "I have split the upper part of the case for my leg, and I am obliged to take the one I had made at Gloucester, it answers pretty well."[140]

It was difficult for a man with a wooden prosthetic leg to walk the tilting deck of a sailing ship. James sometimes fell, and he wrote about those falls to Lydia. "I had had a fall just before I went on shore, and when I came back on board, my head ached very much," he writes to Lydia on March 10, 1813. "The pain went away in the night."[141] People with two legs, however, also fell. Earlier, James pointed out that, as an experienced seaman, he managed better than landsmen with two legs apiece:

Seahorse, December 18, 1812

> I am sure my dear little girl will be happy to hear that I have taken so much care of myself that I have not had a fall yet, nor have I felt inclined to go *to the masthead*. Having so many landsmen on board, poor fellows, they have been tumbling about very much, but I am glad to say without any accident.[142]

He remarks, "I forgot to mention that we were obliged to lash [a passenger] to the table. . . . I was sitting carelessly—the ship gave a roll, and down I went, but I did not hurt myself. We are tumbling about a good deal, with a heavy swell."[143]

Although officers did not work sails, they did go aloft on occasion, another aspect of shipboard life that seems particularly hazardous for a man with only one leg. James replied to Lydia's hope that he would remain on deck—not with a promise to stay out of the rigging, but rather with a promise to go aloft only when moved by "necessity":

Falmouth, December 11 1812

> I perceive, my dear girl, you think I shall run improper risks in going to the masthead. Nothing but necessity will ever oblige me to go above the deck. I think I observe in your letter that you think more of me, my dear, dear wife, than you do of yourself. I hope you will take care of yourself for my sake.[144]

Although he will avoid "improper risks," there is no question of avoiding risk itself. In February 1813, James admits that he has indeed climbed up to the maintop: "A strange sail is just seen from the masthead, which we must chase. I went up to the main-top yesterday for the first time and find I can go up so far with great ease, but I do not think I shall ever go up higher."[145] Lydia hoped that whatever risks James ran in his ship, at least the sea was his "own element," one that he would not leave for the dangers of combat on land. He was, however, on his way to the Battle of New Orleans:

> 3 Oct. 1814
>
> A pretty fellow you are, I think. Not content with the dangers you are constantly exposed to at sea, and the chances of meeting an enemy on your own element, you must also be wishing you had it in your power to join our gallant army in America. Thank God you have no business onshore!

James wrote that he was prudently having a horse-drawn "shore-going" gig constructed to carry him over uneven and swampy ground, difficult terrain for a man with a wooden leg: "I have got on board three horses for myself as I cannot walk and for Christie, and I have wheels to mount a gig (a shore-going one I mean), which will be made in a few days."[146] Lydia was not pleased:

> 24 Oct 1814
>
> What in the world you are to do with a gig and horses I cannot imagine.... I have comforted myself hitherto thinking you had no business out of your ship, and that all your warfare would be carried on in your own element, but now I know not what to think.[147]

On learning on March 21, 1815, that James had indeed left his ship to take on the even more hazardous duty of leading a raid, Lydia writes to him with a touch of frost: "I fancied, nay, I hoped, that you would not (on account of your one leg) be considered eligible to take the command of boats, but being deprived of this imaginary security, I should now be quite miserable but for a firm reliance on a merciful Providence, whose powerful aid on so many occasions I acknowledge with heartfelt gratitude." She concludes, however, with her usual heartfelt sympathy: "I trembled when I read of the difficulties of your landing and the nights you had to pass in a boat during such severe weather."[148]

James writes to Lydia about how his impairment affects their life together with warmth and confidence in her affection, as he writes to her about everything else. For example, he is delighted to hear she enjoyed dancing their favorite dance at a party, even though he was not there to dance with her, and even though he would no longer be able to dance with her even when home. James imagined another scene of dancing, one that acknowledged the loss of his leg with no loss of joy. Having learned to play a drum as a boy on ships beating to quarters before battle, James now pictured himself beating a drum while Lydia danced "to give you music for your steps." Their daughter Hannah would watch and laugh at her parents, a happy "pair of old fools":

> On my word, my dear creature, you have been gay, I am glad of it, for I am sure it will do you good. And so you managed to go down *our* dance, and sing a duet with Eliza. . . . I am glad you have not quite made a resolution not to dance again, for you must remember *I* cannot dance, and I think it will be your duty to amuse our little Hannah, and though I can play on no other instrument than a drum, I can give you music for your steps. Don't you think she will take us for a pair of old fools?[149]

Tobin Siebers points out that "it is a good thing to feel comfortable in one's skin," for people living with an impairment as well as those whose bodies are normative.[150] Few seem to have felt more comfortable in their own skin than James Gordon.

When they were apart from each other on the day he lost his leg, James and Lydia noted the anniversary in their letters. Lydia calls down God's special protection on James on "that never-to-be-forgotten day." She acknowledges suffering, but like James's father, considers November 29 to be the day on which God saved James's life, not the day on which God took his leg:

> 29th November, 1812
>
> This is the anniversary of that memorable, that never-to-be-forgotten day on which you suffered so severely in your country's cause. I trust I may never have such another dreadful trial. May God bless and preserve thee, my beloved James, from all dangers; on His protecting providence we must rest our hopes.[151]

Years later, on the anniversary of the battle, James linked the greatest joy and the greatest pain of his life in a theory of loss and compensation. In his mind, the loss of his leg was redeemed by his marriage with Lydia:

Nov. 29, 1821:

> This is the day I lost my leg, I daresay you will think of me, if I had not lost it I don't think you would have married me, for I should have remained so long in the Mediterranean that you would not have had patience to wait for me. Thank God, it is as it is.[152]

Jane Austen's *Persuasion* reflects on love, loss, time, and happiness. Writing to Lydia, James Gordon reflected on these things as well. However, unlike *Persuasion*, his letters imagine a physically damaged man as the romantic hero of a love story, one who accepts his own impairment as the key to his happy ending: "Thank God, it is as it is."

4

Becoming Victorian

In the summer of 1831, Michael Seymour encountered the eponym of a new age. He led a tour of the Portsmouth Dockyard for the thirteen-year-old Princess Victoria, who showed "a lively sympathy with Sir Michael in the loss of his arm, and expressed great surprise and interest in his ability to do so much with the remaining one."[1] England changed as amputee officers lived on through the middle of the nineteenth century. "Nelson was once Britannia's god of war, / And still should be so, but the tide is turn'd," Byron wrote in 1821, after Waterloo had partially eclipsed Trafalgar in the public consciousness.[2] Trousers replaced the knee breeches of Royal Navy uniforms, and the officers who wore them harried slave ships and led arctic expeditions rather than fighting the French. Steam power heralded a new era at sea where Britannia now reigned supreme; the Great Reform Bill did the same for political life on shore. What did it mean for a body marked by battles that were no longer news but history to live on through the zenith of the British Empire? New views of masculinity, the body, and the mind were promoted by medical and conduct-book writing that increasingly polarized gender difference. While an amputee might have been stigmatized as a "defect" in God's order by the previous century's aesthetic theories or as the object of cruel humor by its jestbooks, Victorian Britain devised a new form of stigma in keeping with its interests: pseudoscientific theorizing.

In addition to making extreme claims about the different natures of men and women, some medical writers lamented the terrifying ease with which such differences could be compromised. Lurid fantasies of "degeneracy" haunted Dr. Henry Maudsley and the new field of psychiatry he helped to establish. Rationality, the crowning glory of civilized man, was always in peril from the low impulses that ruled women and savage men. Infected by such fears, some medical men saw a new meaning in common effects of amputation such as spasms and phantom pain, identifying them as symptoms of hysterical femininity. This remarkable misdiagnosis has understandably attracted considerable attention from cultural historians. Nevertheless, such "rigid and pessimistic somaticism" should not be taken as defining Victorian psychiatry as a whole.[3] Even more importantly, we should remember that nineteenth-century medical theories do not tell the whole story of individual lives lived in that period, any more than eighteenth-century jestbooks or aesthetic treatises do for earlier times. Watkin Owen Pell, for example, was as certain as Henry Maudsley that degeneracy surrounded him, but he saw this degeneracy in the rise of the centralized power of the Victorian state, not in the spasms of his own vestigial limb. As military heroes, as well as gentlemen and the heads of households, surviving amputee officers such as Michael Seymour, James Alexander Gordon, and Watkin Owen Pell appear to have been unaffected by emergent notions that they embodied a pathologized version of femininity. Among their families, friends, colleagues, and doctors, and in public appearances such as Victoria's visit to Portsmouth, they carried on much as they always had. Watkin Owen Pell's diary and *Letters and Records of . . . Gordon's* account of James Gordon's later years represent the medical experiences of two amputee officers' mid-nineteenth-century old age as little changed from those of their eighteenth-century youth.

"Remember Nelson"

On March 13, 1811, William Hoste, the protégé who had been awed to watch Nelson climb aboard ship with his broken right arm dangling at Tenerife, sailed into battle against a French squadron at Lissa, wildly outgunned and outmanned. Hoste had four frigates, one of them the *Active*, commanded by James Alexander Gordon, and nearly nine hundred men. The French had six larger frigates, a brig, two schooners, a xebec, and a gun-boat, and a total of nearly two thousand men. Hoste ordered an unconventional signal to be run up the halyards: "Remember Nelson." The British cheered and won the battle through superior seamanship and gunnery. Such a victory was clearly an excellent way to remember Nelson. But how should Nelson, and other amputee officers, be remembered when there were no more major sea battles to fight? The wartime navy had offered some officers with major physical impairments the chance to establish long and distinguished careers. What would Victorian England make of them once their wars were over?

Some of the era's changes impacted the navy directly. During Seymour's, Pell's, and Gordon's lifetimes, Britain transformed from the world's largest slave-trading nation to its leader in the campaign against slavery. Boys who had joined a navy that escorted slave ships down the African coast grew old in one that harried them. In 1832, Michael Seymour took slave traders to court in Rio de Janeiro, and as the commander of the Jamaica division of the West Indies station from 1833 to 1837, Watkin Owen Pell oversaw the formal emancipation of the enslaved workforce of the plantations of the West Indies. Seymour, Pell, and Gordon also watched steam power change the nature of sailing itself. Although steam engines made many of their hard-won skills archaic, some officers greeted the new era with enthusiasm. On September 22, 1834, Pell's old captain, Henry Duncan, wrote to him from aboard a steam-powered ship, delighted with the new technology: "We don't lose much time nowadays in the journey for I went down to Dundee [from London] within 40 hours," he wrote. "If we had had such as I am now on Board of when you and I were Shipmates what might we not have done." To Duncan's optimistic way of thinking, steam power promised much more than speed alone. "I do not think we shall have another war in our day & I hope not," Duncan continued, "but think . . . this steam will give a new character to war & must tend at all counts to shorten it."[4] On May 20, 1838, Pell himself made a point of traveling to London to admire "the great Steam Vessel at Limehouse."[5]

These officers witnessed other transformations as well. In 1848, as revolutions erupted across Europe, supporters of the People's Charter, Britain's own working-class movement, held their last mass meeting on a rainy day in April on Kennington Common. They planned to assemble there, then march to Parliament to deliver a petition demanding the right to vote for "every male inhabitant of these realms" in a peaceful show of their massive strength.[6] Instead, a worried government led by the Duke of Wellington stationed police, backed up at a discrete distance by cavalry and infantry, to block the bridges to the north side of the Thames. Rather than trying to force their way over Westminster Bridge, the crowd dispersed. The anticlimax of the day, and the dying fall of Chartism as a mass movement, was the leaders' agreement to deliver the petition to Parliament alone in hired cabs. Watkin Owen Pell was there to see it all:

April 10, 1848:

> The great meeting of the Chartists on Kennington Common. I rode right through from the Church to the Bricklayers' Arms at 1 p.m. The great body of the people were dispersing quietly, a few hundreds only attended to the Speeches from the wagons. There were no military or police in sight. Wrote to [my brother] Edwin.[7]

Pell approved of this action to curtail potential working-class unrest. He was less happy about two other major achievements of Victorian government: the centralization of state power and professionalization of domestic security forces, as discussed below.

To naval veterans of the great wars with France, perhaps the strangest change was seeing not only the battles they had fought but also their profession itself fall from the headlines, becoming only one element of an expanding empire. Pell enjoyed living at the center of this empire: his diary mentions visiting the British Museum with his wife "to see the Bull and Lions with human faces and the Nineveh Marbles, &c. &c." in October of 1850, for example, as well as several proud visits to the Great Exhibition in 1851. These cultural triumphs reflected the empire's domination of the oceans throughout the nineteenth century, which allowed it to consolidate control of India, impose the opium trade on China, and colonize countries in Africa. But although Victoria's empire rested on British naval power, the glory of major engagements at sea was a thing of the past. The Royal Navy underwent a massive and permanent postwar downsizing. To veterans like Lieutenant John Marshall, the public's memory of their "many meritorious actions in the warfare of their country" could seem woefully short.[8] Walter Houghton observes that Victorians cherished the image of the Napoleonic war hero—but given the lack of major military mobilization between Waterloo and the Crimea, this image of heroic military masculinity became divorced from the realities of the commercial present.[9] John Tosh sees the "unmistakable imprint" of rising bourgeois values in the decreasing Victorian experience of bearing arms.[10] With the debacle of the Crimean War, the gap between heroic images and the reality of military service became painfully obvious.

To add insult to injury, for naval veterans, "Waterloo" became shorthand for Napoleon's defeat, and the glorious battle of Waterloo was the army's victory. Moreover, while no one disputed that Nelson had died a hero's death, he was also, indisputably, dead—while the Duke of Wellington lived on to 1852, resisting fresh reforms and being loaded with fresh honors each year. Even the great column in Trafalgar Square did not even the score in terms of commemoration, at least to acerbic observers such as Charles Dickens. Dickens reminded what he saw as a forgetful public that Nelson had given "an arm and an eye or so," and his life, for his country:

> If we had, in this time of ours, two great commanders—say one by land and one by sea; one dying in battle (or what was left of him, for we will suppose him to have lost an arm and an eye or so before), and one living to old age—it might be a jest for Posterity if we choked our town with bad Statues to one of the two, and utterly abandoned and deserted the memory of the other.[11]

In addition to choking London with images of himself, Wellington was nearly "ubiquitous" in political life as prime minister and Conservative elder statesman.[12] While Nelson was receding into the past, Wellington was undeniably a "man of the present."[13] When the Duke died at last in 1852, his state funeral was modeled on Nelson's, but was even more grand.[14] Even after death, however, Nelson remained distinctively valuable as a means of rallying the "plebeian patriotism" of the London crowd who threw rocks through the Iron Duke's windows. According to Laurence Brockliss, John Cardwell, and Michael Moss, fear of Chartism was a factor that prompted the establishment of a committee, chaired by the ubiquitous Wellington, to erect a grand monument to Nelson in the new public space of Trafalgar Square.[15]

There are now few national monuments more iconic than Nelson's 170-foot-tall column, with the one-armed admiral at its top, standing

18 feet tall and staring coldly at France. But as Marianne Czisnik points out, when the Trafalgar Square memorial was planned, serious consideration was given to the idea that it should represent Nelson "in his perfect figure," his body unmarked by battle. A symmetrical male figure in classical drapery was proposed as a discrete substitute for the notably asymmetrical body and distinctive uniform of the one-armed Admiral Nelson. John Flaxman suggested that "in the execution of a statue the loss of his arm might so be indicated yet obscured that it would not injure the general effect of the work, or he might be represented . . . in his perfect figure," and drew up a design for a two-armed statue.[16] A critic of an earlier Birmingham monument that represented Nelson without his right arm echoed Flaxman's insistence on "perfect" figure: "Were a great man, Admiral or General, to have both legs shot off in Battle, should we then put up the mutilated trunk—a statue without legs—in the market place? Can we not imagine ourselves as meeting great men in a future state whole and perfect?"[17] This remark about meeting amputees "whole and perfect" in heaven echoes the eighteenth-century aesthetic theories discussed in chapter 2, with their focus on divine order revealed through the beauty of symmetry.

In addition, in *Raw Material: Producing Pathology in Victorian Culture*, Erin O'Connor argues that in the context of Victorian medical thought, "wholeness" became more important as a certain ideal of masculine health became more important. "Dismemberment," she claims, "unmanned amputees": "Victorian ideals of health, particularly of male health, centered on the concept of physical wholeness: a strong, vigorous body was a primary signifier of manliness, at once testifying to the existence of a correspondingly strong spirit and providing that spirit with a vital means of material expression."[18] This idea of masculine health as wholeness might contribute to obscuring an amputee's loss of a limb, or to forgetting the fact that he had indeed fought as an amputee. In addition, by imagining "irregularity," either inherited or acquired, as a marker of vice, Victorian medical theorists added a pseudoscientific gloss to the older insistence on the divine beauty of perfect symmetry. Henry Maudsley, for example, contrasted the "regularity and harmony of beauty" to the irregularity that reveals a "morbid hereditary taint": "A morbid hereditary taint frequently impresses its stamp . . . the physiognomy has not the regularity and harmony of beauty; there is, perhaps, an irregular conformation of the head;

Portrait of Robert Heriot Barclay in oval mat. (Toronto Public Library)

a vicious implantation of the ears, or a deformity of one or both of them, is not uncommon . . . there is sometimes a disproportion between the limbs."[19] As the nineteenth century wore on, images of Napoleonic-era amputee officers other than Nelson became less popular. Some of these images also became less visibly impaired. They were cropped in ways that obscured their empty sleeves. For example, the oval matte around the portrait of Robert Heriot Barclay makes the loss of his left arm unlikely to be noticed by a viewer who is not already aware of that fact—although, on closer look, we can see the white facing and gold braid of the cuff of Barclay's empty left sleeve, which is attached across the chest of his uniform coat in the manner of Nelson.

While James Northcote's original portrait of Michael Seymour shows Seymour's empty left sleeve neatly fastened to a button of his uniform coat, in the manner of Nelson, a later version of the portrait shows traces of an oval matte that would have obscured the loss of Seymour's arm. Portraits are cropped for many reasons, so there is no knowing if this disap-

Colored engraving of Admiral Sir Michael Seymour (wrist restored), Bart. (National Maritime Museum)

pearance was intentional. A later three-quarter length-colored engraving of the same portrait, however, suggests no such ambiguity. It draws in Seymour's missing left wrist, transforming the empty sleeve pinned across his chest into the standard hand-in-waistcoat pose discussed in chapter 2. Marianne Czisnik argues that cheap commemorative goods such as ceramics and engravings had made Nelson's image as the one-armed Admiral too familiar with the public at large for any two-armed "perfect figure" to be acceptable to the Trafalgar Square monument subscription committee.[20] Certainly, Nelson left a strong visual tradition of himself as both an amputee and a hero, the visual tradition chapter 2 explores. In addition to this iconography's possible effect on this committee, however, we should note that the committee itself included a living amputee naval hero, one who seems to have enjoyed few things more than campaigning for his point of view in institutional settings: Watkin Owen Pell. We are not privy to the committee's discussions. Nevertheless, it seems possible that Pell's presence might have put a damper on casually expressing prejudices like those of the critic of the Birmingham statue, who clearly assumed his audience would share his revulsion at the idea of a "mutilated trunk—a statue without legs."

Watkin Owen Pell took part in the process of commemorating Nelson and the Royal Navy as a whole, both in Trafalgar Square and at Greenwich Hospital. Pell was appointed as a commissioner for Greenwich in 1846 and served until his death in 1869. James Gordon became the lieutenant governor of Greenwich Hospital in 1840, then served as governor from 1853 to his death in 1869. On September 6, 1825, Pell enjoyed the view from the top of the Nelson Monument in Edinburgh, which makes no attempt whatsoever to represent Nelson's body. Instead, as described in chapter 2, it takes the form of the piece of technology most strongly linked to Napoleonic-era naval officers: a gigantic upside-down telescope: "Rode to Castle and College, went to the top of Nelson's Monument, clear weather, beautiful view of the city as well as the Firth and high land in Fyffe."[21] Pell worked on preserving the memory of the naval heroes of the Napoleonic Wars in his position as a commissioner of Greenwich Hospital, home of the first National Gallery of Naval Art. Predating by decades the founding of the National Portrait Gallery itself in 1856, this project was instigated by Nelson's old captain, William Locker, when Locker served as lieutenant governor of the hospital. Locker felt that the hall featuring Sir James Thornhill's magnificent frescos glorifying Britain's history from the accession of William and Mary onward "should be appropriated to the service of a National Gallery of Marine Paintings, to commemorate the eminent services of the Royal Navy of England."[22]

In 1806, Nelson's body lay in state for three days in the Painted Hall. Starting in 1824, the hall housed for a century over three hundred paintings by artists such as J. M. W. Turner and Sir Joshua Reynolds. In 1851, Pell took an outspoken role in deciding where in the Painted Hall a bust of Nelson would be placed. In this context, he spoke as a conscientious custodian of the Painted Hall itself. His diary records his first priority, doing right by that "magnificent room" and the characteristically dogged course of investigation, meetings, verbal argument, and written protest he undertook to get his way in committee through May and June. After visiting the Painted Hall "to examine a proper place to put the Bust of

Lord Nelson," he was concerned by a letter "reporting on the bust of Lord Nelson being placed in the Painted Hall to put it up where King William now stands. I object to that, as in my opinion it would be best not to have anything placed where that now stands as it injures the appearance of the magnificent room."[23] Reading a formal protest against this decision at a board meeting and revisiting the Painted Hall with other commissioners, Pell convinced them to reverse their decision and place Nelson's bust in a different location. Pell also took an active role in commemorating Nelson in a wider context: consummate clubman and tireless committee member that he was, he was appointed to the Committee of Management for the Nelson Monument. On February 9, 1838, he "attended the Committee on Nelson's Monument. Left London at 4 p.m. slept at Dr. R. Northampton." On February 22, 1838, he "attended the meeting at the Kitchie House to erect a monument to the memory of Lord Nelson. Dined at James Cavan's."[24]

The significance of the debate of how the Trafalgar Square monument should represent Nelson to naval veterans is suggested by correspondence between Pell and an old shipmate, Lieutenant Edward Bold, who had served with Pell in *La Virginie* 38. Bold said that "altho' very little brought together since we were in a midships. berth, I have not forgotten." Bold had first gone to sea in 1804, helped capture two Spanish privateers and a Dutch frigate, been captured by the French in 1810, and held prisoner until 1814. He wrote to Pell to express his "ardent" wish that Nelson appear in a form that would honor both "our hero" and the nation:

> My dear Pell,
> I am sorry I was ignorant until yesterday of your being in town as I should have had great pleasure in shaking an old ship mate by the hand and at the same time have availed myself of the opportunity your being a member of the Committee of management for the Nelson monument would afford me for suggesting an idea for a monument which I think worthy of the Honorable members consideration. I am not competing for a prize but am enthusiastic on the subject, and ardently wish to do something that will do honour to the memory of our hero and with it to the nation.

Bold cared enough about Nelson's monument to hire a draftsman to draw up plans for his proposed design, which was elaborate indeed. It included

"4 bronze slaves as typical of the nations the hero has defeated"; a British Lion; a frieze of "Nelson being led triumphantly over the sea by Neptune in a fantastiqe car drawn by sea horses, preceded by tritons and followed by a group of Neriads"; and allegorical figures in bronze of "Britannia and Victory crowning the [illegible] hero." Bold's directions about how to represent Nelson himself, however, were simple and straightforward. Rather than an idealized representation like the allegorical figures all around him, the statue of the "hero . . . ought to be an exact likeness of him both in features and dress."[25] By 1844, "features" commonly referred to facial features, although the OED notes an archaic sense of the word as meaning all aspects of the body.[26] Was Bold drawing on this older sense of the word, or for him, did the most well-known of Nelson's "features," the empty right sleeve of his uniform coat, simply go without saying? Alternatively, Bold might have been concerned to stress that this heroic statue should have Nelson's face. In any case, the allegorical bronzes of defeated nations, Neptune, the seahorses, tritons, neriads, Britannia, and Victory did not appear in the finished monument, but the faithful likeness of "our hero" in his naval uniform did.

"What a Degenerated Time We Live In"

Although they served there as dutiful administrators rather than fighting captains, Pell and Gordon in a sense found their last command at Greenwich Hospital. Traditionally, the hospital was organized much like a ship, with the governor exerting something like a captain's authority over the pensioners through his lieutenant governor, commissioners, and other deputies. Another constant was the long-standing tug of war with the Admiralty's central authority. Just as the Admiralty tightened its control over ships' captains through the nineteenth century, so it increased its control over Greenwich Hospital. Greenwich provided long-term residential care for naval veterans who were unable to live on their own. Gordon and Pell took their responsibility for the welfare of these men seriously: for example, when cholera broke out in the hospital while Gordon was in Scotland in 1849, he immediately returned to Greenwich to oversee the response.[27] Pell's diary vociferously protests the erosion of the direct paternalist authority over Greenwich by the forces of centralized state power. In 1851, Pell described a letter from the Admiralty's medical inspector as an outright usurpation of the positions of governor and commissioner of Greenwich Hospital:

August 7, 1851:

> A long statement of Sir John Liddell on the diet of the Pensioners forwarded to us in an abrupt letter from the Admiralty.... It appears to me that the Medical Inspector is intending to become governor and Commissioner of Greenwich Hospital. It is astonishing how he gains his ends with the Governor [Admiral Sir Charles Adam, (1847–1853)].... I wish I could get my brother Commissioners to make a stand against the aggression on the Funds of the Charity and maintain the wishes and intensions of the Founders of this noble establishment.[28]

Pell's greatest fury, and his greatest lament over the "degenerated time we live in," was triggered by the coming to Greenwich Hospital of another Victorian innovation: a professional police force.

Outrage over this issue punctuates his diary. On April 3, 1851, for example, he notes that "the Metropolitan Police Force ordered by the Admiralty and no remonstrance from the Commissioners on the illegality in paying them out of the funds of the Charity."[29] Five days later, when the board dutifully complies with this order, Pell declares that he "cannot find words to express my contempt." But he goes on to express it: "It is sufficient to bring up Lord Hood, Sir R. Healy, Sir Thos. Hardy and Admiral Sir R. Stopford from their graves. Alas! What a degenerated time we live in, it has long been remarked by me that great change has taken place in the minds of Officers, from that high and martial feeling of our forefathers in arms, which I attribute to a long peace and money speculations, &c."[30] January, February, and March are peppered with protests against letters from the Admiralty insisting on the professional police force. "I consider the whole illegal... A most disgraceful contemptible proceeding," Pell complains, and stops trying to overturn the decision only on March 11, when the opinion of the Law Officers of the Crown confirms "that the Commissioners of Greenwich hospital will be justified in applying part of the Revenue of the Hospital for the purpose above mentioned in compliance with the direction of the Lords of Admiralty." On September 16, Pell sees confirmation of his fear that accepting the Admiralty's demand set a terrible precedent: "Attended the Board. A letter from the Admiralty respecting the outlay for the East Lodges, a very uncourteous one and worded in a style not fit to be sent to a petty officer in the Navy. This is the result of my brother Commissioners not maintaining their dignity and independence . . . the governor disgraced himself as an admiral and Royal Pensioners by placing them under the Prohibition Police."[31] In Pell's increasingly archaic view, the Royal Navy was an independent, all-male family of brothers, governed ultimately by "the high and martial feeling of our forefathers in arms." Although by 1851 Lord Hood, Sir R. Healy, Sir Thos. Hardy, and Admiral Sir R. Stopford were in their graves, as long as Pell himself remained above ground he felt their fatherly authority was properly vested in him, not in a centralized bureaucracy.

Even as the state asserted its authority over the everyday life of the Greenwich pensioners, it also questioned what it owed these veterans. Hoping to decrease "the large pension bill" after the demobilization following Waterloo, in 1829 the government appointed a board "to define closely the nature of disabilities qualifying for a pension."[32] These efforts affected Gordon and Pell as administrators responsible for the care of retired seamen. A new scheme encouraged all hospital residents to move out in exchange for a cash pension. By the time the scheme came into effect, the majority of residents were younger men, veterans of the Crimean War with families outside of the hospital, and for them a more independent life was appropriate. Many of the surviving veterans of Gordon and Pell's own generation, however, were infirm and alone in the world aside from their lifelong connection to the navy. Gordon accepted that change was coming, but protested that this innovation put cutting costs over ensuring the well-being of the older veterans: "The Governor had neither complained of, nor put difficulties in the way of reforms or alterations which he knew to be inevitable but his anger was kindled when he heard one who was high in office say that, 'the old men did not die off quick enough.'" Nevertheless, all residents were pressured to leave, and in spring 1864 Greenwich emptied out. According to *Letters and Records of . . . Gordon,* the old men indeed died off quickly once they left Greenwich: "Over 200 of these men died in the workhouses during the winter of 1865–6."[33]

In addition to a generally parsimonious attitude toward military veterans, Victorian debates over pensions reflect changing ideas about impairment and disability. In 1840, a committee of reform-minded members of Parliament encountered the venerable system of smart-money examined in chapter 1. This system had linked pain, impairment, and honor from the seventeenth century through the Napoleonic Wars. This committee did not like what it saw. It objected to one category of injury that smart-money compensated: injuries that did not prevent one from continuing to serve in the navy or from earning one's living as a civilian. That is, smart-money traditionally recognized that impairment had significance separate from disability defined as the inability to work for a living: "In the navy, gratuities, under the denomination of smart-money, have, from a remote period, been given . . . for wounds in battle or hurts accidentally received, either though the man is not so maimed as to require that he should be discharged, or though, being discharged, he is not so maimed as to be entitled to a pension."[34] This committee assumed that injuries should be seen as significant only if they triggered disability, understood as the inability to work. This category of injury was not new. For example, the Greenwich Hospital charter of 1694 identified as deserving of admission seamen who "by reason of Age, Wounds or other disabilities shall be uncapable of further service at sea and . . . unable to maintain themselves." What is striking here is the winnowing away of all the other kinds of injury that smart-money had long recognized, leaving only this single category, an idea of disability that is familiar to us today. These reformers recommended abolishing smart-money in favor of a system of financial compensation for loss of earning power that was more consistent with that used by the army: "In the army, no such grants are made. Non-commissioned officers and soldiers are entitled to no allowance on account of wounds or hurts, until after they are discharged; and they receive no gratuity, either in addition to the Chelsea pensions, or in cases in which they are not considered entitled to a pension. It is therefore most humbly submitted, . . . that it would be desirable that the allowances in the navy, known by the name of smart-money, should cease."[35] In 1846, the War Office took over administration of Greenwich Hospital out-pensioners as well as those of the army's Chelsea Hospital, centralizing power "in the name of establishing 'one uniform System of payment.'"[36] In addition to being consistent with the army's system, the proposal that "smart-money, should cease" was also more consistent with ideas about pain, disability, and the body that we have inherited from the Victorians. While smart-money links pain and honor, the committee focused on the loss of function, understood as a loss of property. If no property, defined as future income, was destroyed by an injury, then there was no wrong to remedy. Under this system, injury either became disability or disappeared.

What had changed? The committee saw smart-money through the frame of tort law and rejected what did not fit within this frame. Founded on the common law principle known as the "made whole doctrine," tort law is distinguished from criminal law by its focus on *restitution* rather than *retribution*. Tort law promises that what has been twisted can be put right again, that what has been injured can be made whole. Central to tort law is the idea of inadvertent injury: harm caused by "negligence" rather than by deliberate intention. From the Middle Ages through much of the eighteenth century, the ways that people could inadvertently injure each other were quite limited. The common law mainly dealt with livestock and fires that escaped from their proper places. The nature of negligence changed when England started to build a network of McAdamized highways and, even more dramatically, when it began constructing steam-powered railroads.[37] A modern transportation system, modern traffic, and modern manufacturing produced inadvertently damaged bodies on an entirely new scale. The ideal form of injury for tort law is property loss: a damaged building, for example, can be made whole again for a certain sum of money. Tort law does its best to imagine human bodies as a kind of real property, translating a person's long-term impairment in form or function—or their experience of pain—into a kind of property damage that can be made whole again with money. "Damages" is legal shorthand for money that is awarded to repair the damaged body, or—failing that—to compensate for this body's permanent loss of wholeness. In the nineteenth century, the legal right to be made whole through compensatory damages became increasingly well established—and this body of law made the system of smart-money that the Royal Navy inherited from the seventeenth century look increasingly odd.[38] Neither smart-money nor the nineteenth-century system of compensation for military injuries included the idea of negligence—but only the latter focused exclusively on lost earning power.

When awarded to those who continued to serve in the military, smart-money linked impairment to honor rather than to disability. When Pell defended his own pension, he pointed to both his injuries and his victories: the loss of his leg in the capture of the French frigate *La Loire* as a midshipman in 1800, and the injuries to his right hand and arm in capturing a Venetian gunboat in 1806. On November 21, 1854, Pell's diary protests that the House of Commons misrepresented his income to the public, in part by ignoring the pension he continued to receive for these services and sufferings: "At home. Mr. Paine sent me Civil Service return ordered by the House of Commons on the motion, Mr. J. Hume. Under the head of Greenwich Hospital they make it appear or wish to do so to the public that I receive as Commissioner of Greenwich Hospital a salary of 1,414:14:4, the return of Greenwich Hospital transmitted by their Secretary shewed separately the amount arrived at this, Commissioner's Salary L658:9:4. Rear Admiral's Half Pay L456:5. Pension for the loss of a leg L300, in taking a French Frigate and for severe wounds in his right hand and arm."[39] Pell's war injuries had not changed, but he felt a new need to assert his sense of their significance for what he was owed by his nation. Interestingly, what Pell sees as a misrepresentation of his own war record draws nothing as strong as the full-hearted outbursts triggered by the encroachment of the state on his authority over Greenwich. Perhaps Pell saw the public misrepresentation of his salary as the Civil Service behaving as badly as he had always expected it to behave, rather than a betrayal by his own "brother officers" degraded by "a long peace and money speculations, &c."

"Completely Degraded"

In 1909, James Richard Thursfield, a former fellow of Jesus College, Oxford, the coauthor of *The Navy and the Nation* (1897), and the founder of the *Times Literary Supplement,* published *Nelson and Other Naval Studies.* This innocuously titled volume presented Horatio Nelson as the hero/villain of one of the most shocking parables of Victorian medicine, *The Strange Case of Dr. Jekyll and Mr. Hyde* (1886). In Thursfield's account, Nelson the commander becomes the virtuous public-minded professional man, Dr. Jekyll, and Nelson the lover becomes Jekyll's bestial alter ego, Mr. Hyde. Nelson's passion for Lady Hamilton was a social scandal in his own day. Thursfield turns it into a case study in the Victorian medical horror genre of degeneracy: "The incomparable Nelson of the Victory's quarter-deck and cockpit is as completely degraded into the sensual, erotic, and frantically jealous paramour of Lady Hamilton as the Dr. Jekyll of Stevenson's story was ever transformed into a Mr. Hyde."[40] What could this urbane man-of-letters and longtime friend of the navy have been thinking when he wrote this sentence? One important context is the legacy of Victorian medical thought that Thursfield inherited. "The ardor of love is a temporary insanity," declared Henry Maudsley in an 1863 issue of the *British Journal of Psychiatry*, striking a similar note.[41] Another of Maudsley's pronouncements suggests the high rhetorical stakes a Nelson biography might have. Maudsley presents a nation's degeneration as such an individual's pathology writ large: "The unhappy tendencies which lead to individual error and degeneration are those which on a national scale conduct peoples to destruction; and the *nisus* of an epoch is summed up in the biography of its great man."[42]

These statements about insanity, degeneration, and great men reflect a habit of seeing bodies, minds, and emotions through certain aspects of nineteenth-century medical science. This medical frame represents a particularly intense chapter in the longer history of ideas about men's nature and women's nature. As John Tosh describes, the Victorian era saw a "growing polarization of sexual difference, embracing body, mind and the gendering of social space."[43] In this era, defining men as the opposite of women had a connection to political reform. As the Chartists' call for "universal manhood suffrage" reminds us, ambitious Englishmen pointed to their gender to support their moral claim to a share in the power of older social elites. This polarization eventually did away with both manly pride in sensibility and knee breeches. Victorian Britain experienced more subtle changes than the abolition of the slave trade, the coming of steam-powered ships, trains, and factories, or the centralization of state power. The meaning of men's tears changed. On the eve of Trafalgar, the tears of military men were an honorable sign of dedication to their profession. The tears shed by Nelson's officers in response to his battle plan for Trafalgar have already been described. Nelson's friend Vice Admiral Cuthbert Collingwood wept openly in the Strand at the end of a command out of sheer fatherly feeling for his disbanded crew. As he explained to a sympathetic

Lord Eldon, "he felt he had lost his children . . . they were dear to him, and he could not refrain."[44] Nelson's own death unleashed weeping of heroic proportions among naval men. Abroad, crying in the street for Nelson was a sign of Englishness. Samuel Taylor Coleridge wrote that "never can I forget the sorrow and consternation that lay on every countenance [when the news reached Naples]. . . . Numbers stopped and shook hands with me, because they had seen tears on my cheek, and conjectured, that I was an Englishman; and several, as they held my hand, burst, themselves into tears."[45] Like Nelson himself, many of his officers were proud to be men of sensibility. By the end of the century, however, tears were part of women's nature, while men were enjoined to stoicism.

As discussed in chapter 2, the eighteenth-century cult of sensibility framed emotion in relatively gender-neutral terms. Despite recurring panic about sensibility's effeminizing effects, such emotion was primarily a marker of social status, a sign of gentility in men as well as in women. Eighteenth-century medical and prescriptive writers joined forces to construct what Mark S. Micale dubs "the Nervous Culture of Georgian Britain," rooting this genteel quality within the very nervous systems of both male and female bodies.[46] From the 1790s through the 1860s, however, medical and prescriptive writing promoted more extreme ideas about sexual difference. Rather than sharing a common nervous system, properly functioning male and female bodies came to be seen as entirely contrasting organisms. Micale writes: "Biomedical knowledge that emphasized the contrasts and oppositions between men and women came to the fore . . . [doctors were] aggressively pressed into the service of discovering and maintaining a regime of difference between the sexes."[47]

Similarly, in 1827, the inherent conservatism of Admiralty regulation dress was at last vanquished by what historians of material culture call "the great masculine renunciation" of splendor in favor of dark, plain clothing.[48] The process of recategorizing embroidery, gold and silver, velvet, silk, wigs, tight body-skimming lines, and other gorgeous aspects of fashion as feminine rather than aristocratic was a long one. It culminated in the drab masculine authority of the Victorian frock coat and trousers. The era's conduct manuals insisted that enjoyment of clothes was natural in women and unnatural in men. What in a woman might be either a commendable eagerness to please or a depraved impulse toward sexual display could now in a man be only one thing: effeminacy.⁴⁹ A service hoping to conform to such gendered ideals preferred its officers to look like businessmen rather than courtiers. Once a mark of pride, by the 1820s the old uniform's deep association with court carried reputational risk.⁵⁰ Many officers had favored trousers for years, but the Admiralty did not relinquish its regulation knee breeches easily. In 1812, a young lieutenant tried to present himself at the Admiralty to receive his first commission but was turned away because he had forgotten to change his white trousers for knee breeches and silk stockings. Only when he returned wearing knee breeches was he allowed to enter.⁵¹ Nevertheless, in 1827, the regulation knee breeches at last officially gave way to trousers and lost their gold lace, and the coat became double-breasted. While the white breeches and silk stockings of Nelson's generation of officers had announced they were not common laborers, the long dark trousers of later nineteenth-century officers proclaimed that they were not women. The separate dress and undress versions were pared down to a single suit of clothes, greatly reducing the expense. Nevertheless, accusations of dandyism dogged even the new uniform, especially protests that young officers, with the help of corsets and padded chests, continued to flaunt their wasp waists.⁵²

This biomedical "regime of difference" is visible in a wide range of texts: medical treatises, conduct books, and novellas, as well as in Thursfield's historical study of Nelson and the Royal Navy. Conduct book writers such as Sarah Stickney Ellis helped popularize such claims about the stark difference between healthy male and healthy female nature, and they were joined by some doctors. In "The Correlation of Mental and Physical Force: or Man, a Part of Nature," Henry Maudsley stressed the power of the thoroughly gendered body over the mind: "Everyday experience . . . will supply hundreds of examples of the direct manner in which moral character is influenced by the physical state."⁵³ Building on this idea of the importance of the body, medical treatises such as Maudsley's *Body and Mind* (1870) claimed that women were naturally prone to insanity because female bodies were naturally subject to "bodily disturbance." Puberty, menstruation, and pregnancy were as dangerous to the minds of women as drinking, sexual exhaustion, and masturbation were to the minds of men. For example, Maudsley matter-of-factly mentions how pregnancy turned one woman into a murdering cannibal who succumbed to her taste for the pickled flesh of her own husband: "The result of the abnormal condition of nerve element is to alter the mode of feeling of impressions ... the morbid appetites and feelings of the hysterical woman and the singular longings of pregnancy are mild examples of a perversion of the manner of feeling and desire, which may reach the outrageous form of morbid appetite exhibited by the pregnant woman who killed her husband and pickled his body in order to eat it."[54] "Bodily disturbance" was the weakness in civilized man's defenses against the forces of irrational passion.

These shifts in thinking about what was "natural" to male and female bodies, and the relation of these bodies to male and female minds, are relevant to Victorian ideas about masculinity and amputation. In the later nineteenth century, some medical theorists interpreted the spasms and pain that amputees had always experienced in light of these theories, presenting male amputees with a new diagnosis: hysterical femininity. For example, John Eric Erichsen's 1854 treatise *The Science and Art of Surgery* asserts that any lingering pain male amputees experience is caused not by the loss of the limb, but what remains: the man's insufficiently masculine constitution. Such a man is like a hysterical woman: "His form of painful stump arises from constitutional causes, and invariably occurs in females, more particularly in those of the hysterical temperament, and who are subject to neuralagic pains elsewhere."[55] That is, rather than being an honorable mark of heroic masculinity, amputation could be described as a sign of hysterical femininity. Erin O'Connor explores such claims, suggesting that if a good Victorian woman knew how to suffer and be still, as Stickney Ellis advised, and a hysterical one suffered from uncontrollable movements, then a male amputee's vestigial limb looked like a hysterical woman: "Thrashing, twitching, and suffering from phantom pain, stumps showed a deep-rooted propensity for theatrical malingering that rivaled that of the hysteric herself."[56]

Such claims, however, tell only part of the story of Victorian psychiatry. They also may not tell us much at all about the lives of particular Victorian amputees. Jenny Bourne Taylor points out that while Maudsley's views are significant, they do not represent all of nineteenth-century psychiatry, much less all of nineteenth-century medical thought. Maudsley is indeed a "prime example of how the medical establishment naturalised and reinforced social divisions and hierarchies during the latter part of the nineteenth century. Yet . . . we cannot regard him as representative of the developing psychiatric profession as a whole."[57] In "Degeneration and Despair," his aptly-titled study, Andrew Scull sees Maudsley as more influential than does Taylor but still regards his founding of Maudsley Hospital as his most significant achievement. It was more influential than all of Maudsley's attempts, through his position as the editor of the *Journal of Medical Science,* to promote his distinctive theories about somatically induced insanity, not to mention his gloomy Lamarkianism.[58] Similarly, Thomas Dixon's *Weeping Britannia* argues that ideals about masculinity in the first half of the nineteenth century are complicated by the social experiences of men in that era. Although much biomedical writing polarized gender identity in terms of rationality and emotion, even as the British Empire expanded, far fewer British men bore arms than during the Revolutionary and Napoleon Wars. Instead, the rising Evangelical middle class promoted domestically oriented ideals for men as well as for women, praising the man whose home was the center of his rich emotional and spiritual life.

The Crystal Palace and Manly Tenderness

Change attracts the historian's eye. Dynamic arcs of social transformation can obscure equally substantial areas of continuity between the eighteenth and nineteenth centuries. As John Tosh suggests, without denying the nineteenth century's distinctive appetite for biomedical fantasizing about masculinity and femininity, we should also recognize "the relative impermeability and endurance" of much gendered experience of daily life.[59] Gordon and Pell died in 1869. They lived through a full half century of increasingly polarized biomedical thought about gender, but male amputees appear to be pathologized in print in specifically gendered terms only in the two decades before their deaths. Even then, this way of thought does not appear to have had much impact on how these amputee officers were seen. For example, Thomas Hughes, author of the Victorian classic *Tom Brown's Schooldays* (1857), was a personal friend of Gordon's daughter Hannah. At Gordon's death, Hughes published a tribute to Gordon calling him "the last survivor of Nelson's captains, the Paladins of the great war... a hale old sea-king of eighty-six." Hughes strove to put the wartime generation of naval officers in historical perspective. He uses the term "Nelson's captains" to describe this cohort as a whole, and what he sees when he contemplates them is a record of military achievement that strains his own sense of the possible: "now that we can look at them as a group of historical personages... were it not for their uniform success, and the thoroughness with which they carried through that work, one might be inclined to call them foolhardy disciples of the chief who 'did not know Mr. Fear.'" Hughes describes Gordon as a "very formidable man" rather than a feminized one: "Even with a wooden leg, he must have been a very formidable man... for he stood six feet three inches, and had been all his life famous for feats of strength and activity."[60]

James Gordon's daughters published *Letters and Records . . . of Gordon* in 1890, well into the period O'Connor describes, but they represent their father as the head of their household rather than as a victim of pathologized femininity. That is, his patriarchal authority is not in doubt. Rather, the question is whether he was a merciful master or a tyrant. Interestingly, his daughters describe his spasms and his nerves in some detail, noting that Gordon's nervous system was "extremely sensitive," despite his "strong, vigorous frame." Much like John Erichsen, they claim this sensitivity was partly caused by the loss of his leg: "Owing, partly, to the loss of his leg, which (as is usual) caused him to suffer from periodical attacks of tic-douloureux in the stump, of which the spasms were so severe that he would start violently, as he sat in his chair—and which, ordinarily, lasted for three days; his nerves were extremely sensitive—and this to an extent which seemed incompatible with his strong, vigorous frame."[61] They acknowledge that in his old age, Gordon's sensitive nerves made him difficult to live with: "Any sudden noise, or sharp, loud speaking, gave him positive pain, and his servants had to be trained to avoid slamming of doors, and rattling of plates. To those who were unaware or unmindful of this sensitiveness, he often appeared unreasonably irritable." However, instead of seeing this sensitive amputee, with his spasms and his irritable nerves, as pathologically feminine, they consider how well he measured up to his responsibilities as the head of the household. Gordon's daughters stress that even when in pain, he tried not to abuse his power: "He was very considerate to his servants and dependents; and, although quick and hasty in speech, he was never unreasonable or severe in action."⁶²

As a young man, James Gordon had been distressed by witnessing a patriarch behaving badly on his sick bed. Close to death, Lord Glenbervie, James's patron and the most powerful member of his family, refused to let James read the Bible to him. He instead spent his last weeks on earth making "ill-natured" remarks and bullying his dependents. James was disturbed by this behavior, so disturbed that he sought comfort in describing it to his wife: "I tell you all, only to ease my own mind, by writing to my best beloved." Glenbervie required his younger relatives and his servants to sit in the hallway outside of his door waiting on his whims, and threatened to fire the servants. James tried to protect them:

April 6, 1823

> Now I am in disgrace for trying to save his servants; he has Milne, myself, Charles [Charles Birch, the second son of James's sister], and a servant sitting outside his door, and he has told the man if he moves, he will turn him away directly. Ah! My dear Lydia, what a lesson I have had. I trust in God my mind at my last hour may be in a better and more tranquil state.⁶³

Whether or not Gordon remembered this scene, his daughters indeed describe his last years, days, and hours as "better and more tranquil," despite the considerable pain he experienced.

The lasting importance of Gordon's role as head of the household, in sickness and in health, reminds us that even in a time of new biomedical theories about gender, many assumptions about masculinity remained the same. Among those that survived from the childhood of these amputee officers through to their deaths, one that continued to shape their lives most clearly was the identification of mature masculinity with the obligation to provide financially for their daughters and to launch the careers of their sons. Although Michael Seymour conscientiously attacked slave traders at sea and in the courts of Rio de Janeiro until his death, for example, he accepted this commission in hopes of doing his duty as a father by promoting his son Michael's career during the postwar stagnation of the Navy List. In this regard he was the most successful of the amputee officers who are the focus of this study. Seymour founded a naval dynasty. Rising to the rank of admiral, the second Sir Michael Seymour had an active career and fostered in turn the careers of his family, including a nephew Sir Michael Culme-Seymour, who brought needed reforms to the Mediterranean Fleet at the end of the nineteenth century and whose son commanded the battleship *Centurion* in World War I and became Second Sea Lord. This Sir Michael Culme-Seymour's son and heir, also named Michael, served in the Royal Navy during World War II.[64] In contrast, as noted, Horatio Nelson's stepson Josiah Nisbet left the navy in disgrace after failing in the command positions Nelson secured for him and became instead a successful Parisian stockbroker. James Gordon took his son and namesake, James Alexander Gordon, to sea with him, but this son died as the commander of a sloop in January 1847.[65] Watkin Owen Pell's son Owen Spencer Pell was accepted as a naval cadet in 1867 but had no career.[66]

O'Connor takes the Great Exhibition of 1851 as the inaugural moment for a later nineteenth-century pathologizing of male amputees. It forms a convenient bookend for considering a "discourse of amputation" that she posits arising between the Crystal Palace's exhibition of cutting-edge prosthetic limbs and the newly widespread exposure to "bodily mutilation" brought by World War I.[67] Now recognized as a milestone in the history of prosthetics, among its other technological wonders, the Great Exhibition displayed the Palmer Patent Leg, one of the first modern prosthetic limbs with articulated knee, ankle, and toe joints. The Palmer Leg won a silver medal, was praised by the *Times*, and was lampooned by *Punch*. Watkin Owen Pell was present at this inaugural moment. He and his wife held season tickets to the Great Exhibition at the Crystal Palace: he visited fifteen times, Lady Pell, twelve. What impression did the Palmer Leg, or the rising "discourse of amputation" it now signifies, make on this man who had already lived as an amputee for half a century?

It is tempting to imagine that Pell responded to the invention with a personal interest, just as it is tempting to imagine that he responded as a collector with a personal interest in Maltese marble mosaic table tops to the items displayed by the workshop of J. Darmanin & Sons, craftsmen who exhibited and won a prize medal for "their accuracy of work with a very skillful use of material." In 1841, Pell had bought two marble mosaic tables in Malta from Darmanin's workshop, items now in the collection of the Victoria and Albert museum. Furniture historian Kate Hay speculates how "one can imagine that [Pell and his wife] paid great attention to the Malta stand showing four Darmanin mosaic tables including the splendid example now in the Royal Collection."[68] Pell may indeed have been engaged by both of these prize-winning exhibits, but his diary makes no mention of either Darmanin's mosaics or Palmer's leg. Rather than a response to new technology or to Italian artistry, it records longstanding family and professional preoccupations. Now in his early sixties, Pell's fashion sense, and his testy relationship with his older brother Owen, remained as strong as ever: "Lady P. and I went to the great Exhibition, we met my brother Owen and his wife. He was dressed in an old coat and looked as if he had come from the back Woods of America."[69]

Pell's entry on the Great Exhibition in the "splendid and unrivalled Crystal Palace" records the thoughts of a patriotic British naval officer and gentleman. He strongly approved of the opening ceremonies and the public's loyal response on May 1, 1851: "The Great Exhibition of the Works of Industry of all Nations opened by Her Majesty in person. Lady Pell and I went having season tickets. The splendid and unrivalled Crystal Palace was opened in a manner becoming its splendor by prayer and thanksgiving to the Almighty for his blessing on one and all Nations. The whole arrangements were very creditable to all concerned in them, the People who had assembled in many thousands listened with the greatest quietness and respect, and showed the best feelings towards Her Majesty."[70] On the day of the opening, Pell also notes seeing Wellington walk arm-in-arm with another famous military amputee, the Marquess of Anglesey, who lost a leg at Waterloo—but Pell makes no mention of the fact that Anglesey was a fellow amputee. Rather, Pell writes as a naval officer sensitive to a perceived slight to his service. He does not begrudge Wellington another moment in the spotlight but feels the public honor should have been shared by a representative of the navy: "It was highly gratifying to see the two old veteran Field Marshalls walking arm in arm, the Duke of Wellington and Marquess of Anglesey, where was the Admiral of the Fleet."[71] "Admiral of the Fleet" was an honorary title given to the most senior admirals: in 1851, there were two: Admiral Sir George Cockburn, whose active career included burning Washington, D.C., during the War of 1812, as well as promoting the adoption of improved gunnery and steam technology; and Admiral Sir

Byam Martin, who fought in the Napoleonic Wars and was investigating possible uses of poison gas in the Crimean War up to his death in 1854. Pell sought recognition for Martin in another form: on November 5, 1851, he writes, "Sir Wm Hall Gage asked me to speak to Sir Jas. Gordon to get up a subscription to get a portrait of the other Admiral of the Fleet, Sir Byam Martin, he being with Sir G. Cockburn the only two surviving Admirals who had their flags afloat during the War."[72] For Pell, the battles he fought in his youth are still simply "the War." Similarly, when Wellington and Anglesey appear at a United Servicers Club dinner in 1848, Pell's diary does not reflect a sense of fellow-feeling with Anglesey as an amputee, merely noting "the dinner [was] well served and the whole meeting went off most satisfactorily."[73]

In his later years, Pell's diary often mentions "spasms." He records his attacks in brief and matter-of-fact terms, often together with another unpleasant condition of interest to naval officers: bad weather. May 18, 1856, for example, notes "squally with rain. Spasms," and December 20, 1856, saw "snow in the night. Squally and a heavy gale. I was attacked with spasm at 5 am. Rain at pm strong breezes." By December 30, both the spasms and the weather have improved: "Fine. I rode out, much better."[74] This is the same matter-of-fact tone James Gordon took in his letters during the 1820s about the spasms and pain he experienced. For example, on October 17, 1821, he wrote to Lydia: "When I was writing to you yesterday my stump pained me so much that I could not have written more had I the time to have done so. Now, I am happy to say, the spasms have left me."[75]

When Pell and Gordon were unwell, the medical care they received seems far removed from newer medical theories that pathologized or objectified amputees. On October 25, 1850, Pell does make note of a medical novelty: a fellow naval officer was about to "undergo a serious operation under the influence of Chloroform."[76] Overall, however, rest, leeches, and poultices figure most prominently—along with "kind and attentive" medical visits, often by Pell's brother-in-law, Dr. Robertson. Commonly, Pell fell off horses, injured himself, and took to his bed or sofa until he felt better. For example, he reports being "laid up with broken shin" from March 21 to March 23, 1829, after a fall while riding; "on the sofa all day" after hurting his knee riding to hounds on October 20, 1829; and getting his blood drawn by leeches after another fall from a horse on January 12, 1830: "Chestnut horse threw me in the road, hurt my back, sent to Northampton for some leeches, received 5 only." On December 7, with no specifics, he reports himself "very unwell. At Dr Robertson's. Mr Terry attending me."[77] In 1832, an interesting series of concise diary entries chronicle the progress of the Great Reform Bill together with the progress of his hemorrhoids:

April 9:

At home. Called on Dr. Wright. The Reform Bill to be read a second time in the House of Peers, adjourned debate.

April 9:

At home. The second reading of the Reform Bill was carried in the House of peers by a majority of nine. . . .

May 16:

Unwell in bed at the St. Albany, wrote to O'Brien.

May 19:

Called on Mr. Copeland, Golden Square, consulted him.

May 25:

Mr. Copeland put a ligature on me. Rt. Jones was present.

May 29:

Mr. Copeland cut me for the Piles, very large and severe operation. Mr. Copeland called to see me at 9 p.m., in great pain, took a pill.

May 31:

Admiral Brace called on me, wrote a note to Capt. Duncan letters to Edwin and Dr. R.

June 4:

The Reform Bill passed the House of Lords by a majority of 84.[78]

In 1833, Pell returned to his usual routine of hounds, falls, and leeches. On January 22, for example, he sprained his ankle in a fall from his favorite horse while riding in a severe frost, then spent several days at home applying leeches to the swelling before riding to hounds again on February 4. On February 19, running a fox to earth at Overstone, he fell hurt "his forehead, &c." but notes that a Colonel Bouverie also had a fall. Two days later Pell was still "at home with a black eye and broken nose" but met the hounds at Harrington by the end of the week. On December 5, 1841, Pell "broke my shin" while hunting in the rain and spent the next several days at home on the sofa. In June 1844, Dr. Robertson informed Pell that the "severe pain in my foot" was gout. January 24, 1849, found both Pell and his wife resting at home, he nursing yet another injury from a fall, and she with a bad cold: "Cold and stormy. Confined to house both of us, one with cold the other with a broken shin." September, 26, 1849, is "a day of fast and humiliation for the cholera."[79] Intriguingly, in 1852, Pell underwent some form of medical "discipline" at the hands of his brother-in-law Dr. Robertson for an attack of spasms, although what sort of discipline is unclear. He rode to London on March 15, stayed at Dr. Robertson's on the 27th and 28th while "undergoing discipline to get well of the spasms," then reported himself "much better."[80] He left Dr. Robertson and returned to Greenwich on March 29, apparently satisfied with the treatment. When Pell suffered further attacks of spasms, however, he simply waited them out.

On March 15, 1860, something more dramatic happened: Pell was "taken very ill in bed. Lady Pell sent for medical assistance, Dr. Stewart came immediately, I was quite sensible when he arrived and began to vomit. At 9 am Dr Wilson and Dr Stewart came to me and did the needful."[81] The following day, Pell was "in bed all day. Dr. Wilson and Dr. Stewart visited me 4 times. It appears I had two attacks, one at 3 am and 6 am. Dr. Stewart came. I had two Epilepsy fits."[82] It is unclear if these "Epilepsy fits" were related to his more common attacks of spasms, but they could have brought on a host of faddish and dehumanizing medical responses. Psychiatry, neurology, and psychology had not yet emerged as fields with clear disciplinary boundaries. Instead, symptoms such as Pell's belonged to the broad study of "nervous disorders," which included everything from amorphously defined conditions such as neurasthenia and hysteria, problems of the nervous system such as paralysis and epilepsy, and laboratory experiments on the brains of animals.[83] Nevertheless, the treatment Pell received on this occasion was respectful and compassionate. March 17 finds Pell "in bed. Dr Wilson and Dr Stewart very kind and attentive. Dr. and Mrs. Baird came." On March 30, he "received a very kind letter from Dr Robertson with instructions for my future guidance as regard my late attack." The final medical event in Pell's diary was more mundane, although painful: a carbuncle on the neck. Blistering, then lancing, was the treatment from June 4 to June 16, when Pell notes hopefully that "Sarah ferments it twice day, improving."[84]

Pell's "kind and attentive" doctors seem to embody what Roy Porter has described as a relatively gender-neutral Victorian ideal, one that cut against stereotypes about feeling, gender, and medicine as a profession. While scientists such as Maudsley were austerely masculine professional figures, kind attention at a sickbed could take the form of either a post-Nightingale female nurse or a conscientious, hard-worked male G.P.: "In the devoted nurse or general practitioner, Victorians found or fantasized medical personnel" who brought comfort.[85] Moreover, in *Military Men of Feeling: Emotion, Touch, and Masculinity in the Crimean War* (2016), Holly Furneaux points to the robust survival of a specifically military "manly tenderness" as a value among the generation of officers and soldiers who fought in the Crimean War.[86] "Every woman is a nurse," declares the famous first sentence of Florence Nightingale's 1859 *Notes on Nursing*. To some later Victorians' way of thinking, if every woman was a nurse, then no man ought to be one. That is, one justification for the feminization as well as professionalization of the field of nursing that Nightingale instigated was the claim that women's feeling nature, in contrast to the rational nature of men, gave women unique sympathy for those in pain. The rise of nursing as a respectable profession for middle-class woman may have helped obscure the ongoing contribution of male nurses. Nevertheless, both the letters Crimean-era military men themselves wrote and popular representations of them still praise the manly tenderness they showed in nursing wounded or sick comrades.

In the prominence it gives to such manly sympathy, the medical care Gordon received toward the end of his life recalls strongly the scenes of nursing from Nelson's time. The physician who attended him, Sir John Liddell, had served in battle with the Royal Navy. A fellow Scot, he was a graduate of the University of Edinburgh, a Fellow of the Royal Society, a Companion of the Order of the Bath, and director-general of the navy's

Medical Department (the office formerly known as Physician-General) during the Crimean War. After Crimea, Liddell solicited Nightingale's help to improve the quality of care in navy hospitals. Liddell took care of Gordon with "strong and tender sympathy." As Gordon's daughters recount, Liddell was not only Gordon's physician, a figure of professional authority, but also his friend and his nurse:

> To our Father, Sir John Liddell was friend, physician and nurse in one. Nothing was too slight or unimportant, where he was concerned, for Sir John to attend to, and with his own hands he often performed services which in many cases would have been left to a servant. . . . Never did he hesitate to come at any hour, early or late, if he thought his presence, either as physician or friend, could be of comfort and help to him. And the moral influence of his strong and tender sympathy, his cheerfulness and confidence, had the happiest effect on his patient.[87]

Liddell's predecessor as the chief medical officer of the Royal Navy was Sir William Burnett, the old friend whom Gordon remembered nursing him through a life-threatening illness in 1806, "when I could not go to rest without his hand being in mine."[88] Nearly half a century later, in Gordon's last days, the navy's new director-general showed the same compassion.

The history of those who returned to active military service after serious injury, from Nelson's era to our own, offers an opportunity for further research. From the time of James Gordon's death to the emergence of the modern disability rights movement in the later twentieth century, the histories of war and disability have been intertwined. Through their sheer numbers, the men who lived on with profoundly damaged bodies after the Civil War and two world wars had a massive cultural impact on their homelands. At the same time, the wider study of disability has often lived at a distance from the study of military disability, a distance that mirrors the different social and political experiences of those in each group. Twentieth-century military service, combat, and injury established for disabled veterans a distinctive moral claim on the state for assistance. Through their military experiences, disabled veterans also developed a distinctive sense of solidarity, a collective identity furthered by their own penchant for organizing to support each other and to enforce their moral claim on the state.[89] Furthermore, as David Gerber points out, while disability studies as practiced by academics and political activists today often focuses on destabilizing traditional hierarchies of identity, disabled veterans' groups have been more likely to focus on reclaiming a stable place within such hierarchies for their members.[90]

This book's stories of amputee officers who continued to serve on active duty do not fit comfortably into the oppositional stance of contemporary disability studies. Nor do they fit comfortably into the history of collective lobbying for state assistance through which disabled veterans, determined to better their own chances at rehabilitation, helped propel the modern welfare state out for a trial run. In the ways in which their loss affected their lives, the four amputee officers who are the focus of this book were very much men of their particular era, social class, and profession. How they lived on after the loss of an arm or a leg was shaped by such factors: their status as gentlemen, their fame as national heroes, and their secure place within a network made of personal bonds of patronage and naval "brotherhood." They continued to seize glory, wealth, love, and friendship because the navy of their day continued to offer them the possibility of a meaningful military career. Nevertheless, their stories suggest the continued relevance of considering the particular abilities of individuals rather than generalizations about broad categories of persons when deciding who is the right candidate to fill a given job. Few professions can make a more legitimate claim than the military to require a uniform standard of physical ability, so it is important to note how the military has also benefited from the talents of some people with unusual bodies.

Moreover, although so much about warfare has changed, the history of combat-related injury is increasingly a survivor's story, and one that now may more often include continued service on active duty. In World War II, one out of every two wounded or sick military personnel died. In contrast, in the United States' war in Iraq, the number of deaths was one out of sixteen.[91] The great length of the wars of our time has also increased the potential for injured service members to consider returning to active duty rather than to civilian life. The Napoleonic Wars lasted for twelve years; at the time of writing this book, the United States has been at war in Afghanistan for nineteen. In the contemporary United States, although returning to active duty after the loss of a limb is an unusual path for a military career, it is also one that is becoming more familiar. In the 1980s, only a little more than 2 percent of U.S. amputee soldiers returned to duty, and that number included partial-foot, partial-hand, and below-knee amputation. More recently, more of those whose injuries in Afghanistan and Iraq required amputation have continued to serve with success, including a greater number of above-the-knee amputees. Between 2001 and 2006, the overall rate of return was 16.5 percent, with amputee officers returning at a much higher rate than all other service members: 35.3 percent.[92] A 2010 study found that those who return to active duty show a level of function like that of an athlete who uses a prosthesis, a level of function that allows them to perform the duties of their military occupation to a reasonable standard.[93] Their athleticism recalls Midshipman Pell skylarking high in his ship's rigging after adapting to his wooden leg. To the surprise of the investigators in this study, amputees from combat units were not less likely but rather slightly more likely to return to active duty than amputees from combat support or combat service roles, despite the greater physical demands on combat units. Such surprise is a reminder that we have more to learn about the abilities of individual peculiar bodies.

APPENDIX

Short Biographies of Amputee Officers Who Returned to Active Duty

Unless otherwise noted, information in these biographies is drawn from John Marshall's *Royal Navy Biography* and William Richard O'Byrne's *Naval Biographical Dictionary*.

Captain Robert Heriot Barclay

The son of Reverend Peter Barclay and a nephew of Rear Admiral William Duddingstone, Robert Heriot Barclay was born at Kettlehill, Scotland, on September 18, 1786. He joined the *Anson* 44 as midshipman in 1798, at the age of eleven. He was promoted to lieutenant on October 11, 1805, and served at the Battle of Trafalgar in the *Swiftsure* 74, under Captain William Gordon Rutherford. In addition to fighting the French ship *l'Achille*, Barclay helped to rescue French sailors from the sea after the battle. In 1807 or 1808, he lost his left arm while commanding a detachment of boats in an attack upon a French convoy. In 1809, Barclay was granted a pension for the loss of his arm and sent to Halifax with the expectation of promotion, which was delayed for four years due to a change in naval administration. He served as first lieutenant of the frigates *Aeolous* and *Iphigenia*. In 1813, Barclay was appointed to the naval command on the Canadian lakes, facing superior American forces. Ordered to break an American blockade without an adequate supply of either guns or trained seamen, Barclay fought and lost the Battle of Lake Erie, September 10, 1813: "Never in any action was the loss more severe. Every officer commanding a vessel, and his second, was either killed, or wounded so severely as to be unable to keep the deck."[1] As was customary after any defeat or loss of a ship, Barclay stood trial at a court-martial and was honorably acquitted of all fault. Nevertheless, Barclay was not promoted to post-rank. For the next ten years, the remainder of his active career, he remained a commander and was employed for only four or five months. In August 1815, he married his first cousin, Agnes Cosser, and they had several children. He was promoted to captain on October 14, 1824, and his pension for wounds was raised to 400 *l* per year. He died May 8, 1837.

Captain John Bedford

Bedford passed the lieutenant's exam in 1794. He was a lieutenant in the *Tonnant* 80 at Trafalgar and the commander of the *Swallow* 16 in 1810. While in command of the *Swallow*, he captured the French privateer *General Ottoway* and lost a leg. In 1812, he became commander of the *Childers* 16 and captain in 1813. He married and had two sons who joined the Royal Navy, one named Lieutenant Delbouf Baker Bedford. He died in 1814.

Commander John Holmes Bond

Bond became a lieutenant on February 20, 1815. He lost a leg while serving in the *Penguin* brig sloop, under Captain James Dickinson, in an unequal and unsuccessful action with the United States ship *Hornet*, under Captain James Biddle, near the island of Tristan-d'Acunha, March 23, 1815. The captain, boatswain, and four seamen of the *Penguin* were killed. A master's mate, one midshipman (John Noyes, who also lost a leg), and twenty-nine seamen were wounded, four of them fatally. Bond was granted a pension of 91 *l* 5 s. for the loss of his leg and was appointed to the *Bulwark* 76, the flagship of Sir Benjamin H. Carew, in the River Medway, on June 29, 1821. He was promoted to commander on September 5, 1828. He died in 1836.

Captain Charles Worsley Boys

Charles Worsley (also appears as William) Boys was the son of John Boys, M.D., of Mortimer Street, Mary-le-Bone, born in 1778. He joined his first ship at the age of eleven and lost a leg on the Glorious First of June, 1794, serving as a midshipman in the *Royal George* 100. Boys was promoted to lieutenant on June 16, 1795. He commanded the *Harpy* sloop at the Battle of Copenhagen, 1801, and was promoted to post-captain on April 29, 1802. He then commanded the following ships: the *Amaranthe* 28 (1804), the *Orpheus* 32 (1805), the *Regulus* 44 (1807), and the *Statira* 38 (1809). On June 10, 1809, Boys, in command of the *Statira*, together with Captain Irby of the *Amelia* 38, captured *La Mouche*, a French courvette; *la Rejouie*, a brig; and a schooner. From July 28 to December 1809, Boys, in command of the *Statira*, joined the Walcheren Expedition, which included Michael Seymour, in command on the *Amethyst*. On August 11, 1809, Boys's *Statira*, together with nine other frigates, including Seymour's *Amethyst*, helped to establish a blockade of Flushing, taking heavy enemy fire for two hours.[2] Boys died in 1809 while in command of the *Statira*, after a brief illness, leaving his widow with two young children.[3]

Flag Captain David Colby

Colby was second lieutenant of the *Latona* 38 and first lieutenant of the *Robust* 74, both under the command of Captain Edward Thornbrough. He lost his right arm on October 12, 1798, off Tory island on the coast of Ireland, in an action with French ships carrying supplies for Irish rebels. He commanded the *Dido* 28, then was promoted to post-captain on April 29, 1802. When Thornbrough was promoted to rear admiral, Colby served as Thornbrough's flag captain on the North Sea and Mediterranean stations. Colby married a Mrs. Costin on May 2, 1806, and died in 1834.

Captain William Cuppage

William Cuppage was the son of Lieutenant General William Cuppage of the Royal Artillery and a cousin of two Royal Navy officers: Commander Adam Cuppage and Lieutenant James Heyland. Cuppage lost a leg in a skirmish with the French near Toulon on November 5, 1813, while serving as signal midshipman in the *San Josef* 120, the flagship of Rear Admiral Sir Richard King. He was awarded a pension of 91 *l* 5 s. per year on April 4, 1815, and a lieutenant's commission on April 6, 1815. Between 1815 and 1827, Cuppage served in eight ships and sailed to the East Indies, the West Indies, and South America. He was promoted to commander of the *Java* on December 24, 1827, and to post-captain on July 22, 1830, but did not go to sea again. He died on January 3, 1856.

Rear-Admiral William Bateman Dashwood

Dashwood was born September 1, 1790, and joined his first ship, the *Defiance* 74, in 1799. As an eleven-year-old first-class volunteer, he served at the Battle of Copenhagen, April 2, 1801, on the *Defiance* 74, then the flagship of Rear Admiral Thomas Graves. From 1802 to 1811, he served as a midshipman in a number of ships, cruising to the East Indies and Newfoundland and serving at the Siege of Cadiz. He was invalided home in July 1809. He was commissioned as first lieutenant into the *Active* 46, under Captain James Alexander Gordon, in October 1811. On November 29, 1811, Dashwood's right arm was shot off in the same action that cost Captain Gordon his leg, the capture of *La Pomone* 40. Dashwood was promoted to commander on May 19, 1812, and on July 31, 1812 or 1813, was awarded a pension of 200 *l* a year for the loss of his arm. Dashwood remained a lifelong friend of Gordon. He gained command of the *Snap* 16 on July 23, 1813, and captured a French privateer, *Le Lion* 16, off the coast of France on November 1, 1813. In August 1816, he took part in Admiral Exmouth's bombardment of Algiers, attracting particular notice for rescuing the wife and daughter of the British consul of Algiers before the battle started. The women boarded Dashwood's ship dressed as midshipmen. The bombardment of Algiers lasted for nine hours, and, according to Exmouth, "so devoted was every creature in the fleet, that even British women served at the same guns with their husbands, and during a contest of many hours never shrank from danger, but animated all around them."[4] British casualties were 128 killed and 690 wounded. More than 1,200 Neapolitan and Sicilian slaves were liberated. Dashwood was promoted to post-captain of the *Amphion* 32 on October 21, 1818. From 1819, he remained on shore on half-pay, marrying Louisa Henrietta Bode on April 17, 1820. He retired with the rank of rear admiral in 1857 and died in 1869.

Captain Joseph Ellison

Ellison went to sea at the age of nine with Admiral Sir Joseph Hawke. He served in several different ships and was repeatedly in action during the American Revolutionary War. He was commissioned lieutenant on July 29, 1778. On July 4, 1780, he lost his right arm while capturing the French frigate *Capricieuse* 32, serving in the *Prudente* 36, commanded by Captain Hon. William Waldegrave, in conjunction with the *Licorne* 32, commanded by Captain Hon. Thomas Cadogen. Because he was junior to the senior lieutenants of both the *Prudente* and the *Licorne*, Ellison was not promoted for his gallantry in this battle. He was assigned to the impress service and awarded a pension of 5 shillings a day for the loss of his arm. He made post-captain in 1783 and commanded a number of ships, including the *Druid* 32 from 1790 to 1795. In 1795, Ellison transferred with all of his officers and some of the *Druid*'s crew to the *Standard* 64 and commanded it at the Battle of Groix, June 23, 1795. In August 1797, he was given command of the *Marlborough* 74, whose disaffected crew had managed to get their loathed captain, Henry Nicholls, removed from the ship at the Spithead Mutiny. Ellison won the confidence of this crew but displeased St. Vincent, ending his active career. His pension was not raised in accordance with his rank when he made post-captain, possibly because St. Vincent regarded him as a "driveller." He married Esther Collis of Gosport in 1779. He became third captain in Greenwich Hospital, promoted in 1805 to second captain and director of the chest. He died in 1816, at the age of sixty-three.

Commander James Henry Garrety

Garrety became a lieutenant on May 23, 1801. On July 15, 1805, he commanded the gun-brig *Plumper* in the blockade of the coast of northern France. Together with its sister ship, the gun-brig *Teazer*, the *Plumper* was becalmed and anchored off Chausey. Eight French vessels attacked and outgunned the two ships. Garrety's arm was shot off, his leg crippled by grapeshot, and his chest lacerated by langrage. The sublieutenant who had assumed command surrendered after another hour of fighting. Garrety stood court-martial for the loss of his ship and was honorably acquitted.[5] On February 5, 1806, Garrety was granted a pension for the loss of his arm; it amounted to 200 *l* a year at the time of his death. He was promoted to the rank of commander on May 3, 1811, and given command of the *Parthian* sloop, on the North Sea Station, in January 1812. He died in 1827.

Captain Thomas Gill

Gill was born February 19, 1782, a direct descendent of the Reverend Alexander Gill, who was high master of St. Paul's School and John Milton's teacher. On January 15, 1794, Gill became captain's servant on board the *Swan* 18, commanded by Captain Hugh Pigot. He served as master's mate on the *Racoon* brig, under Captain Austin Bissell; the *Racoon's* first lieutenant was James Alexander Gordon. Early in July 1803, while Gill had command of a merchant schooner that the *Racoon* had taken as a prize, he captured a much more heavily manned French cutter. Later that month, on July 11, 1803, Gill lost his left arm near the shoulder while capturing the French brig *Lodi*. He had already lost a finger and received three other wounds in the battle but had refused to leave his place. Bissell recommended Gill to the commander-in-chief, Sir J. T. Duckworth, as "a very worthy, promising young man who has served his time in the navy, and will, if he survives, do credit to your patronage." In the same letter, Bissell also recommends his first lieutenant, James Alexander Gordon: "The conduct of Mr. James Alexander Gordon, the first Lieutenant, on this as well as many other recent occasions, has been highly exemplary and praiseworthy."[6] On August 17, 1803, off Cuba, the *Racoon* defeated the 18-gun brig *La Mutine*; on October 14, with only 42 men, it captured a French gunbrig, cutter, and schooner carrying altogether between 300 and 400 men. Gill played a valuable part in this second battle, which occurred four months after the loss of his arm. His gallantry was recognized by a 50-guinea award from the Patriotic Society. Soon afterward, Bissell was made captain of the *Creole* 38 and took Gill with him as a lieutenant. Gill's promotion was confirmed by a commission dated May 8, 1804, and he served in seven different ships before the conclusion of the war in 1814. While serving as lieutenant of the *Aurora* 28, Gill took part in a three-hour battle with several Spanish gunboats near Tarifa, three of which were captured. He also demonstrated gallantry in a number of boat operations on the coast of Italy. In December 1806, in command of two boats belonging to the *Kingfisher* 16, King captured a prize and conducted a raid on shore against steep odds. He "chased an armed felucca on shore, then landed at the head of a party of 40 officers, seamen, and marines, secured the prize, plundered a neighbouring village, and ultimately brought off the spoil, although the enemy had rallied, and had brought together a force of 500 men to oppose him."[7] On June 27, 1808, Gill was wounded once again while capturing the letter-of-marque *Le Hercule* 12. After being promoted to commander, Gill commanded the *Sparrowhawk* 19, on the West India station, and the *Magnificent* 74, at Port Royal, Jamaica. Gill married on August 16, 1816, and eventually had six daughters and three sons, of whom the eldest, Thomas Cadman Roberts, also joined the Royal Navy. Gill was promoted to captain on January 10, 1837, and subsequently was unemployed. He received a pension of 200 *l* a year for wounds.

Admiral Sir James Alexander Gordon

Gordon was born October 6, 1782, a nephew of Lord Glenbervie, who married Lady Katharine North, daughter of Prime Minister Frederick North. These relations wielded considerable political influence. Gordon became first lieutenant in the *Racoon* 18 in 1802, and on March 3, 1804, became the *Racoon's* captain, in which position he captured a number of prizes. On March 13, 1811, as captain of the *Active* 38, Gordon combined with three other frigates under the command of Captain Hoste, carrying a total of 156 guns, for a battle off Lissa. They defeated a Franco-Venetian armament, whose force amounted to 284 guns. On November 29, 1811, the *Active* captured *La Pomone* 44. Although casualties in this battle were relatively light, Lieutenant William Bateman Dashwood lost his right arm and Gordon lost his leg. In July 1812, he was awarded a pension of 300 *l* a year; he married Lydia Ward that August. The Gordons had seven daughters and one son who survived infancy. As captain of the *Seahorse* 38, Gordon destroyed *Le Subtile*, a privateer, on September 14, 1812. In August 1814, Gordon lead a squadron up the Potomac River and captured Fort Washington and the city of Alexandria. He then joined the expedition against New Orleans. For his services in America, Gordon was awarded the KCB. In July 1832, he became superintendent of Chatham Dockyard; in July 1840, he became lieutenant governor of the Royal Hospital at Greenwich, and on January 30, 1868, he retired as Admiral of the Fleet. Gordon died in January 1869.

Admiral Alexander Graeme

Graeme was born on December 9, 1741, the second son of the Laird of Graemeshall in Orkney, Scotland. He was commissioned as a lieutenant on August 24, 1760, into the *Temple* 68, and commanded the sloop *Kingfisher* at the Battle of Turtle Gut Inlet in June 1776. He lost his right arm as captain of the *Preston* 50 in 1781 in the Battle of Dogger Bank, an action guarding British merchant ships from a Dutch squadron,. He was awarded a pension of 300 *l* a year in 1790 and was given command of the *Glory* in January 1795, although he left the ship after a month to return home at his mother's death.[8] From June 1799 to July 1802, he was commander-in-chief at Sheerness, the Nore. Graeme was Admiral of the Red at the time of his death on August 4, 1818.

Vice Admiral John Hackett

Hackett entered the navy on December 16, 1799, as A.B., in the *Raisonnable* 64, commanded by Captain Charles Boyles. As a midshipman, he participated in the Battle of Copenhagen, April 2, 1801. He passed his lieutenant's exam in 1808 and was commissioned as a lieutenant in *Barfleur* 98, the flagship of George Cranfield Berkeley, on May 11, 1811. He was employed on the North America and West India station in the *Epervier* 18, under Captain Richard Walter Wales. On April 29, 1814, the *Epervier* was taken by the U.S. sloop *Peacock* 22, and Hackett lost his left arm in the battle. On October 23, 1815, Hackett was awarded a pension for his wounds of 182 *l* 10 s. He served as a lieutenant in two more ships, then was promoted to commander on September 2, 1828. He commanded the *Jaseur* 16 sloop in the Mediterranean from November 1833 to the spring of 1837, and his services during the civil war in Spain were rewarded with the first class of the order of Charles III. He was promoted to captain on June 28, 1838. He died a vice admiral on March 29, 1865.

Lord John Hay

The third son of the seventh marquis of Tweeddale, Hay was born on April 1, 1793. In December 1806 he joined the *Seahorse* 42, going to the Mediterranean. He saw a good deal of active service, losing his left arm in a cutting-out expedition in Hyères Roads in 1807 and sharing in the capture of a Turkish ship of 52 guns on July 5, 1808. On April 1, 1812, he was made lieutenant and in June was appointed to the *Pique,* in which he went to the West Indies; on May 31, 1814 he was transferred to the *Venerable,* carrying the flag of Sir Philip Durham, and from it was promoted on June 15 to the rank of commander. In November he was appointed to the *Bustard* at Lisbon and in the following year commissioned the *Opossum* 10, which he commanded in the Channel and on the Halifax station till August 1818. On December 7, 1818, he was promoted to captain; he was member of Parliament for Haddington from 1826 to 1830 and had no employment afloat till September 1832, when he was appointed to the *Castor* frigate. In November 1836 he was transferred to the sloop *Phœnix* 6 and in March 1837 to the *North Star* 28, which he left in 1840. He commanded a small squadron on the north coast of Spain during the civil war and was frequently landed in command of a naval and marine brigade. On February 17, 1837, he received the CB (Companion) and the Grand Cross of Charles III in acknowledgment of his services. From August 1841 to October 1843 Hay commanded the *Warspite* 50 on the North America and West Indies Station; in 1846 he acted as superintendent of Woolwich dockyard. In 1847 he was returned to Parliament as member for Windsor and from 1847 to 1850 was one of the lords of the Admiralty. On February 9, 1850, he was appointed commodore-superintendent of Devonport dockyard, where he still was at the time of his death on September 9, 1851, two days after he had hoisted his flag as rear admiral on board the *St. George.* He married in 1846 Mary Anne, the eldest daughter of Donald Cameron of Lochiel. They had no children.

Vice Admiral Sir Samuel Hood

Born in 1762, Hood was a cousin of the more famous Admiral Samuel Hood, the first Viscount Hood. He entered the navy in 1776 and was present at the First Battle of Ushant, July 27, 1778, and a number of actions in the West Indies, under the command of his cousin. In 1797, in command of the *Zealous* 74, he was present at Horatio Nelson's unsuccessful attack on Santa Cruz de Tenerife and negotiated for the squadron in the aftermath of this failure. As captain of the *Zealous* 74, he played an important role at the Battle of the Nile, then commanded the blockade of Alexandria and Rosetta. He was awarded the KC for his actions against the French in the West Indies in 1802. In September 1805, Hood lost an arm in an action blockading Rochefort from a French frigate squadron. A few days after this action, Hood was promoted to rear admiral and in 1807 was put in command of operations against Madeira. King Gustav IV Adolf of Sweden awarded Hood the Grand Cross of the Order of the Sword for his actions in the Baltic Sea during the Russo-Swedish War. Hood married Mary Elizabeth Frederica Mackenzie, the heiress of Baron Seaforth. He commanded a division of the British fleet in the Mediterranean and became a vice admiral in 1811; his final command was the East Indies Station. He died at Madras on December 27, 1814.

Commander Joshua Kneeshaw

Kneeshaw was commissioned as a lieutenant in September 1800 and commanded and lost the cutter *Georgiana* near Honfleur, on the river Seine, on September 25, 1804. He commanded the *Martial* 12 gun-brig on the Walcheren expedition, then the *Piercer* 12, under the orders of Captain Arthur Farquar. Farquar praised him in this official dispatch announcing the fall of Gluckstadt on January 5, 1814: "Lieutenant Kneeshaw, who will have the honor of carrying home this despatch, is an officer of great merit—his attention to his duty since he has been under my command, claims my warmest approbation. He is an old officer, and has lost his right arm in the service of his country."[9] The day he arrived at the Admiralty, January 12, 1814, Kneeshaw was promoted to the rank of commander and given command of the *Piercer*, rated as a sloop of war. In 1815 he was given command of the *Censor* 14. His pension was originally granted in 1802 and raised to 200 *l* per year. He died on September 3, 1843.

Mr. Phillip LeVesconte

Phillip LeVesconte lost a leg on the Glorious First of June, 1794. He died a purser on the *Royal William* 84 at Spithead on May 25, 1807. His two sons both became commanders in the navy.

Captain Sir Robert Mends

Mends came from a well-established Pembrokeshire family. His younger brother, William Bowen Mends (1781–1864), died an admiral. Robert joined the *Culloden* 74 under Captain George Balfour and was present at the action off Cape St. Vincent. In the frigate *Guadeloupe* 28, under the command of Captain Hugh Robinson, Mends took part in the action at the mouth of the Chesapeake on March 16, 1781, and at Yorktown, where the *Guadeloupe* was destroyed and Mends lost his right arm, in addition to being wounded in the knee. He was thirteen years old. Because of difficulties with his recovery, he endured two separate amputation procedures. He was awarded a pension of 7 *l* a year. In 1786, Mends was back at sea, serving in the *Grampus* 50 on the coast of Africa, under Commodore Edward Thompson. On August 26, 1789, he was commissioned as a lieutenant to the *Childers* sloop of war, under the command of Sir Robert Barlow. He took part in the Battle of Groix on June 23, 1795, as a lieutenant of the *Colossus* 74 and was badly burned by a gunpowder explosion from a defective cannon. On March 3, 1797, Mends commanded the *Diligence* 16 and captured *La Nativetas*. He was made a post-captain on May 2, 1800, and continued to serve in the West Indies, capturing another ship. On September 29, 1802, Mends married a Miss Butler, of Bagshot, Surrey. In 1805, Mends was appointed to the Sea Fencible service in Ireland, and as captain of the *Arethusa* frigate, in November 1808, he captured the *General Ernouf*, a French privateer. On April 6, 1809, the *Arethusa* joined the *Amethyst* 36, commanded by Sir Michael Seymour, in the capture of a French frigate. In this action Mends was knocked unconscious by a block that struck him on the back of his head. Mends commanded a squadron stationed on the north coast of Spain, cooperating with Spanish patriots in a number of actions. He was knighted by Spain on May 25, 1815, and also made a Knight of the Bath the same day. In April 1816, his pension for the loss of his arm (originally 7 *l*) was increased to 300 *l*. In June 1821, Mends was given the chief command on the coast of Africa. He died of cholera on board the *Owen Glendower* frigate at Cape Coast, on September 4, 1823.

Captain Joseph Packwood

A native of Bermuda, Packwood joined the *Virginia* 28 frigate at the invitation of its captain, Sir John Orde. He witnessed the capture and destruction of an American fleet in the Penobscot River and lost his arm during the siege of Charlestown in 1780. When he recovered his health, Packwood followed Captain Orde into the *Chatham* 50 and *Roebuck* 44, on the American, North Sea, and Channel stations, until peace came in 1783, when he was placed in an academy abroad. He served in the *Camilla* 20, commanded by Captain J. Hutt, until he returned to his patron Orde, then serving as governor of Dominica. Orde gave Packwood command of the colonial brig that belonged to the island, and in it he took part in actions against Martinique and Guadeloupe conducted by Sir John Jervis and Sir Charles Grey. In 1792, Packwood was commissioned as a lieutenant into the *Perdrix* 22, under Captain William C. Fahie. He served in a number of other ships, under different captains, and took part in the battle off Algeziras, July 6, 1801. Packwood rejoined Captain Orde as senior lieutenant of the *Glory* 98. In spring of 1805, Orde gave Packwood command of the *Wasp* sloop, and he was promoted to the rank of commander on January 22, 1806. He was appointed to the *Childers* brig in 1808 and captured a Danish privateer, as well as a British merchant ship that the privateer had seized. He was made a post-captain on February 14, 1811.

Admiral Sir Watkin Owen Pell

Pell was born in 1788, the son of Samuel Pell of Sywell Hall, Northamptonshire, and Mary Owen, a Welsh gentleman's daughter. Under the patronage of Earl Spencer, Pell joined the *Loire* 38 in 1799 and lost his left leg on February 6, 1800, in the capture of the French frigate *Pallas*. After two years on shore, Pell served on various ships, and then on November 11, 1806, he was made Lieutenant into the *Mercury* 28. He served under several captains, including James Alexander Gordon, at Bermuda, Newfoundland, and in the Mediterranean. On April 4, 1808, First Lieutenant Pell commanded a boarding party that used small boats to capture and destroy a Spanish convoy in cooperation with two other ships, one of them the *Alceste,* commanded by James Alexander Gordon. Pell again took to small boats in battle on April 1, 1809, capturing a Venetian gunboat, *La Leda,* which was armed with a long 24-pounder and 6 large swivels, displaying gallantry under heavy fire. He became a commander on March 29, 1810; a captain on November 1, 1813; Knight Commander of the Bath in April 1837; and rear admiral of the Blue on September 5, 1848. In 1847, at the age of sixty, he married Sarah Dorothea Owen, who was thirty-four. They had several children. He died December 19, 1869.

Captain Sir John Strutt Peyton

Peyton was born on January 14, 1786, connected to the navy on both sides of his family. His father was a long-serving official in the Navy Office; his grandfather was Admiral Joseph Peyton; three of his uncles were officers (one died a rear admiral in 1809); and his mother was a captain's sister, a commander's daughter, and the daughter of the matron of Greenwich Hospital. Peyton went to sea under Horatio Nelson's patronage in the 1790s and served in the *Emerald* 36 under Captain Thomas Moutray Waller. He was in Nelson's ship at two of Nelson's most important battles: the Nile (1798) and Copenhagen (1801). He sailed with Nelson in the Baltic, off Cadiz, and in the West Indies, served in several different frigates in the Channel and the North Sea, and then in August 1803 joined Nelson in the *Victory*. In March 1805 he was appointed acting lieutenant of the *Canôpus* 80. Peyton's commission as lieutenant is dated October 7, 1805. In July 1807 he was sent to destroy a vessel run ashore near Ortona and was wounded in the right elbow by a musket bullet. His right arm was amputated. A family memoir notes that "the bullet struck a button at his wrist, and ran up his arm splintering the bone. The button saved his life, by diverting the bullet from his heart. He became marvelously expert in the use of his left hand, and was a good shot, and a good whip. His combined knife and fork is still preserved."[10] Peyton's daughters also reported that he was "habitually reticent about the particulars of the casualty."[11] He was promoted to commander in December 1807, and from June 1809 to February 1811 he commanded the *Ephira* 10 in the North Sea, in the Walcheren expedition, and off Cadiz. He commanded three other ships off the coast of Valencia and Catalonia till near the end of the war, repeatedly engaging with the enemies' batteries and privateers. He conveyed the Archduke Francis from Smyrna to Sardinia, where he gave a ball celebrating King George's birthday on his ship, the *Weazle* 16, for the king and queen of Sardinia and the Austrian prince. He married, in 1814, a daughter of Lieutenant Woodyear, R.N., of St. Christopher's Island, and had three daughters and two sons. On January 25, 1836, Peyton was nominated a Knight Commander of Hannover, and in June 1836 he was appointed to the *Madagascar* 46 and went out to the West Indies. In the spring of 1838, he invalided out of active service and died in London on May 20 that year. His oldest son, Lumley Woodyear, died a retired commander in 1885.

Captain Sir Wilson Rathbourne

Rathbourne was born in Ireland in 1748, the nephew of John Wilson Croker, secretary to the Admiralty. He joined the *Niger* 32 as a midshipman in 1763 under the patronage of Sir Thomas Adams. He served under Adams in two more ships until Adams's death in 1770. Rathbourne became a lieutenant on March 18, 1780, commissioned into the *Bedford* 74, commanded by Sir Edmund Affleck. He served in a number of ships. In Vice Admiral Hotham's action on March 14, 1794, he lost the sight in his right eye, and his right arm was so severely injured that he permanently lost most of its function. The arm was not amputated. Rathbourne became a commander on November 9, 1795. In 1799, he took command of the *Racoon* 18, employed off Boulongne, in the Channel, the Mediterranean, and the West Indies. He made post-captain on October 18, 1802. He commanded the frigate *Santa Margaritta* as part of the Channel Fleet and played a lead role in Sir Richard Strachan's capture of four French line-of-battle ships on November 4, 1805. In 1805 he also married a daughter of John French, of Loughrea, in Galway. Commanding the *Santa Margaritta,* Rathbourne was employed on the Channel, Lisbon, West Indian, and Irish stations. When his ship became so decayed as to be put out of commission in 1807, Rathbourne was put in command of the Essex Sea Fencibles. On May 19, 1810, he was granted a pension for the loss of his eye, which was later raised to 300 *l* a year. He became a Companion of the Bath on June 4, 1815, and died in 1831.

Lieutenant William Rivers

William Rivers was born sometime between 1786 and 1788, the son of the *Victory*'s gunner, who was also named William Rivers. From 1795 to 1799, he was a first-class volunteer on the *Victory* 100. Rivers was wounded in the right arm by pieces of ship's timber shattered in Hotham's second partial action on July 13, 1795, and at the Battle off Cape St. Vincent February 14, 1797. When Rivers was a sixteen-year-old midshipman in the *Victory*, his left foot or left leg was injured, and three of his teeth were knocked out by shot during the Battle of Trafalgar. When his leg was amputated, he is reported to have tried to hearten the injured men waiting in the surgeon's cockpit with him by urging them, "My men, it is nothing to have a limb off, you will find pleasure when you come here, men, to get rid of your shattered limb."[12] Rivers returned to duty in the *Victory* a few weeks after the amputation and was promoted to lieutenant on January 8, 1806, into the *Princess of Orange* 74, under Captain Thomas Rogers. He also received a gratuity from the Patriotic Fund.

For the next twelve years, Rivers served as a lieutenant or a first lieutenant on a number of ships. He served on the *Otter* sloop, under Captain John Davies, from April 1, 1806, to January 1807, and the *Cossack* 24, under Captain George Digby, from April 1, 1806, to April 11, 1807, as part of Admiral Gambier's expedition to Copenhagen. While in the *Cossack*, Rivers took part in a number of boat actions. On July 9, 1809, Lieutenant Rivers married a niece of Joseph Gibson, Esq. of Long Bennington, County Lincoln, with whom he eventually had two sons (one of whom, William Thomas Rivers, also became a lieutenant R.N.) and six daughters. He joined the *Cretan* 16 on October 18, 1809, as first lieutenant, under Captain Charles Frederick Payne, then served in the *Raisonnable* 64 under Captains Thomas New, Charles Hewitt, and Edward Sneyd Clay. On June 16, 1814, he joined the *Namur* 74, under Sir Thomas Williams, commander-in-chief at the Nore, whom he served as flag lieutenant. He continued to serve as first lieutenant in the *Namur*, and then, on August 24, 1815, joined the *Bulwark* 74 under Sir Charles Rowley, until paid off in April 1818. In 1816, Rivers was granted a pension of 91 *l* 5 s a year. In November 1824, he was appointed warden at Woolwich Dockyard. He continued in that position until April 28, 1826, when he joined the Royal Hospital at Greenwich, where he became the governor's adjutant lieutenant. His exemplary service in that role was commemorated in 1857 with a marble bust paid for by friends and shipmates, displayed in the Painted Hall.

Commander George Robinson

Robinson was first commissioned as a lieutenant in 1790. He lost a leg on October 24, 1793, while serving as the second lieutenant of the *Thames* 32, under Captain James Cotes, in an action against the French frigate *Uranie*, which had superior force. After being severely damaged in this inconclusive battle, the *Thames* was captured by a French squadron. On June 23, 1795, Robinson was promoted to commander. In January 1796, he was granted a pension of 91 *l* 5 s. On May 8, 1816, this pension was increased to 200 *l*.

Rear Admiral Sir Michael Seymour

Michael Seymour was born on November 8, 1768, at Glebe House, Pallas, County Limerick, the second son of the Reverend John Seymour, who was related to the dukes of Somerset who settled in Ireland under Elizabeth I. In November 1780 he joined the sloop *Merlin* 18 under Captain James Luttrell, whom he followed in March 1781 to the *Portland* 50; in April 1782 to the *Mediator* 44; and in April 1783 to the *Ganges* 74. As a midshipman in the *Mediator,* Seymour took part in Luttrell's successful action against a French squadron of superior force. Seymour was commissioned as a lieutenant into the *Magnificent* 74 in November 1790 and served in the *Marlborough* 74 at the Glorious First of June, 1794, in which action he lost his arm. He took a number of prizes as the commander of the *Spitfire* sloop of war and was made a post-captain on August 11, 1800. He served as acting captain of a number of ships and frigates and then became captain of the *Amethyst* 43, in which ship, on November 10, 1808, he captured *la Thetis,* a French frigate of superior force. On April 6, 1809, he captured *La Niemen,* another French ship of superior force. Seymour commanded several other ships, won further battles, and was awarded the title of baronet in 1809, then Knight Commander of the Bath in 1816. His pension for the loss of his arm was raised to 300 *l.* He married Jane Hawker, the daughter of another naval captain, and they had a large family. He served as commissioner of Portsmouth Dockyard from 1829 to 1832 and was named Rear Admiral of the Blue, June 27, 1832. In poor health, Seymour went back to sea to be of service to his son's career and died there on July 9, 1834.

Captain Edward Stopford

Stopford was a nephew of Admiral the Honorable Sir Robert Stopford, KCB, who was himself a younger son of the Earl of Courtown. In August 1811, when Stopford was acting captain of the *Otter,* his right arm was carried off by a cannon ball in a successful attack on the island of Java. Stopford arrived at the Admiralty Office in London on December 17, 1811, bearing a dispatch and letters from his uncle, who had commanded the expedition, recommending his promotion.

Stopford was promoted to post rank on the second day after his arrival in London. He was given command of the *Rosamond* 20 in the spring of 1814 and convoyed three merchantmen to the coast of Labrador. Stopford lost command of the *Rosamond* in 1814, when it was found to be so damaged by the ice of Hudson's Straits that it was put out of commission. He retained a pension of 300 *l* per year for the loss of his arm. He died on April 19, 1837.

Commander Henry Clements Thompson

Thompson lost an arm during the French Revolutionary Wars and was commissioned as a lieutenant on September 14, 1802. He commanded the boats belonging to the *Merlin* 16 sloop under Captain Edward P. Brenton and aided in destroying a French privateer on October 27, 1803. In August 1808, Gustavus Adolphus IV awarded him the Order of the Sword for his distinguished services on the Baltic station. He was promoted to commander the next month. Thompson became deeply involved in a parliamentary election campaign and fell into debt. He was committed to the King's Bench Prison on March 11, 1824, and died there in May.

NOTES

Abbreviations

ADM Admiralty Records held by the National Archives
BL British Library
NMM National Maritime Museum
NA Northumberland Archives (formerly known as the Northumberland Record Office)

Introduction

1. Francis Bacon, "42. Of Deformity," in *The Essays Or Counsels Civil and Moral, of Francis Lord Verulam, Viscount St. Alban* (London: printed by John Hanland for Hanna Barret, and Richard Whitaker, 1625), 47.
2. Douglas C. Baynton, "Disability and the Justification of Inequality in American History," in Paul K. Longmore and Lauri Umansky, eds., *The New Disability History: American Perspectives,* History of Disability Series (New York: New York University Press, 2001), 52.
3. Colin White, ed., *Nelson: The New Letters* (Rochester: Boydell Press, 2005), 67.
4. Colin White, *The Nelson Companion* (Annapolis, MD: Naval Institute Press, 1995), 33.
5. Rina Prentice, *The Authentic Nelson,* illustrated ed. (London: National Maritime Museum, 2005), 61.
6. Jubilee Sailing Trust, "Our History," http://jst.org.uk/about-us/history.
7. Katherine Ott, "Disability and the Practice of Public History: An Introduction," *Public Historian* 27, no. 2 (2005): 12, https://doi.org/10.1525/tph.2005.27.2.9.
8. John Sugden, *Nelson: The Sword of Albion,* illustrated reprint ed. (London: Bodley Head, 2014).
9. See Roger Knight, "Changing the Agenda: The 'New' Naval History of the British Sailing Navy," *Mariner's Mirror* 97, no.1 (February 2011), 225–42.

10. Maev Kennedy, "Nelson Put in His Place by New Maritime Museum Exhibition," *The Guardian*, October 14, 2013, sec. Culture, https://www.theguardian.com/culture/2013/oct/14/nelson-maritime-museum-exhibition.
11. R. J. B. Knight, *The Pursuit of Victory: The Life and Achievement of Horatio Nelson* (New York: Basic Books, 2005), xxii.
12. N. A. M. Rodger, introduction to *The Command of the Ocean: A Naval History of Britain, 1649–1815* (New York: W. W. Norton, 2005), lxiv.
13. Lawrence Stone, *An Imperial State at War: Britain from 1689 to 1815* (London: Routledge, 1994), 120; N. A. M. Rodger, "Commissioned Officers' Careers in the Royal Navy, 1690–1815," *Journal for Maritime Research* 3, no. 1 (December 2001): 86, https://doi.org/10.1080/21533369.2001.9668314.
14. Leigh Allen and Ceri Boston, eds., *Safe Moor'd in Greenwich Tier: A Study of the Skeletons of Royal Navy Sailors and Marines Excavated at the Royal Hospital Greenwich* (Oxford: Oxford Archaeology, 2008), 13.
15. Nicholas Roe, *John Keats: A New Life* (New Haven, CT: Yale University Press, 2012), 5.
16. David A. Gerber, ed., introduction to *Disabled Veterans in History*, Corporealities: Discourses of Disability (Ann Arbor: University of Michigan Press, 2000), 1; Gerber, "Disabled Veterans, the State, and the Experience of Disability in Western Societies, 1914–1950," *Journal of Social History* 36, no. 4 (Summer 2003): 899; Stephen R. Ortiz, ed., *Veterans' Policies, Veterans' Politics: New Perspectives on Veterans in the Modern United States* (Gainesville: University Press of Florida, 2012); Paul K. Longmore and Lauri Umansky, eds., *The New Disability History: American Perspectives*, History of Disability Series (New York: New York University Press, 2001).
17. See Timothy Jenks, *Naval Engagements: Patriotism, Cultural Politics, and the Royal Navy, 1793–1815* (Oxford: Oxford University Press, 2006); Margarette Lincoln, *Representing the Royal Navy: British Sea Power, 1750–1815* (Burlington VT: Ashgate, 2002); David Carradine, ed., *Admiral Lord Nelson: Context and Legacy* (Houndsmill, Bassingstoke, Hampshire, UK: Palgrave Macmillan, 2005).
18. "World Health Organization, "Disabilities," http://www.who.int/topics/disabilities/en/.
19. Martin Wilcox, "The 'Poor Decayed Seamen' of Greenwich Hospital, 1705–1763," *International Journal of Maritime History* 25, no. 1 (June 1, 2013): 66, https://doi.org/10.1177/084387141302500104.
20. Lennard J. Davis, *The Disability Studies Reader*, 5th ed. (New York: Routledge, 2016), 2, https://doi.org/10.4324/9781315680668.
21. Tom Shakespeare, "Nasty, Brutish, and Short? On the Predicament of Disability and Embodiment," in *Disability and the Good Human Life,* ed. Jerome Birckenbach, Franziska Felder, and Barbara Schmitz (New York: Cambridge University Press, 2013), 93–112; Alison Kafer, *Feminist, Queer, Crip* (Bloomington: Indiana University Press, 2013).
22. David M. Turner, "Disability History and the History of Emotions: Reflections on

Eighteenth-Century Britain," *Asclepio*, 68, no. 2 (2016): 146, http://dx.doi.org/10.3989/asclepio.2016.08.
23. Steven L. Kurzman, "Performing Able-Bodiness: Amputees and Prosthetics in America" (PhD thesis, University of California, Santa Cruz, 2003), 90.
24. "Miscellaneous Papers" (n.d.), PLL /88/53, National Maritime Museum Caird Archive, Greenwich, London, UK.
25. John I. Knight, "Telescope Holder for One-Handed Persons," *Mechanics' Magazine and Journal of Science, Arts, and Manufactures* 20 (January 1834): 351, Google Books, https://play.google.com/books/reader?id=-I5fAAAAcAAJ&hl=en&pg=GBS.PA351.
26. Knight, *Pursuit of Victory*, 487.
27. Richard Seymour, *Memoir of Rear-Admiral Sir Michael Seymour, Bart., K.C.B.* (London: Spottiswoode, 1878; Internet Archive, 2008), 101, http://archive.org/details/memoirrearadmirooseymgoog.
28. United States Department of Labor, Office of Disability Employment Policy, "Focus on Ability: Interviewing Applicants with Disabilities," https://www.dol.gov/odep/pubs/fact/focus.htm.
29. Tobin Siebers, *Disability Theory*, Corporealities: Discourses of Disability (Ann Arbor: University of Michigan Press, 2008), 6.
30. Evan Wilson, *A Social History of British Naval Officers, 1775–1815* (Woodbridge, Suffolk, UK: Boydell Press, 2017), 3.
31. Wilson, *Social History*, 3.
32. See Helen Deutsch and Felicity Nussbaum, *"Defects": Engendering the Modern Body*, Corporealities: Discourses of Disability (Ann Arbor: University of Michigan Press, 2000).
33. Simon Dickie, *Cruelty and Laughter: Forgotten Comic Literature and the Unsentimental Eighteenth Century* (Chicago: University of Chicago Press, 2011), 93.
34. Rosemarie Garland-Thomson, "Opinion | Becoming Disabled," *New York Times*, August 19, 2016, https://www.nytimes.com/2016/08/21/opinion/sunday/becoming-disabled.html.
35. Siebers, *Disability Theory*, 5.
36. David M. Turner, "Disability and Crime in Eighteenth-Century England," *Cultural and Social History* 9, no. 1 (March 1, 2012): 59, https://doi.org/10.2752/147800412X13191165982953.
37. White, *Nelson: The New Letters*, 60.
38. Wilson, *Social History*, 4.
39. Evan Wilson, "Social Background and Promotion Prospects in the Royal Navy, 1775–1815," *English Historical Review* 131, no. 550 (June 2016): 578, https://doi.org/10.1093/ehr/cew174.
40. John Kirkup, *A History of Limb Amputation* (London: Springer, 2007).
41. Sir James Watt, "Surgery at Trafalgar," *Mariner's Mirror* 91, no. 2 (January 1, 2005): 266–83, https://doi.org/10.1080/00253359.2005.10656949.

42. Sir James Watt, "Naval and Civilian Influences on Eighteenth- and Nineteenth-Century Medical Practice," *Mariner's Mirror* 97, no. 1 (February 2011): 280.
43. Watt, "Surgery at Trafalgar," 280. See also Christopher Lloyd and Jack L. S. Coulter, *Medicine and the Navy, 1200–1900: 1714–1815*, vol. 3. (Edinburgh: Livingstone, 1957).
44. William R. O'Byrne, "Bedford. (Lieut., 1799. F-P., 10; H-P., 44.)," in *A Naval Biographical Dictionary: Comprising the Life and Services of Every Living Officer in Her Majesty's Navy, from the Rank of Admiral of the Fleet to That of Lieutenant, Inclusive, Compiled from Authentic and Family Documents* (London: J. Murray, 1849), 65 (available in digital collection, *Sabin Americana: History of the Americas, 1500–1926*, GALE | CY0102755979).
45. O'Byrne, "Bedford," in *Naval Biographical Dictionary*, 65.
46. Great Britain Parliament, House of Lords, *Journals of the House of Lords*, vol. 52 (n.p.: H.M. Stationery Office, 1818–19), 886, *HathiTrust*, https://hdl.handle.net/2027/uc1.c0000029280?urlappend=%3Bseq=890.
47. Great Britain Parliament, , *Journals of House of Lords* 52: 887.
48. O'Byrne, "Bedford," in *Naval Biographical Dictionary*, 69.
49. David J. Hepper, *British Warship Losses in the Age of Sail, 1650–1859*, (Rotherfield, East Sussex, UK: Jean Boudriot, 1994), 147.
50. Marshall, "Barclay, Robert Herriot [sic]," in *Royal Naval Biography*, 3: 187.
51. United States Department of the Interior, National Park Service, "Robert Heriot Barclay," https://www.nps.gov/people/robert-heriot-barclay.htm.
52. Brian Lavery, *Nelson's Navy: The Ships, Men, and Organisation, 1793–1815* (Annapolis, MD: Naval Institute Press, 1989), 117.
53. Rodger, "Commissioned Officers' Careers in the Royal Navy, 1690–1815," *Journal for Maritime Research* 3, no. 1 (December 2001): 104, https://doi.org/10.1080/21533369.2001.9668314.
54. N. A. M. Rodger, *The Wooden World: An Anatomy of the Georgian Navy* (Annapolis: Naval Institute Press, 1986), 275.
55. Wilson, *Social History*, 225.
56. Wilson, *Social History*, 225.
57. Charles Consolvo, "The Prospects and Promotion of British Naval Officers 1793–1815," *Mariner's Mirror* 91, no. 2 (January 1, 2005): 151, https://doi.org/10.1080/00253359.2005.10656942.
58. See Christopher Lloyd, ed., *The Health of Seamen: Selections from the Work of Dr. James Lind, Sir Gilbert Blane, and Dr. Thomas Trotter* (London: Navy Records Society, 1965).
59. Michael Lewis, *A Social History of the Navy, 1793–1815* (London: Allen & Unwin, 1960), 423.
60. Lewis, *Social History of the Navy*, 395.
61. Sir Gilbert Blane, "Statements of the Comparative Health of the British Navy, from the Year 1779 to the Year 1814, with Proposals for Its Farther Improvement," *Medico-Chirurgical Transactions* 6 (1815): 526. Blane offers a rousing defense of tea as an alter-

native drink. He challenges those who fear tea's "supposed relaxing property . . . [on] British courage and hardihood . . . [on] whether there is to be found in the results of the battles of Trafalgar and Waterloo, any proof of British nerves being unbraced by the habitual use of this beverage" (526).

62. Lewis, *Social History of the Navy*, 398.
63. Great Britain Parliament, "Parl. Debates, May 11, 1810.- Navy Estimates," in *The Parliamentary Debates from the Year 1803 to the Present Time*, vol. 16 (London: published under the superintendence of T.C. Hansard, 1812), 1007–08, *HathiTrust*, https://hdl.handle.net/2027/njp.32101019449006?urlappend=%3Bseq=638.
64. Great Britain Parliament, "Parl. Debates," 16: 1011, 1015.
65. Marshall, *Royal Naval Biography*. This edition is accessible and searchable online through Wikisource, as is J. Murray's edition of O'Byrne, *Naval Biographical Dictionary*. A full searchable version of Marshall's work with page and volume numbers can also be found in the HathiTrust virtual catalog Gale's Sabin Americana, the latter of which was used for citations in this text..
66. Wilson, *Social History*, 230. Wilson has also recently compiled a statistical database of 556 commissioned naval officers from the period based on a random sample of lieutenants' passing certificates. He estimates that there were over 5,000 officers in the navy during the Great Wars and notes that "only 185 officers in my database have entries in Marshall, and a mere 123 are described in O'Byrne."
67. Lewis, *Social History of the Navy*, 423.
68. Wilson, *Social History*, 86.
69. "Miscellaneous Papers" (n.d.), PLL /84.
70. Lieutenant William Phippard Haydon to O'Byrne, October 18, 1844, in William R, O'Byrne, "Correspondence and Biographical Notes upon Which William Richard O'Byrne Based His Naval Biographical Dictionary of All Living Officers (1849), Compiled during the Years 1843–1849. 16 vols. Paper. Folio" (unpublished manuscript chapters), Add MS 38044, 503, BL.
71. Marshall, preface to *Royal Naval Biography*, 1: viii.
72. Nicholas Tracy, *Who's Who in Nelson's Navy* (London: Chatham, 2006), 9.
73. Marshall, "Williams, Richard," in *Royal Naval Biography*, 4: 312.
74. Great Britain Parliament, House of Commons, *Parliamentary Papers: 1780–1849*, vol. 17 (n.p.: H.M. Stationery Office, 1831), 18, Google Books, https://books.google.com/books?id=f8FDAQAAMAAJ&printsec=frontcover#v=onepage&q&f=false.
75. Marianne Czisnik, *Horatio Nelson: A Controversial Hero* (London: Hodder Arnold, 2005).
76. Ellen Gill, *Naval Families, War and Duty in Britain, 1740–1820* (Woodbridge, Suffolk, UK: Boydell Press, 2016); Mary Favret, *War at a Distance: Romanticism and the Making of Modern Wartime* (Princeton, NJ: Princeton University Press, 2010).
77. Homer, *The Iliad of Homer*, trans. Alexander Pope (London: Cassel, 1909) book 11, pp. 214, line 574.

78. Basil Hall, *Fragments of Voyages and Travels*, 2nd series, vol. 2 (Edinburgh: R. Cadell, 1832–34), 24.
79. Brian Lavery, *Royal Tars: The Lower Deck of the Royal Navy, 875–1850* (Annapolis, MD: Naval Institute Press, 2010), 268.
80. White, *Nelson: The New Letters*, 114.
81. Viscount Horatio Nelson, *The Dispatches and Letters of Vice Admiral Lord Viscount Nelson: With Notes*, ed. Nicholas Harris Nicolas, 7 vols. (London: H. Colburn, 1845), vol. 2: 405.
82. ADL/T/16, NMM.
83. Hall, *Fragments of Voyages and Travels*, 2:35.

1. Patrons and Followers

1. Seymour, *Memoir* 33.
2. Evan Wilson, "British Naval Administration and the Quarterdeck Manpower Problem in the Eighteenth Century," in *Strategy and the Sea: Essays in Honour of John B. Hattendorf*, ed. N.A.M. Rodger et al., rev. ed. (Woodbridge, Suffolk, UK: Boydell and Brewer, 2016), 65, http://www.jstor.org/stable/10.7722/j.ctt19x3j3g.13.
3. Denis A. Orde, *Nelson's Mediterranean Command: Concerning Pride, Preferment & Prize Money* (Edinburgh: Pentland Press, 1997), 94.
4. Rodger, "Commissioned Officers' Careers," 105.
5. Consolvo, "Prospects and Promotion," 149.
6. Royal Statistical Society of London, "On the Mortality Arising from Naval Operations," *Journal of the Royal Statistical Society: General*, vol. 18 (London: John William Parker and Son, 1855), 204–5, HathiTrust Digital Library, https://hdl.handle.net/2027/mdp.39015036988460?urlappend=%3Bseq=214.
7. ADM 82 126, National Archives.
8. ADM 82 126, National Archives.
9. Great Britain Parliament, Lords, *Journals of House of Lords*, 52: 887.
10. Rodger, "A Note on Conventions," in *Command of the Ocean*, xxv.
11. Robert D. Hume, "The Value of Money in Eighteenth-Century England: Incomes, Prices, Buying Power—and Some Problems in Cultural Economics," *Huntington Library Quarterly* 77, no. 4 (Winter 2014): 373–416, https://doi.org/10.1525/hlq.2014.77.4.373.
12. Rodger, *Command of the Ocean*. For a complete list of naval pay scales through 1815, see Appendix 4.
13. In celebration of Waterloo, an 1815 Act by the Prince Regent decreed that pensions should be augmented by rank in this manner. *Niles' Weekly Register*, vol. 9 (Baltimore: H. Niles, September 1815–Feb. 1816), 74, HathiTrust Digital Library, https://hdl.handle.net/2027/pst.000055571128?urlappend=%3Bseq=88.
14. Tracy, *Who's Who in Nelson's Navy*, 1335.

15. Great Britain Parliament, "Parl. Debates," 16: 1007.
16. ADL/T/8, NMM.
17. ADL/T/8, NMM.
18. Czisnik, *Horatio Nelson*, 183.
19. James Harrison, *The Life of the Right Honourable Horatio Lord Viscount Nelson*, vol. 1 (London: Ranelagh Press, 1806; Project Gutenberg, 2005), 356, http://www.gutenberg.org/ebooks/16912.
20. Robert Southey, *The Life of Nelson*, vol. 1 (London: J. Murray, 1813), 199–201.
21. Jenks, *Naval Engagements*, 218.
22. "Parliamentary Paper: Sixth Report from the Select Committee of Finance," *Naval Chronicle* 39 (January–June 1818): 71, HathiTrust Digital Library, https://hdl.handle.net/2027/umn.319510007440670?urlappend=%3Bseq=93 .
23. Great Britain Parliament, Lords, *Journals of House of Lords*, 52: 887.
24. Rodger, "Commissioned Officers' Careers," 95.
25. Consolvo, "Prospects and Promotion," 155.
26. Consolvo, "Prospects and Promotion," 155.
27. R. J. B. Knight, *Pursuit of Victory*, 664.
28. Collingwood to Parker, Nov 1, 1805, NMM, RUSI/NM/214(i).
29. See, for example, Thomas Malcomson, *Order and Disorder in the British Navy, 1793–1815: Control, Resistance, Flogging and Hanging* (Woodbridge, Suffolk, UK: Boydell Press, 2016).
30. Wilson, *Social History*, 4.
31. S. A. Cavell, *Midshipmen and Quarterdeck Boys in the Royal Navy, 1771–1831* (London: Boydell Press, 2012), 215.
32. Cavell, *Midshipmen and Quarterdeck Boys*, 211.
33. Nelson, *Dispatches and Letters*, 2: 406.
34. Edward Pelham Brenton, *Life and Correspondence of John, Earl of St. Vincent, etc. [With a portrait]*, vol. 2 (London: H. Colbourn, 1838), 53.
35. Marshall, "Duncan, Henry," in *Royal Naval Biography*, vol. 2, bk. 2, 984.
36. Rodger, "Commissioned Officers' Careers," 104.
37. Seymour, *Memoir*, 55.
38. White, *Nelson: The New Letters*, October 1804, 90.
39. Lincoln, *Representing the Royal Navy*, 177.
40. Katherine Ott, "The Sum of Its Parts: An Introduction to Modern Histories of Prosthetics," in *Artificial Parts, Practical Lives: Modern Histories of Prosthetics*, ed. Katherine Ott, David Serlin, and Stephen Mihm (New York: New York University Press, 2002), 27.
41. Marshall, "Gordon, James Alexander," in *Royal Naval Biography*, vol 2 bk. 2: 938.
42. O'Byrne, "Gill. (Captain, 1837. F-P., 16; H-P., 37.)," in *Naval Biographical Dictionary*, 397.
43. White, *Nelson: The New Letters*, 99.
44. *London Gazette*, "Page 1006 | Issue 15397, 15 August 1801 | London Gazette | The Gazette," https://www.thegazette.co.uk/London/issue/15397/page/1006.

45. Marshall, "Stopford, Edward," in *Royal Naval Biography*, 6: 454.
46. Marshall, "Stopford, Edward," in *Royal Naval Biography*, 6: 454.
47. Marshall, "Sayer, George," in *Royal Naval Biography*, 2: 356.
48. Marshall, "Stopford, Edward," in *Royal Naval Biography*, 6: 454.
49. Roy and Lesley Adkins, *Jack Tar: Life in Nelson's Navy*, digital original ed. (London: Abacus, 2009), 304.
50. O'Byrne, "Correspondence and Biographical Notes," Add MS 38044, BL.
51. O'Byrne, "Correspondence and Biographical Notes," Add MS 38044, BL.
52. A. H. Bullen and Rebecca Mills, "Barker, Matthew Henry [pseud. the Old Sailor] (1790–1846), Sailor and Writer," in *Oxford Dictionary of National Biography*.
53. Matthew Henry Barker, *Greenwich Hospital: A Series of Naval Sketches, Descriptive of the Life of a Man-of-War's Man* (London: James Robins, 1826), 94–95.
54. Barker, *Greenwich Hospital*, 93.
55. J. K. Laughton and Andrew Lambert, "Seymour, Sir Michael, First Baronet (1768–1834), Naval Officer," in *Oxford Dictionary of National Biography*, https://doi.org/10.1093/ref:odnb/25177.
56. Seymour, *Memoir*, 94.
57. Wilson, *Social History*.
58. Seymour, *Memoir*, 12.
59. See Rodger, "Following and Advancement," in *Wooden World*, 119.
60. Sir Lewis Namier and John Brooke, eds., *The History of Parliament: The House of Commons, 1754–1790*, vol. 3 (London: Boydell and Brewer, 1985), 66.
61. Namier and Brooke, *History of Parliament*, 3: 66.
62. Michael Partridge, "Luttrell, James (c.1751–1788), Naval Officer and Politician," in *Oxford Dictionary of National Biography*, https://doi.org/10.1093/ref:odnb/17224.
63. Seymour, *Memoir*, 1.
64. Consolvo, "Prospects and Promotion," 158.
65. Seymour, *Memoir*, 8.
66. *The Annual Biography and Obituary, 1835*, vol. 19 (London: Longman, Hurst, Rees, Orme, and Brown, 1835), 192.
67. Namier and Brooke, *History of Parliament*, 3: 66.
68. Seymour, *Memoir*, 9.
69. Seymour, *Memoir*, 9–10.
70. David R. Fisher, "Berkeley, Hon. George Cranfield (1753–1818), of Wood End, nr. Chichester, Suss," History of Parliament Online, historyofparliamentonline.org/volume/1790-1820/member/berkeley-hon-george-cranfield-1753-1818.
71. Brian Mark de Toy, "Berkeley, Sir George Cranfield (1753–1818), Naval Officer and Politician," in *Oxford Dictionary of National Biography*, https://doi.org/10.1093/ref:odnb/2213.
72. Seymour, *Memoir*, 12.
73. Seymour, *Memoir*, 13.

74. Seymour, *Memoir*, 13.
75. Seymour, *Memoir*, 15.
76. Seymour, *Memoir*, 15.
77. Seymour, *Memoir*, 13.
78. Seymour, *Memoir*, 16.
79. Rodger, *Command of the Ocean*, 430.
80. *Annual Biography and Obituary*, 19: 197.
81. Seymour, *Memoir*, 17.
82. Seymour, *Memoir*, 17.
83. George Cranfield Berkeley, *Biographical Memoir of the Hon. George Cranfield Berkeley, Rear Admiral of the Red Squadron. [Extracted from "The Naval Chronicle." With a Portrait.]* (London: J. Gold, 1805), 108, Google Books, https://play.google.com/books/reader?id=LUJiAAAAcAAJ&hl=en&pg=GBS.PA88.
84. Seymour, *Memoir*, 19.
85. Seymour, *Memoir*, 18.
86. Seymour, *Memoir*, 19.
87. Seymour, *Memoir*, 20.
88. Seymour, *Memoir*, 19.
89. Seymour, *Memoir*, 22.
90. Seymour, *Memoir*, 23.
91. Seymour, *Memoir*, 93.
92. Brian Murphy and R. Thorne, eds., "Douglas, Sylvester (1743–1823), of The Pheasantry, Bushey Park, Mdx.," *History of Parliament Online*, http://www.historyofparliamentonline.org/volume/1790-1820/member/douglas-sylvester-1743-1823.
93. Sir James Alexander Gordon, *Letters and Records of Admiral Sir J. A. Gordon, G.C.B., 1782–1869*, comp. Elizabeth, Adelaide, and Sophia Gordon (London: printed for private circulation, 1890), 435.
94. J. A. Gordon, *Letters and Records*, 5.
95. J. A. Gordon, *Letters and Records*, 9.
96. J. A. Gordon, *Letters and Records*, 9.
97. Bryan Perrett, *The Real Hornblower: The Life and Times of Admiral Sir James Gordon* (New York: Skyhorse, 2014), 32.
98. Perrett, *Real Hornblower*, 39. Also see J. K. Laughton and Roger Morriss, "Gordon, Sir James Alexander (1782–1869), Naval Officer," in *Oxford Dictionary of National Biography*, https://doi.org/10.1093/ref:odnb/11054.
99. William James, *The Naval History of Great Britain, from . . . 1793, to . . . 1820, with an Account of the Origin and Increase of the British Navy* (London: Harding, Lepard, 1826), 55–56.
100. J. A. Gordon, *Letters and Records*, 58.
101. J. A. Gordon, *Letters and Records*, 58.
102. J. A. Gordon, *Letters and Records*, 61.

103. Marshall, "Gordon, Sir James Alexander," in *Royal Naval Biography*, 2: 938.
104. J. A. Gordon, *Letters and Records*, 44–45.
105. J. A. Gordon, *Letters and Records*, 68.
106. J. A. Gordon, *Letters and Records*, 68.
107. J. A. Gordon, *Letters and Records*, 75–76.
108. Nick Draper, "'Possessing Slaves': Ownership, Compensation and Metropolitan Society in Britain at the Time of Emancipation, 1834–40," *History Workshop Journal*, no. 64 (2007): 77, www.jstor.org/stable/25472936.
109. Draper, "'Possessing Slaves,'" 77–78.
110. "Owen Pell: Profile and Legacies Summary," Legacies of British Slave-Ownership, University College London, https://www.ucl.ac.uk/lbs/person/view/218.
111. PLL/86, NMM.
112. PLL/81 36 MS 06080 (a), NMM.
113. Marshall, "Duncan, Henry," in *Royal Naval Biography*, 2: 1001, GALE | CY0111483233.
114. "Watkin Owen Pell, Autograph Memorial of His Services," 36 MS. 0669, PLL/37, NMM.
115. PLL/81 36 MS 06080 (a), NMM.
116. PLL/9.b, NMM.
117. PLL/9/G, NMM.
118. PLL/9.a, NMM.
119. Great Britain Parliament, Commons, *Parliamentary Papers*, 17: 16.
120. NMM, PLL/19a.b.
121. PLL/9.F, NMM.
122. Marshall, "Pell, Watkin Owen," in *Royal Naval Biography*, 7: 164.
123. PLL/9.h; PLL/g/m, NMM.
124. PLL/51, NMM.
125. ZB 1381/4, Northamptonshire Record Office and Archives, Northampton, England.
126. Bolton House Dec 13th, 1811, ZB 1381/5, Northamptonshire Archives.
127. August 8, 1812, ZB 1381/6, Northamptonshire Archives.
128. October 27, 1813, ZB 1381/10, Northamptonshire Archives.
129. ZB 1381/29, Northamptonshire Archives.
130. PLL/88/53, NMM.
131. For more on the planter class's attempts to imagine life after slavery, see Anita Rupprecht, "From Slavery to Indenture: Scripts for Slavery's Endings," in *Emancipation and the Remaking of the British Imperial World*, ed. Catherine Hall, Nicholas Draper, and McClelland Keith (Manchester: Manchester University Press, 2014), 77–97, www.jstor.org/stable/j.ctt18mvmt2.11.
132. *London Gazette*, September 2, 1797.
133. Nelson to St. Vincent, 27/7/2797, ADM 1/396, National Archives.
134. Nelson and Nicolas, *Dispatches and Letters*, 2: 435.
135. Nelson and Nicolas, *Dispatches and Letters*, 2: 436.
136. Nelson and Nicolas, *Dispatches and Letters*, 2: 436.

137. Nelson and Nicolas, *Dispatches and Letters*, 2: 439.
138. White, *Nelson: The New Letters*, 190.
139. See also Orde, *Nelson's Mediterranean Command*, 94.

2. Looking Like a Hero

1. J. A. Gordon, *Letters and Records*, 78.
2. Amy Miller, *Dressed to Kill: British Naval Uniform, Masculinity and Contemporary Fashions, 1748–1857* (London: National Maritime Museum, 2007), 8.
3. Miller, *Dressed to Kill*, 7.
4. Beverly Lemire, "A Question of Trousers: Seafarers, Masculinity and Empire in the Shaping of British Male Dress, c. 1600–1800," *Cultural and Social History* 13, no. 1 (January 2, 2016): 2, https://doi.org/10.1080/14780038.2016.1133493.
5. Lemire, "Question of Trousers," 3.
6. Amy Miller, "Clothes Make the Man: Naval Uniform and Masculinity in the Early Nineteenth Century.," *Journal for Maritime Research* 17, no. 2 (November 2015): 148.
7. Miller, "Clothes Make the Man," 150.
8. Tobias Smollett, "Chapter 34," in *The Adventures of Roderick Random*, ed. James G. Basker, Nicole Seary, and Paul-Gabriel Boucé, 168–69. The Works of Tobias Smollett Series, ed. O. M. Brack Jr. and Alexander Pettit (Athens: University of Georgia Press, 2012), www.jstor.org/stable/j.ctt46nbth.45.
9. Tom Pocock, *Remember Nelson: The Life of Sir William Hoste* (n.p.: Thistle, 2013), 65.
10. Rodger, *Wooden World*, 246.
11. Douglas W. Allen, "The British Navy Rules: Monitoring and Incompatible Incentives in the Age of Fighting Sail," *Explorations in Economic History* 39, no. 2 (April 2002): 210, https://doi.org/10.1006/exeh.2002.0783.
12. Terry Coleman, *The Nelson Touch: The Life and Legend of Horatio Nelson* (Oxford: Oxford University Press, 2002), 320.
13. Rodger, *Wooden World*, 244.
14. Catriona Kennedy, *Narratives of the Revolutionary and Napoleonic Wars: Military and Civilian Experience in Britain and Ireland*, War, Culture and Society, 1750–1850 (New York: Palgrave Macmillan, 2013), 76.
15. Dickie, *Cruelty and Laughter*, 13.
16. Turner, "Disability and Crime," 48.
17. Turner, "Disability and Crime," 60.
18. Linda Colley, *Britons: Forging the Nation, 1707–1837* (New Haven, CT: Yale University Press, 2005), 177.
19. Colley, *Britons*, 177.
20. Perrett, *Real Hornblower*, chapter 11.
21. Perrett, *Real Hornblower*, 27–43.
22. Kurzman, "Performing Able-Bodiness," 170.

23. Mrs Elizabeth Wynne Fremantle and Mrs Eugenia Wynne Campbell, *The Wynne Diaries*, vol. 2 (Oxford University Press, H. Milford, 1935), 281.
24. Kurzman, "Performing Able-Bodiness," 167.
25. Rosemarie Garland-Thomson, "The Story of My Work: How I Became Disabled," *Disability Studies Quarterly* 34, no. 2 (March 18, 2014), https://doi.org/10.18061/dsq.v34i2.4254.
26. Kurzman, "Performing Able-Bodiness," 200.
27. Lennard Davis, "Dr. Johnson, Amelia, and the Discourse of Disability in the Eighteenth Century," in *"Defects": Engendering the Modern Body*, ed. Helen Deutsch and Felicity Nussbaum, 56, Corporealities: Discourses of Disability (Ann Arbor: University of Michigan Press, 2000).
28. Steven L. Kurzman, "Presence and Prosthesis: A Response to Nelson and Wright," *Cultural Anthropology* 16, no. 3 (2001): 381.
29. Coleman, *Nelson Touch*, 139.
30. R. J. B. Knight, *Pursuit of Victory*, 257.
31. White, *Nelson: The New Letters*, 67.
32. Horatio Nelson Nelson (Viscount), *The Letters of Lord Nelson to Lady Hamilton: With a Supplement of Interesting Letters*, vol. 1 (London: Macdonald and Son, 1814), 140.
33. Pocock, *Remember Nelson*, 160.
34. White, *Nelson: The New Letters*, 96.
35. White, *Nelson: The New Letters*, 96.
36. Nelson, *Letters of Lord Nelson*, 2: 47.
37. Seymour, *Memoir*, 101.
38. Seymour, *Memoir*, 100.
39. Seymour, *Memoir*, 25–26.
40. Miscellaneous Papers, PLL /88/53, NMM.
41. Charles Croslegh, *Descent and Alliances of Croslegh, or Crossle, or Crossley, of Scaitcliffe* (London: private printing, De La More press, 1904), 393, http://archive.org/details/descentandalliaoocrosgoog.
42. Croslegh, *Descent and Alliances*, 393.
43. NMM PLL /88/53 Miscellaneous Papers.
44. NMM PLL /88/53 Miscellaneous Papers.
45. Gordon et al., *Letters and Records of Gordon*, 508.
46. J. A. Gordon, *Letters and Records*, 508.
47. J. A. Gordon, *Letters and Records*, 236.
48. J. A. Gordon, *Letters and Records*, 91.
49. J. A. Gordon, *Letters and Records*, 140.
50. J. A. Gordon, *Letters and Records*, 384.
51. J. A. Gordon, *Letters and Records*, 98.
52. Coleman, *Nelson Touch*, 143.

53. Sugden, *Nelson*, 348.
54. Pocock, *Remember Nelson*, 66.
55. R. J. B. Knight, *Pursuit of Victory*, 248.
56. R. J. B. Knight, *Pursuit of Victory*, 249.
57. Seymour, *Memoir*, 100–101.
58. Seymour, *Memoir*, 105.
59. Seymour, *Memoir*, 101.
60. NMM, PLL/85.
61. NMM, PLL/85.
62. NMM, PLL/85.
63. J. A. Gordon, *Letters and Records*, 268.
64. J. A. Gordon, *Letters and Records*, 361.
65. J. A. Gordon, *Letters and Records*, 504.
66. J. A. Gordon, *Letters and Records*, 378.
67. J. A. Gordon, *Letters and Records*, 431.
68. J. A. Gordon, *Letters and Records*, 393.
69. J. A. Gordon, *Letters and Records*, 395.
70. J. A. Gordon, *Letters and Records*, 435.
71. Seymour, *Memoir*, 101.
72. Seymour, *Memoir*, 89.
73. Siebers, *Disability Theory*, 31.
74. Matthew McCormack, "Boots, Material Culture and Georgian Masculinities," *Social History* 42, no. 4 (November 2017): 461–79.
75. J. A. Gordon, *Letters and Records*, 256.
76. Carolyn Steedman, *Labours Lost: Domestic Service and the Making of Modern England* (Cambridge University Press, 2009), 28. Steedman also reveals that in the later eighteenth century, the "contemporary domestic labour force was at least 75 per cent female . . . but . . . all commentators on the service economy . . . figured the servant as a man. Contemporary debates about the deleterious effects of 'luxury,' of which keeping a liveried manservant was a prime example, made it difficult to conceptualise the much greater number of young women labouring in the back kitchens of modest households as 'servants', even if there was not the conventions of a gendered language to make imagined men in powdered wigs stand in for them. The servant taxes, inaugurated in 1777 to extract a payment from employers who displayed their opulence by means of a liveried man-servant, reinforced this gendered linguistic usage" (13).
77. Seymour, *Memoir*, 80.
78. Seymour, *Memoir*, 128.
79. Seymour, *Memoir*, 79.
80. Jean-Jacques Rousseau, *Emile; or, On Education* (1762; repr., New York: Basic Books, 1979), 236.

81. Rousseau, *Emile*, 268.
82. Carolyn Steedman, "Servants and Their Relationship to the Unconscious," *Journal of British Studies* 42, no. 3 (July 2003): 326.
83. Steedman, *Labours Lost*, 18.
84. Maria and R. L. Edgeworth, *Practical Education*, 2nd ed., vol. 1 (1798; repr., London: J. Crowder, Warwick Square, for J. Johnson, St. Paul's Church-yard, 1801), 195, https://books.google.com/books?id=OrUVyWAyMCYC&printsec=frontcover&source=gbs_ge_summary_r&cad=0#v=onepage&q&f=false.
85. Mary Wollstonecraft, *Original Stories from Real Life; with Conversations, Calculated to Regulate the Affections, and Form the Mind to Truth and Goodness* (1787; repr., London: Henry Crowder, 1906; Project Gutenberg, 2011), 52, https://www.gutenberg.org/files/36507/36507-h/36507-h.htm.
86. Leonore Davidoff and Catherine Hall, introduction to *Family Fortunes: Men and Women of the English Middle Class 1780–1850*, 3rd ed. (London: Routledge, 2018).
87. Sugden, *Nelson*, 352.
88. Sugden, *Nelson*, 26.
89. Sugden, *Nelson*, 23.
90. Sugden, *Nelson*, 26.
91. Nelson, *Dispatches and Letters*, 4: 457.
92. Sugden, *Nelson*, 487.
93. R. J. B. Knight, *Pursuit of Victory*, 370.
94. Sugden, *Nelson*, 468.
95. R. J. B. Knight, *Pursuit of Victory*, 620.
96. "Nelson, His Valet, and His Native Coast," *The United Service Magazine: With Which Are Incorporated the Army and Navy Magazine and Naval and Military Journal* 20 (February 1836) (London: H. Colburn, February 1836), 202, https://hdl.handle.net/2027/nyp.33433081656971?urlappend=%3Bseq=212.
97. George Samuel Parsons, *Nelsonian Reminiscences; or Leaves from Memory's Log* (Boston: Little, Brown, 1843), 250.
98. R. J. B. Knight, *Pursuit of Victory*, 357.
99. White, *Nelson: The New Letters*, 44–45.
100. R. J. B. Knight, *Pursuit of Victory*, 358.
101. Sugden, *Nelson*, 344.
102. Sugden, *Nelson*, 375.
103. Colin White, *Nelson: The Admiral* (Thrupp, Stroud, Gloucestershire: Sutton, in association with the Royal Navy and the Royal Naval Museum, 2005), 87.
104. R. J. B. Knight, *Pursuit of Victory*, 662.
105. White, *Nelson: The Admiral*, 95.
106. R. J. B. Knight, *Pursuit of Victory*, 662.
107. White, *Nelson: The Admiral*, 96.

108. "Threatened Invasion," *Naval Chronicle* 6 (July–December 1801): 73–74, https://hdl.handle.net/2027/uc1.b2990327?urlappend=%3Bseq=95.
109. Ott, "Sum of Its Parts," *Artificial Parts*, 25.
110. Mary Louisa Boyle, *Mary Boyle: Her Book* (J. Murray, 1902), 24.
111. Boyle, *Her Book*, 24.
112. NMM, PLL/85.
113. NMM, PLL/85.
114. NMM, PLL/85.
115. J. A. Gordon, *Letters and Records*, 93.
116. J. A. Gordon, *Letters and Records*, 134.
117. J. A. Gordon, *Letters and Records*, 268.
118. J. A. Gordon, *Letters and Records*, 508.
119. J. A. Gordon, *Letters and Records*, 495.
120. "Powerful Incentives to Victory," *The Naval Chronicle* 15 (January–July 1806): 400, https://hdl.handle.net/2027/uc2.ark:/13960/t16m34z4d?urlappend=%3Bseq=426. See also *Annual Biography and Obituary*, vol. 1949.
121. London Gazette, "Page 371 | Issue 15902, 24 March 1806 | London Gazette | The Gazette," https://www.thegazette.co.uk/London/issue/15902/page/371.
122. Lemire, "Question of Trousers," 3.
123. Marcia R. Pointon, *Hanging the Head: Portraiture and Social Formation in Eighteenth-Century England* (New Haven, CT: Yale University Press, 1993), 1.
124. Kurzman, "Performing Able-Bodiness," 75.
125. Jonathan Richardson, *An Essay on the Theory of Painting*, 2nd ed. (London: Printed for A. C. and sold by A. Bettesworth in Pater-noster Row, 1725), 21, Google Books, https://play.google.com/books/reader?id=e9NPAQAAIAAJ&printsec=frontcover&pg=GBS.PA21.
126. On the idea of "defect," see Deutsch and Nussbaum, *"Defects."*
127. Lemire, "Question of Trousers," 3.
128. Richard Brilliant, *Portraiture* (Cambridge, MA: Harvard University Press, 1991), 25.
129. Sir Joshua Reynolds, "A Discourse Delivered to the Students of the Royal Academy on the Distribution of the Prizes, December 10, 1771, by the President.," in *Seven Discourses on Art* (London: Cassell, 1901); Project Gutenberg, http://www.gutenberg.org/files/2176/2176-h/2176-h.htm.
130. Lincoln, *Representing the Royal Navy*, 23.
131. Favret, *War at a Distance*.
132. Jenks, *Naval Engagements*, 28.
133. Wilcox, "'Poor Decayed Seamen,'" 66.
134. Lincoln, *Representing the Royal Navy*, 197.
135. Adam Smith, *The Theory of Moral Sentiments*, ed. Dugald Stewart (Edinburgh: A. Miller, A. Kincaid, and J. Bell, 1769), 42.

136. Barker, *Greenwich Hospital*, 87.
137. Barker, *Greenwich Hospital*, 93.
138. Barker, *Greenwich Hospital*, 88.
139. Barker, *Greenwich Hospital*, 90.
140. Barker, *Greenwich Hospital*, 88.
141. Barker, *Greenwich Hospital*, 89.
142. Barker, *Greenwich Hospital*, 93.
143. Barker, *Greenwich Hospital*, 93.
144. Barker, *Greenwich Hospital*, 93.
145. Barker, *Greenwich Hospital*, 80.
146. Perrett, *Real Hornblower*, chapter 2.
147. Arline Meyer. "Re-Dressing Classical Statuary: The Eighteenth-Century 'Hand-in-Waistcoat' Portrait." *Art Bulletin* 77, no. 1 (March 1995): 27.
148. Czisnik, *Horatio Nelson*, 3.
149. "The Naval Gallery, or Painted Hall, in Greenwich Hospital," *Penny Magazine of the Society for the Diffusion of Useful Knowledge* 7 (January 6, 1838): 2.
150. McGrath and Barton suggest that Nelson acquired a sword with a blade shortened to facilitate drawing it from the scabbard with the left hand, as he continued to wear it on the left, as does a right-handed swordsman. See Hoppner's full-length portrait of Nelson. Mark Barton and John McGrath, *British Naval Swords and Swordsmanship* (Havertown, PA: Seaforth, 2013).
151. Meyer, "Re-Dressing Classical Statuary," 40.
152. See R. J. B. Walker, *The Nelson Portraits: An Iconography of Horatio, Viscount Nelson, Vice Admiral of the White* (London: Royal Naval Museum, 1998).
153. Peter Harrington, *British Artists and War: The Face of Battle in Paintings and Prints, 1700–1914* (London: Greenhill Books; Mechanicsburg, PA: Stackpole Books in association with Brown University Library, Rhode Island, 1993), 29.
154. Harrington, *British Artists and War*, 30.
155. Czisnik, *Horatio Nelson*, 39.
156. Czisnik, *Horatio Nelson*, 3.
157. J. A. Gordon, *Letters and Records*, 78.
158. J. A. Gordon, *Letters and Records*, 78.
159. J. A. Gordon., *Letters and Records*, 155.
160. J. A. Gordon, *Letters and Records*, 93.

3. Love and Friendship

1. Thomas Dixon, *Weeping Britannia: Portrait of a Nation in Tears* (Oxford: Oxford University Press, 2015), 215.
2. Mark S. Micale, "Hysterick Women and Hypochondriac Men," in *Hysterical Men: The*

Hidden History of Male Nervous Illness (Cambridge, MA: Harvard University Press, 2008), 25.
3. J. A. Gordon, *Letters and Records*, 456.
4. Siebers, *Disability Theory*, 10.
5. J. A. Gordon, *Letters and Records*, 50.
6. Gordon, *Letters and Records*, 427.
7. Nelson, *Dispatches and Letters*, 1:15.
8. Coleman, *Nelson Touch*, 6.
9. R. J. B. Knight, *Pursuit of Victory*, 557.
10. Southey, *Life of Nelson*, 2: 206.
11. R. J. B. Knight, *Pursuit of Victory*, 506.
12. White, *Nelson: The New Letters*.
13. R. J. B. Knight, *Pursuit of Victory*, 368.
14. Czisnik, "Nelson's Circles: Networking in the Navy during the French Wars," in *Liberty, Property and Popular Politics: England and Scotland, 1688–1815; Essays in Honour of H. T. Dickinson*, ed. Gordon Pentland and Michael T. Davis (Edinburgh: Edinburgh University Press, 2016), 196, http://www.jstor.org/stable/10.3366/j.ctt1bgzd27.19.
15. Marshall, "Mends, Robert," in *Royal Naval Biography*, 2: 270.
16. J. A. Gordon, *Letters and Records*, 62.
17. Seymour, *Memoir*, 26.
18. Seymour, *Memoir*, 127.
19. Seymour, *Memoir*, 127.
20. J. A. Gordon, *Letters and Records*, 130.
21. J.A. Gordon, *Letters and Records*, 375.
22. J. A. Gordon, *Letters and Records*, 434.
23. Seymour, *Memoir*, 101.
24. J. A. Gordon, *Letters and Records*, 135.
25. London Gazette, "Page 1790 | Issue 17173, 15 September 1816 | London Gazette | The Gazette," https://www.thegazette.co.uk/London/issue/17173/page/1790.
26. J. A. Gordon, *Letters and Records*, 494.
27. PLL/86, NMM.
28. PLL/86, NMM.
29. Frances Burney, *Evelina, or, A Young Lady's Entrance Into the World In a Series of Letters*, 4th ed., vol. 3 (London: T. Lowndes, 1779), 78.
30. Boyle, *Mary Boyle*, 24.
31. Gill, *Naval Families, War and Duty*, 5.
32. Wilson, *Social History*, 2.
33. White, *Nelson: The New Letters*.
34. PLL/84, NMM.
35. PLL/85, NMM.

36. PLL/36, NMM.
37. PLL/36, NMM.
38. PLL/36, NMM.
39. c. 1869, PLL/44, NMM.
40. PLL/5.
41. PLL/86/NMM.
42. PLL/84, NMM.
43. PLL/85, NMM.
44. PLL/36, NMM.
45. PLL/84, NMM.
46. Davidoff and Hall, introduction to *Family Fortunes*.
47. Davidoff and Hall, introduction to *Family Fortunes*.
48. Seymour, *Memoir*, 89.
49. Seymour, *Memoir*, 80.
50. Seymour, preface to *Memoir*, 1.
51. Laughton and Lambert. "Seymour, Sir Michael."
52. *Annual Biography and Obituary*, 19: 200.
53. *Annual Biography and Obituary*, 19: 195.
54. J. A. Gordon, *Letters and Records*, 93.
55. J. A. Gordon, *Letters and Records*, 412.
56. J. A. Gordon, *Letters and Records*, 434.
57. Fremantle and Campbell, *Wynne Diaries*, 310.
58. Pryse Lockhart Gordon, *Personal Memoirs; or, Reminiscences of Men and Manners*, vol. 2 (London: H. Colburn and Richard Bentley, 1830), 386.
59. Czisnik, *Horatio Nelson*, 141.
60. Parsons, *Nelsonian Reminiscences*, 7.
61. P. L. Gordon, *Personal Memoirs*, 2: 217–23.
62. Czisnik, *Horatio Nelson*, 134.
63. James, *Naval History of Great Britain*, 2: 54.
64. Thomas Joseph Pettigrew, *Memoirs of the Life of Vice-Admiral, Lord Viscount Nelson, K. B., Duke of Bronté, Etc., Etc., Etc*, 2 vols. (London: T. & W. Boone, 1849), 1:140.
65. Czisnik, *Horatio Nelson*, 490.
66. Alfred Morrison, *The Collection of Autograph Letters and Historical Documents Formed by Alfred Morrison (Second Series, 1882–1893); The Hamilton & Nelson Papers*, 2 vols. (printed for private circulation, 1893), 2:123.
67. White, *Nelson: The New Letters*, "Family," 4.
68. Nelson, *Dispatches and Letters*, 5: 198.
69. Laurence Brockliss, John Cardwell, and Michael Moss, *Nelson's Surgeon: William Beatty, Naval Medicine, and the Battle of Trafalgar* (Oxford: Oxford University Press, 2008).
70. J. A. Gordon, *Letters and Records*, 443.
71. J. A. Gordon, *Letters and Records*, 62.

72. J. A. Gordon, *Letters and Records*, 508.
73. Perrett, *Real Hornblower*, 57.
74. J. A. Gordon, *Letters and Records*, 395.
75. J. A. Gordon, *Letters and Records*, 63.
76. J. A. Gordon, *Letters and Records* 71–72.
77. J. A. Gordon, *Letters and Records*, 71.
78. J. A. Gordon, *Letters and Records*, 73.
79. J. A. Gordon, *Letters and Records*, 68–69.
80. J. A. Gordon, *Letters and Records*, 79.
81. J. A. Gordon, *Letters and Records*, 75–76.
82. J. A. Gordon, *Letters and Records*, 76.
83. J. A. Gordon, *Letters and Records*, 141.
84. J. A. Gordon, *Letters and Records*, 126.
85. J. A. Gordon, *Letters and Records*, 228.
86. Gill, *Naval Families, War and Duty*, 15.
87. Perrett, *Real Hornblower*.
88. J. A. Gordon, *Letters and Records*, 189.
89. J. A. Gordon, *Letters and Records*, 365.
90. J. A. Gordon, *Letters and Records*, 77.
91. J. A. Gordon, *Letters and Records*, 100.
92. J. A. Gordon, *Letters and Records*, 100.
93. J. A. Gordon, *Letters and Records*, 271.
94. J. A. Gordon, *Letters and Records*, 326.
95. J. A. Gordon, *Letters and Records*, 105.
96. J. A. Gordon, *Letters and Records*, 132.
97. J. A. Gordon, *Letters and Records*, 131.
98. J. A. Gordon, *Letters and Records*, 107.
99. J. A. Gordon, *Letters and Records*, 155.
100. J. A. Gordon, *Letters and Records*, 127.
101. J. A. Gordon, *Letters and Records*, 235.
102. J. A. Gordon, *Letters and Records*, 398.
103. J. A. Gordon, *Letters and Records*, 399.
104. J. A. Gordon, *Letters and Records*, 315.
105. J. A. Gordon, *Letters and Records*, 94.
106. J. A. Gordon, *Letters and Records*, 416.
107. J. A. Gordon, *Letters and Records*, 101.
108. J. A. Gordon, *Letters and Records*, 130.
109. "Wonderful Preservation of the Meander," *Naval Chronicle* 37 (January–June 1817): 25, HathiTrust Digital Librar, https://hdl.handle.net/2027/uc1.b2990359?urlappend=%3Bseq=37.
110. J. A. Gordon, *Letters and Records*, 247.

111. J. A. Gordon, *Letters and Records*, 100.
112. J. A. Gordon, *Letters and Records*, 101.
113. J. A. Gordon, *Letters and Records*, 102.
114. J. A. Gordon, *Letters and Records*, 107.
115. J. A. Gordon, *Letters and Records*, 107.
116. J. A. Gordon, *Letters and Records*, 107.
117. J. A. Gordon, *Letters and Records*, 110.
118. J. A. Gordon, *Letters and Records*, 112.
119. J. A. Gordon, *Letters and Records*, 111.
120. J. A. Gordon, *Letters and Records*, 115.
121. J. A. Gordon, *Letters and Records*, 117.
122. J. A. Gordon, *Letters and Records*, 118.
123. J. A. Gordon, *Letters and Records*, 118.
124. J. A. Gordon, *Letters and Records*, 50.
125. Geoffrey Chamberlain, "British Maternal Mortality in the 19th and Early 20th Centuries," *Journal of the Royal Society of Medicine* 99, no. 11 (November 2006): 562, https://doi.org/10.1177/014107680609901113.
126. Chamberlain, "British Maternal Mortality," 559.
127. Chamberlain, "British Maternal Mortality," 559.
128. J. A. Gordon, *Letters and Records*, 443.
129. J. A. Gordon, *Letters and Records*, 50.
130. J. A. Gordon, *Letters and Records*, 50.
131. J. A. Gordon, *Letters and Records*, 68.
132. J. A. Gordon, *Letters and Records*, 93.
133. J. A. Gordon, *Letters and Records*, 195.
134. J. A. Gordon, *Letters and Records*, 83.
135. J. A. Gordon, *Letters and Records*, 140.
136. J. A. Gordon, *Letters and Records*, 88.
137. J. A. Gordon, *Letters and Records*, 95.
138. J. A. Gordon, *Letters and Records*, 143.
139. J. A. Gordon, *Letters and Records*, 147.
140. J. A. Gordon, *Letters and Records*, 134.
141. J. A. Gordon, *Letters and Records*, 140.
142. J. A. Gordon, *Letters and Records*, 91.
143. J. A. Gordon, *Letters and Records*, 384.
144. J. A. Gordon, *Letters and Records*, 86.
145. J. A. Gordon, *Letters and Records*, 98.
146. J. A. Gordon, *Letters and Records*, 182.
147. J. A. Gordon, *Letters and Records*, 206.
148. J. A. Gordon, *Letters and Records*, 22.

149. J. A. Gordon, *Letters and Records*, 150.
150. Siebers, *Disability Theory*, 5.
151. J. A. Gordon, *Letters and Records*, 84.
152. J. A. Gordon, *Letters and Records*, 389.

4. Becoming Victorian

1. Seymour, *Memoir*, 105.
2. Lord Byron, *Don Juan: In Sixteen Cantos, with Notes*, (Halifax, NS: Milner and Sowberry, 1837; Project Gutenberg, 2007), canto 1, st. 4, https://www.gutenberg.org/files/21700/21700-h/21700-h.htm.
3. Andrew Scull, Charlotte MacKenzie, and Nicholas Hervey, "Degeneration and Despair: Henry Maudsley (1835–1918)," in *Masters of Bedlam: The Transformation of the Mad-Doctoring Trade*, Princeton Legacy Library (Princeton, NJ: Princeton University Press, 1996), 254, https://doi.org/10.2307/j.ctt7zvbsw.12.
4. PLL/9, NMM.
5. PLL/84, NMM.
6. William Lovett and the Working Men's Association, *The People's Charter: With the Address to the Radical Reformers of Great Britain and Ireland, and a Brief Sketch of Its Origin* (London: C. H. Helt and Charles Fox, 1848), 11, Google Books, https://books.google.com/books?id=kvlZuAEACAAJ&printsec=frontcover#v=onepage&q&f=false.
7. PLL/84, NMM.
8. Marshall, preface to *Royal Naval Biography*, 1: vii–viii.
9. Walter E. Houghton, *The Victorian Frame of Mind, 1830–1870* (New Haven, CT: Yale University Press, 1957).
10. John Tosh, *A Man's Place: Masculinity and the Middle-Class Home in Victorian England* (New Haven, CT: Yale University Press, 2007), 66.
11. Charles Dickens, *Gone Astray and Other Papers from Household Words, 1851–59*, The Dent Uniform Edition of Dickens' Journalism, vol. 3, ed. Michael Slater (Columbus: Ohio State University Press, 1999), 123.
12. Cornelia D. J. Pearsall, "Burying the Duke: Victorian Mourning and the Funeral of the Duke of Wellington," *Victorian Literature and Culture* 27, no. 2 (1999): 365.
13. Laurence Brockliss, John Cardwell, and Michael Moss, "Nelson's Grand National Obsequies," *English Historical Review* 121, no. 490 (2006): 180.
14. Brockliss, Cardwell, and Moss, "Nelson's Grand National Obsequies," 180.
15. Brockliss, Cardwell, and Moss, "Nelson's Grand National Obsequies," 180.
16. Quoted in Czisnik, *Horatio Nelson*, 113.
17. Quoted in Czisnik, *Horatio Nelson*, 116.
18. Erin O'Connor, *Raw Material: Producing Pathology in Victorian Culture*, Body, Commodity, Text (Durham, NC: Duke University Press, 2000), 104.

19. Henry Maudsley, *The Physiology and Pathology of the Mind* (New York: Appleton, 1867; Internet Archive, 2009), 300–301, http://archive.org/details/physiologyandpa03maudgoog.
20. Czisnik, *Horatio Nelson*, 116.
21. PLL/88, NMM.
22. "The Royal Hospital for Seamen, Greenwich: 'A Refuge for All,'" Port Cities London, http://www.portcities.org.uk/london/server/show/ConNarrative.148/chapterId/3048/The-Royal-Hospital-for-Seamen-Greenwich-A-Refuge-for-All.html.
23. PLL/88, NMM.
24. PLL/88, NMM.
25. Letter from Lieut. E. Bold, RN, to Sir W. O. Pell, May 14, 1844, PLL/9, NMM.
26. See "feature, n.", OED Online (Oxford University Press: 2020).
27. J. A. Gordon, *Letters and Records*, 462.
28. PLL 88, NMM.
29. PLL/88, NMM.
30. PLL/88, NMM.
31. PLL/88, NMM.
32. Bernard D. Rostker, "Chapter Three: Evolution of the European System of Providing for Casualties in the Age of Enlightenment: France and Britain as the Antecedents of the American System of Care," in *Providing for the Casualties of War: The American Experience through World War II* (Santa Monica: RAND Corporation, 2013), 95.
33. J. A. Gordon, *Letters and Records*, 485.
34. Great Britain Parliament, House of Commons, "Minutes of Evidence Taken before the Commissioners for Inquiring into Naval and Military Promotion and Retirement," in *Parliamentary Papers: 1780–1849*, vol. 22 (London: H. M. Stationery Office, 1818–19), 148, Google Books, https://books.google.com/books?id=nVoSAAAAYAAJ&pg=PA148&lpg=PA148&dq#v=onepage&q&f=false.
35. Great Britain Parliament, Commons, "Minutes of Evidence," 22: 148.
36. J. E. Cookson, "Alexander Tulloch and the Chelsea Out-Pensioners, 1838–43: Centralisation in the Early Victorian State," *English Historical Review* 125, no. 512 (2010): 79.
37. Henson Moore and Jeffrey O'Connell, "Foreclosing Medical Malpractice Claims by Prompt Tender of Economic Loss," *Louisiana Law Review* 44, no. 5 (1984): 1271–72, https://digitalcommons.law.lsu.edu/cgi/viewcontent.cgi?article=4833&context=lalrev.
38. Johnny Parker, "The Made Whole Doctrine: Unraveling the Enigma Wrapped in the Mystery of Insurance Subrogation," *Missouri Law Review* 70, no. 3 (June 1, 2005), https://scholarship.law.missouri.edu/mlr/vol70/iss3/3.
39. PLL/88, NMM.
40. James Richard Thursfield, *Nelson and Other Naval Studies* (London: J. Murray, 1920; Internet Archive, 2008), 125, http://archive.org/details/nelsonothernavaloothur.

41. Henry Maudsley, "Delusions," *Journal of Mental Science* 9, no. 45 (April 1863), 11, https://archive.org/details/britishjournalof09roya/page/10/mode/2up?view=theater.
42. Maudsley, *Physiology and Pathology*, 28.
43. Tosh, *Man's Place*, 62.
44. Max Adams, *Trafalgar's Lost Hero: Admiral Lord Collingwood and the Defeat of Napoleon* (Hoboken, NJ: John Wiley & Sons, 2005), 23.
45. Samuel Taylor Coleridge, "Essay VI," in *The Collected Works of Samuel Taylor Coleridge*, vol. 4 (pt. 1): *The Friend*, ed. Barbara E. Rooke, 574–75, Princeton Legacy Library (Princeton, NJ: Princeton University Press, 1969), https://www.jstor.org/stable/j.ctt1b3h9k5.73.
46. Micale, "Hysterick Women and Hypochondriac Men," 22.
47. Mark S. Micale, "The Great Victorian Eclipse," in Micale, *Hysterical Men*, 49.
48. David Kuchta, *The Three-Piece Suit and Modern Masculinity: England, 1550–1850* (Berkeley: University of California Press, 2002), 164.
49. Kuchta, *Three-Piece Suit*, 168.
50. Miller, *Dressed to Kill*, 9.
51. Lemire, "Question of Trousers," 14.
52. Miller, "Clothes Make the Man," 148–49.
53. Henry Maudsley, "The Correlation of Mental and Physical Force: or Man, a Part of Nature," *Journal of Mental Sciences* 6, no. 31 (1859): 60, doi:10.1192/bjp.6.31.50.
54. Maudsley, *Physiology and Pathology of Mind*, 303–4.
55. John Eric Erichsen, *The Science of Art and Surgery, Being a Treatise on Surgical Injuries, Disease, and Operations*, ed. John H. Brinton (Philadelphia: Blanchard and Lea, 1854), 87, https://www.google.com/books/edition/The_Science_and_Art_of_Surgery/fgFuMsrstToC?hl=en&gbpv=1.
56. O'Connor, *Raw Material*, 104.
57. Jenny Bourne Taylor, "Psychology at the Fin de Siècle," in *The Cambridge Companion to the Fin de Siècle*, ed. Gail Marshall (Cambridge: Cambridge University Press, 2007), 13.
58. Scull, Mackenzie, and Harvey, "Degeneration and Despair," 254.
59. Tosh, *Man's Place*, 62.
60. Thomas Hughes, "The Last of Nelson's Captains," *Macmillan's Magazine* 19, no. 112 (February 1869): 354.
61. J. A. Gordon, *Letters and Records*, 502.
62. J. A. Gordon, *Letters and Records*, 502.
63. J. A. Gordon, *Letters and Records*, 404.
64. *Oxford Dictionary of National Biography*.
65. Laughton and Morriss, "Gordon," in *Oxford Dictionary of National Biography*, .
66. "Royal Naval College," *The Times* (London, England), Wednesday, August 28, 1867, 10, https://www.thetimes.co.uk/archive/article/1867-08-28/10/4.html.

67. O'Connor, *Raw Material*, 105.
68. Kate Hay, "Mosaic Marble Tables by J. Darmanin & Sons of Malta," *Furniture History* 46 (2010): 184.
69. PLL/88, NMM.
70. PLL/88, NMM.
71. PLL/88, NMM.
72. PLL/88, NMM.
73. PLL/88, NMM.
74. PLL/88, NMM.
75. J. A. Gordon, *Letters and Records*, 383.
76. PLL/88, NMM.
77. PLL/88, NMM.
78. PLL/88, NMM.
79. PLL/88, NMM.
80. PLL/88, NMM.
81. PLL/88, NMM.
82. PLL/88, NMM.
83. Taylor, "Psychology at Fin de Siècle."
84. PLL/88, NMM.
85. Roy Porter, *Bodies Politic: Disease, Death and Doctors in Britain, 1650–1900* (London: Reaktion Books, 2001), 273.
86. Holly Furneaux, "'Our Poor Colonel Loved Him as if He Had Been His Own Son': Family Feeling in the Crimea," in *Military Men of Feeling: Emotion, Touch, and Masculinity in the Crimean War* (Oxford: Oxford University Press, 2016), Oxford Scholarship Online, doi: 10.1093/acprof:oso/9780198737834.003.0005.
87. J. A. Gordon, *Letters and Records*, 488.
88. J. A. Gordon, *Letters and Records*, 456.
89. Gerber, "Disabled Veterans, the State,"; David A. Gerber, "Creating Group Identity: Disabled Veterans and American Government," *OAH Magazine of History* 23, no. 3 (July 2009).
90. David Gerber, preface to *Disabled Veterans in History,* enlarged and revised ed. (Ann Arbor: University of Michigan Press: 2012).
91. Daniel J. Stinner, Travis C. Burns, Kevin L. Kirk, and James R. Ficke. "Return to Duty Rate of Amputee Soldiers in the Current Conflicts in Afghanistan and Iraq." *Journal of Trauma and Acute Care Surgery* 68, no. 6 (June 2010):1476–79. doi:10.1097/TA.0b013e3181bb9a6c.
92. Stinner et al., "Return to Duty Rate."
93. Stinner et al., "Return to Duty Rate."

Appendix

1. Marshall, "Barclay, Robert Heriot." in *Royal Naval Biography*, 3: 191.
2. James, *Naval History of Great Britain*, 5: 136.
3. Edward Cave [Sylvanus Urban, pseud.], "Obituary, with Anecdotes, of Remarkable Persons.," *The Gentleman's Magazine, and Historical Chronicle, for the Year 1809* 79, pt. 2 (July–December 1809): 1236, HathiTrust Digital Library, https://hdl.handle.net/2027/njp.32101077261921?urlappend=%3Bseq=682.
4. *London Gazette*, "Page 1790 | Issue 17173, 15 September 1816 | London Gazette | The Gazette," https://www.thegazette.co.uk/London/issue/17173/page/1790.
5. Hepper, *British Warship Losses*.,
6. Marshall, "Gordon, Sir Alexander James," in *Royal Naval Biography*, 2: 938.
7. O'Byrne, "Gill," in *Naval Biographical Dictionary*, 397.
8. Rif Winfield, *British Warships in the Age of Sail, 1714–1792: Design, Construction, Careers and Fate* (Barnsley, South Yorkshire, UK: Seaforth, 2007).
9. Marshall, "Joshua Kneeshaw, Esq.," in *Royal Naval Biography*, 4:149.
10. Croslegh, *Descent and Alliances*, 393.
11. Croslegh, *Descent and Alliances*, 400.
12. Adkins, *Jack Tar*, 303–4.

BIBLIOGRAPHY

Adams, Max. *Trafalgar's Lost Hero: Admiral Lord Collingwood and the Defeat of Napoleon.* Hoboken, NJ: John Wiley & Sons, 2005.

Adkins, Roy, and Lesley Adkins. *Jack Tar: Life in Nelson's Navy.* Digital original ed. London: Abacus, 2009.

Allen, Douglas W. "The British Navy Rules: Monitoring and Incompatible Incentives in the Age of Fighting Sail." *Explorations in Economic History* 39, no. 2 (April 2002): 204–31. https://doi.org/10.1006/exeh.2002.0783.

Allen, Leigh, and Ceri Boston, eds. *"Safe Moor'd in Greenwich Tier": A Study of the Skeletons of Royal Navy Sailors and Marines Excavated at the Royal Hospital Greenwich.* Oxford: Oxford Archaeology, 2008.

Annual Biography and Obituary, 1835, The. Vol. 19. London: Longman, Hurst, Rees, Orme, and Brown, 1835.

Bacon, Francis. "42. Of Deformity." In *The Essays Or Counsels Civil and Moral, of Francis Lord Verulam, Viscount St. Alban.* London: John Hanland for Hanna Barret and Richard Whitaker, 1625.

Barker, Mathew Henry. *Greenwich Hospital: A Series of Naval Sketches, Descriptive of the Life of a Man-of-War's Man, By an Old Sailor.* London: J. Robins and Company, 1826.

Barton, Mark, and John McGrath. *British Naval Swords and Swordsmanship.* Havertown, PA: Seaforth, 2013.

Baynton, Douglas C. "Disability and the Justification of Inequality in American History." In *The New Disability History: American Perspectives,* edited by Paul K. Longmore and Lauri Umansky, 33–57. History of Disability Series. New York: New York University Press, 2001.

Berkeley, George Cranfield. *Biographical Memoir of the Hon. George Cranfield Berkeley, Rear Admiral of the Red Squadron. [Extracted from "The Naval Chronicle." With a Portrait.]* London: J. Gold, 1805. Google Books. https://play.google.com/books/reader?id=LUJiAAAAcAAJ&hl=en&pg=GBS.PA88.

Blane, Gilbert. "Statements of the Comparative Health of the British Navy, from the Year

1779 to the Year 1814, with Proposals for Its Farther Improvement." *Medico-Chirurgical Transactions* 6 (1815): 490–573.

Boyle, Mary Louisa. *Mary Boyle: Her Book*. London: J. Murray, 1902.

Brenton, Edward Pelham. *Life and Correspondence of John, Earl of St. Vincent, etc. [With a portrait]*. Vol. 2. London: H. Colbourn, 1838.

Brilliant, Richard. *Portraiture*. Cambridge, MA: Harvard University Press, 1991.

Brockliss, Laurence, John Cardwell, and Michael Moss. "Nelson's Grand National Obsequies." *English Historical Review* 121, no. 490 (2006): 162–82.

———. *Nelson's Surgeon: William Beatty, Naval Medicine, and the Battle of Trafalgar*. Oxford: Oxford University Press, 2008.

Bullen, A. H., and Rebecca Mills. "Barker, Matthew Henry [pseud. the Old Sailor] (1790–1846), Sailor and Writer." In *Oxford Dictionary of National Biography*. Oxford University Press, 2004–. https://doi.org/10.1093/ref:odnb/1408.

Burney, Frances. *Evelina, or, A Young Lady's Entrance Into the World In a Series of Letters*. 4th ed., vol. 3. London: T. Lowndes, 1779.

Byron, Lord. *Don Juan: In Sixteen Cantos, with Notes*. Halifax: Milner and Sowberry, 1837; Project Gutenberg, 2007. https://www.gutenberg.org/files/21700/21700-h/21700-h.htm.

Carradine, David, ed. *Admiral Lord Nelson: Context and Legacy*. Houndsmill, Bassingstoke, Hampshire, UK; New York: Palgrave Macmillan, 2005.

Cave, Edward [Sylvanus Urban, pseud.]. "Obituary, with Anecdotes, of Remarkable Persons." *The Gentleman's Magazine, and Historical Chronicle, for the Year 1809* 79, pt. 2 (July–December 1809): 1236. HathiTrust Digital Library. https://hdl.handle.net/2027/njp.32101077261921?urlappend=%3Bseq=682.

Cavell, S. A. *Midshipmen and Quarterdeck Boys in the Royal Navy, 1771–1831*. London: Boydell Press, 2012.

Chamberlain, Geoffrey. "British Maternal Mortality in the 19th and Early 20th Centuries." *Journal of the Royal Society of Medicine* 99, no. 11 (November 2006): 559–63. https://doi.org/10.1177/014107680609901113.

Coleman, Terry. *The Nelson Touch: The Life and Legend of Horatio Nelson*. Oxford: Oxford University Press, 2002.

Coleridge, Samuel Taylor. *The Collected Works of Samuel Taylor Coleridge*. Vol. 4, pt. I, *The Friend*. Princeton, NJ: Princeton University Press, 2016.

Colley, Linda. *Britons: Forging the Nation, 1707–1837*. New Haven, CT: Yale University Press, 2005.

Consolvo, Charles. "The Prospects and Promotion of British Naval Officers, 1793–1815." *Mariner's Mirror* 91, no. 2 (January 1, 2005): 137–59. https://doi.org/10.1080/00253359.2005.10656942.

Cookson, J. E. "Alexander Tulloch and the Chelsea Out-Pensioners, 1838–43: Centralisation in the Early Victorian State." *English Historical Review* 125, no. 512 (2010): 60–82.

Croslegh, Charles. *Descent and Alliances of Croslegh, or Crossle, or Crossley, of Scaitcliffe*. London: private printing, De La More Press, 1904; Internet Archive, 2009. http://archive.org/details/descentandallia00crosgoog.

Czisnik, Marianne. *Horatio Nelson: A Controversial Hero*. London: Hodder Arnold, 2005.

———. "Nelson's Circles: Networking in the Navy during the French Wars." In *Liberty, Property and Popular Politics: England and Scotland, 1688–1815; Essays in Honor of H. T. Dickinson,* edited by Gordon Pentland and Michael T. Davis, 194–206. Edinburgh: Edinburgh University Press, 2016. http://www.jstor.org/stable/10.3366/j.ctt1bgzd27.19.

Davidoff, Leonore, and Catherine Hall. *Family Fortunes: Men and Women of the English Middle Class, 1780–1850*. 3rd ed. London: Routledge, 2018.

Davis, Lennard J. *The Disability Studies Reader*. 5th ed. New York: Routledge, 2016. https://doi.org/10.4324/9781315680668.

———. "Dr. Johnson, Amelia, and the Discourse of Disability in the Eighteenth Century." In *"Defects": Engendering the Modern Body,* edited by Helen Deutsch and Felicity Nussbaum, 54–74. Corporealities: Discourses of Disability. Ann Arbor: University of Michigan Press, 2000.

Deutsch, Helen, and Felicity Nussbaum, eds. *"Defects": Engendering the Modern Body*. Corporealities: Discourses of Disability. Ann Arbor: University of Michigan Press, 2000.

Dickens, Charles. *Gone Astray and Other Papers from Household Words, 1851–59*. The Dent Uniform Edition of Dickens' Journalism, vol. 3. Columbus: Ohio State University Press, 1999.

Dickie, Simon. *Cruelty and Laughter: Forgotten Comic Literature and the Unsentimental Eighteenth Century*. Chicago: University of Chicago Press, 2011.

DiNardo, R. L., and David Syrett, eds. *The Commissioned Sea Officers of the Royal Navy, 1660–1815*. 2nd ed. Edited by Michael Slater. Occasional Publications of the Navy Records Society. Aldershot, Hants, UK: Scolar Press for the Navy Records Society, 1994; Brookfield, VT: Ashgate, 1994.

Dixon, Thomas. *Weeping Britannia: Portrait of a Nation in Tears*. Oxford: Oxford University Press, 2015.

Draper, Nick. "'Possessing Slaves': Ownership, Compensation and Metropolitan Society in Britain at the Time of Emancipation, 1834–40." *History Workshop Journal*, no. 64 (Autumn 2007): 74–102. www.jstor.org/stable/25472936.

Edgeworth, Maria, and R. L. Edgeworth. *Practical Education*. 2nd ed. Vol. 1. 1798; repr., London: J. Crowder, Warwick Square, for J. Johnson, St. Paul's Church-yard, by 1801. Google Books. https://books.google.com/books?id=OrUVyWAyMCYC&printsec=frontcover&source=gbs_ge_summary_r&cad=0#v=onepage&q&f=false.

Erichsen, John Eric. *The Science of Art and Surgery, Being a Treatise on Surgical Injuries, Disease, and Operations*. Edited by John H. Brinton. Philadelphia: Blanchard and Lea, 1854. https://www.google.com/books/edition/The_Science_and_Art_of_Surgery/fgFuMsrstToC?hl=en&gbpv=1.

Favret, Marie. *War at a Distance: Romanticism and the Making of Modern Wartime*. Princeton, NJ: Princeton University Press, 2010.

"Feature, n." Oxford English Dictionary Online. Oxford: Oxford University Press, 2020.

Fisher, David R. "Berkeley, Hon. George Cranfield (1753–1818), of Wood End, nr. Chichester, Suss." History of Parliament Online. historyofparliamentonline.org/volume/1790-1820/member/berkeley-hon-george-cranfield-1753-1818.

Fremantle, Mrs Elizabeth Wynne, and Mrs Eugenia Wynne Campbell. *The Wynne Diaries*. London: H. Milford, Oxford University Press, 1935.

Furneaux, Holly. "'Our Poor Colonel Loved Him as if He Had Been His Own Son': Family Feeling in the Crimea." In *Military Men of Feeling: Emotion, Touch, and Masculinity in the Crimean War*. Oxford: Oxford University Press, 2016. Oxford Scholarship Online. doi: 10.1093/acprof:oso/9780198737834.003.0005.

Garland-Thomson, Rosemarie. "Opinion | Becoming Disabled." *New York Times*, January 20, 2018, sec. Opinion. https://www.nytimes.com/2016/08/21/opinion/sunday/becoming-disabled.html.

———. "The Story of My Work: How I Became Disabled." *Disability Studies Quarterly* 34, no. 2 (March 18, 2014): https://doi.org/10.18061/dsq.v34i2.4254.

Gerber, David A. "Creating Group Identity: Disabled Veterans and American Government." *OAH Magazine of History* 23, no. 3 (July 2009): 23–28.

———. "Disabled Veterans, the State, and the Experience of Disability in Western Societies, 1914–1950." *Journal of Social History* 36, no. 4 (Summer 2003): 899–916.

———. *Disabled Veterans in History*. Corporealities: Discourses of Disability. Ann Arbor: University of Michigan Press, 2000.

Gill, Ellen. *Naval Families, War and Duty in Britain, 1740–1820*. Woodbridge, Suffolk, UK: Boydell Press, 2016.

Gordon, Sir Admiral James Alexander. *Letters and Records of Sir Admiral J. A. Gordon, G.C.B., 1782–1869*. Compiled by Elizabeth, Adelaide, and Sophia Gordon. London: printed for private circulation, 1890.

Gordon, Pryse Lockhart. *Personal Memoirs; or, Reminiscences of Men and Manners*. Vol. 2. London: H. Colburn and Richard Bentley, 1830.

Great Britain Parliament. "Parl. Debates, May 11, 1810.- Navy Estimates." In *The Parliamentary Debates from the Year 1803 to the Present Time*, 1007–15. Vol. 16. London: published under the superintendence of T. C. Hansard, 1812.: HathiTrust Digital Library. https://hdl.handle.net/2027/njp.32101019449006?urlappend=%3Bseq=638.

Great Britain Parliament, House of Commons. *Parliamentary Papers: 1780–1849*. Vol. 17. n.p.: H.M. Stationery Office, 1831. Google Books. https://books.google.com/books?id=f8FDAQAAMAAJ&printsec=frontcover#v=onepage&q&f=false.

———. "Minutes of Evidence Taken before the Commissioners for Inquiring into Naval and Military Promotion and Retirement." In *Parliamentary Papers: 1780–1849*. Vol. 22. n.p.: H.M. Stationery Office, 1829. Google Books. https://books.google.com/books?id=nVoSAAAAYAAJ&pg=PA148&lpg=PA148&dq#v=onepage&q&f=false.

Great Britain Parliament, House of Lords. *Journals of the House of Lords* 52 (1818–19): 896.

n.p.: H.M. Stationery Office, 1818–1819. HathiTrust Digital Library. https://hdl.handle.net/2027/uc1.c0000029280?urlappend=%3Bseq=890.

Hall, Basil. *Fragments of Voyages and Travels*. 2nd series. Vol. 2. Edinburgh: Robert Cadell, 1832.

Harrington, Peter. *British Artists and War: The Face of Battle in Paintings and Prints, 1700–1914*. London: Greenhill Books; Mechanicsburg, PA: Stackpole Books in association with Brown University Library, Rhode Island, 1993.

Harrison, James. *The Life of the Right Honourable Horatio Lord Viscount Nelson*. Vol. 1. London: Ranelagh Press, 1806; Project Gutenberg, 2005. http://www.gutenberg.org/ebooks/16912.

Hay, Kate. "Mosaic Marble Tables by J. Darmanin & Sons of Malta." *Furniture History* 46 (2010): 157–88.

Hepper, David J. *British Warship Losses in the Age of Sail, 1650–1859*. 1st ed. Rotherfield, East Sussex, UK: Jean Boudriot, 1994.

Homer. *The Iliad of Homer*. Translated by Alexander Pope. London: Cassel, 1909.

Houghton, Walter E. *The Victorian Frame of Mind, 1830–1870*. New Haven, CT: Yale University Press, 1957.

Hughes, Thomas. "The Last of Nelson's Captains." *Macmillan's Magazine* 19, no. 112 (February 1869): 353–54.

Hume, Robert D. "The Value of Money in Eighteenth-Century England: Incomes, Prices, Buying Power—and Some Problems in Cultural Economics." *Huntington Library Quarterly* 77, no. 4 (Winter 2014): 373–416. https://doi.org/10.1525/hlq.2014.77.4.373.

James, William. *The Naval History of Great Britain, from . . . 1793, to . . . 1820, with an Account of the Origin and Increase of the British Navy*. London: Harding, Lepard, 1826.

Jenks, Timothy. *Naval Engagements: Patriotism, Cultural Politics, and the Royal Navy, 1793–1815*. Oxford: Oxford University Press, 2006.

Jubilee Sailing Trust. "Our History." jst.org.uk/about-us/history.

Kafer, Alison. *Feminist, Queer, Crip*. Bloomington: Indiana University Press, 2013.

Kennedy, Catriona. *Narratives of the Revolutionary and Napoleonic Wars: Military and Civilian Experience in Britain and Ireland*. War, Culture and Society, 1750–1850. New York: Palgrave Macmillan, 2013.

Kennedy, Maev. "Nelson Put in His Place by New Maritime Museum Exhibition." *The Guardian*, October 14, 2013, sec. Culture. https://www.theguardian.com/culture/2013/oct/14/nelson-maritime-museum-exhibition.

Kirkup, John. *A History of Limb Amputation*. London: Springer, 2007.

Knight, John I. "Telescope Holder for One-Handed Persons." *Mechanics' Magazine and Journal of Science, Arts, and Manufactures* 20 (January 1834): 351. Google Books. https://play.google.com/books/reader?id=-I5fAAAAcAAJ&hl=en&pg=GBS.PA351.

Knight, R. J. B. *The Pursuit of Victory: The Life and Achievement of Horatio Nelson*. New York: Basic Books, 2005.

Knight, Roger. "Changing the Agenda: The 'New' Naval History of the British Sailing Navy." *Mariner's Mirror* 97, no. 1 (February 2011): 225–42.

Kuchta, David. *The Three-Piece Suit and Modern Masculinity: England, 1550–1850*. Studies on the History of Society and Culture. Berkeley: University of California Press, 2002.

Kurzman, Steven L. "Performing Able-Bodiedness: Amputees and Prosthetics in America." PhD thesis, University of California, Santa Cruz, 2003.

———. "Presence and Prosthesis: A Response to Nelson and Wright." *Cultural Anthropology* 16, no. 3 (2001): 374–87. https://www.jstor.org/stable/656681.

Laughton, J. K., and Andrew Lambert. "Seymour, Sir Michael, First Baronet (1768–1834), Naval Officer." In *Oxford Dictionary of National Biography*. Oxford University Press, 2004. https://doi.org/10.1093/ref:odnb/25177.

Laughton, J. K., and Roger Morriss, "Gordon, Sir James Alexander (1782–1869), Naval Officer." In *Oxford Dictionary of National Biography*. Oxford University Press, 2004-. https://doi.org/10.1093/ref:odnb/11054.

Lavery, Brian. *Nelson's Navy: The Ships, Men, and Organisation, 1793–1815*. Annapolis, MD: Naval Institute Press, 1989.

———. *Royal Tars: The Lower Deck of the Royal Navy, 875–1850*. Annapolis, MD: Naval Institute Press, 2010.

Lemire, Beverly. "A Question of Trousers: Seafarers, Masculinity and Empire in the Shaping of British Male Dress, c. 1600–1800." *Cultural and Social History* 13, no. 1 (January 2, 2016): 1–22. https://doi.org/10.1080/14780038.2016.1133493.

Lewis, Michael Arthur. *A Social History of the Navy, 1793–1815*. London: Allen & Unwin, 1960.

Lincoln, Margarette. *Representing the Royal Navy: British Sea Power, 1750–1815*. Burlington, VT: Ashgate, 2002.

Lloyd, Christopher, ed. *The Health of Seamen: Selections from the Work of Dr. James Lind, Sir Gilbert Blane, and Dr. Thomas Trotter*. London: Navy Records Society, 1965.

Lloyd, Christopher, and Jack L. S. Coulter. *Medicine and the Navy, 1200–1900: 1714–1815*. Vol. 3. Edinburgh: Livingstone, 1957.

London Gazette. "Page 371 | Issue 15902, 24 March 1806 | London Gazette | The Gazette." https://www.thegazette.co.uk/London/issue/15902/page/371.

———. "Page 1006 | Issue 15397, 15 August 1801 | London Gazette | The Gazette." https://www.thegazette.co.uk/London/issue/15397/page/1006.

———. "Page 1790 | Issue 17173, 15 September 1816 | London Gazette | The Gazette." https://www.thegazette.co.uk/London/issue/17173/page/1790.

Longmore, Paul K., and Lauri Umansky, eds. *The New Disability History: American Perspectives*. History of Disability Series. New York: New York University Press, 2001.

Lovett, William, and the Working Men's Association. *The People's Charter: With the Address to the Radical Reformers of Great Britain and Ireland, and a Brief Sketch of Its Origin*. London: C.H. Helt and Charles Fox, 1848. https://books.google.com/books?id=kvlZuAEACAAJ&printsec=frontcover#v=onepage&q&f=false.

Malcomson, Thomas. *Order and Disorder in the British Navy, 1793–1815: Control, Resistance, Flogging and Hanging*. Woodbridge, Suffolk, UK: Boydell Press, 2016.
Mark de Toy, Brian. "Berkeley, Sir George Cranfield (1753–1818), Naval Officer and Politician." In *Oxford Dictionary of National Biography*. Oxford University Press, 2004-. https://doi.org/10.1093/ref:odnb/2213.
Marshall, John. *Royal Naval Biography: or, Memoirs of the services of all the flag-officers, superannuated rear-admirals, retired-captains, and post-captains, whose names appeared on the Admiralty list of sea officers at the commencement of the present year, or who have been promoted, illustrated by a series of historical and explanatory notes . . . with copious addenda*. 8 vols. (4 plus 4 supplemental bks). London: Longman, Hurst, Rees, Orme, and Brown, 1823–35. Available in digital collection, *Sabin Americana: History of the Americas, 1500–1926*. GALE | CY0111484263.
Maudsley, Henry. "The Correlation of Mental and Physical Force; or, Man, a Part of Nature." *Journal of Mental Science* 6, no. 31 (1859): 50–78. doi:10.1192/bjp.6.31.50.
———. "Delusions." *Journal of Mental Science* 9, no. 45 (April 1863): 1–24. https://archive.org/details/britishjournalof09roya/page/10/mode/2up?view=theater.
———. *The Physiology and Pathology of the Mind*. New York: D. Appleton, 1867; Internet Archive, 2009. http://archive.org/details/physiologyandpa03maudgoog.
McCormack, Matthew. "Boots, Material Culture and Georgian Masculinities." *Social History* 42, no. 4 (November 2017): 461–79.
Meyer, Arline. "Re-Dressing Classical Statuary: The Eighteenth-Century 'Hand-in-Waistcoat' Portrait." *Art Bulletin* 77, no. 1 (March 1995): 45–63.
Micale, Mark S. "The Great Victorian Eclipse." In Micale, *Hysterical Men*, 49–116.
———. *Hysterical Men: The Hidden History of Male Nervous Illness*. Cambridge, MA: Harvard University Press, 2008. www.jstor.org/stable/j.ctt13x0fj4.6.
———. "Hysterick Women and Hypochondriac Men." In Micale, *Hysterical Men*, 8–48.
Miller, Amy. "Clothes Make the Man: Naval Uniform and Masculinity in the Early Nineteenth Century." *Journal for Maritime Research* 17, no. 2 (November 2015): 147–54.
———. *Dressed to Kill: British Naval Uniform, Masculinity and Contemporary Fashions, 1748–1857*. London: National Maritime Museum, 2007.
"Miscellaneous Papers." N.d. PLL /88/53. Caird Archive, National Maritime Museum, Greenwich, London.
Moore, Henson, and Jeffrey O'Connell. "Foreclosing Medical Malpractice Claims by Prompt Tender of Economic Loss." *Louisiana Law Review* 44, no. 5 (1984): 1267–88. https://digitalcommons.law.lsu.edu/cgi/viewcontent.cgi?article=4833&context=lalrev.
Morrison, Alfred. *The Collection of Autograph Letters and Historical Documents Formed by Alfred Morrison (Second Series, 1882–1893); The Hamilton & Nelson Papers*. 2 vols. Printed for private circulation, 1893.
Murphy, Brian, and R. G. Thorne. "Douglas, Sylvester (1743–1823), of The Pheasantry, Bushey Park, Mdx." History of Parliament Online. http://www.historyofparliamentonline.org/volume/1790-1820/member/douglas-sylvester-1743-1823.

Namier, Sir Lewis, and John Brooke, eds. *The History of Parliament: The House of Commons, 1754–1790.* Vol. 3. London: Boydell and Brewer, 1985.

Naval Chronicle, The: Containing a General and Biographical History of the Royal Navy of the United Kingdom, with a Variety of Original Papers on Nautical Subjects. 40 vols. London: J. Gold, 1799–1818. HathiTrust Digital Library. https://catalog.hathitrust.org/Record/000550825/Home.

"The Naval Gallery, or Painted Hall, in Greenwich Hospital." *Penny Magazine of the Society for the Diffusion of Useful Knowledge* 7 (January 6, 1838): 2.

"Nelson, His Valet, and His Native Coast." *The United Service Magazine: With Which Are Incorporated the Army and Navy Magazine and Naval and Military Journal* 20 (February 1836): 201–8. London: H. Colburn, February 1836. HathiTrust Digital Library. https://hdl.handle.net/2027/nyp.33433081656971?urlappend=%3Bseq=212.

Nelson, Viscount Horatio. *The Dispatches and Letters of Vice Admiral Lord Viscount Nelson: With Notes,* edited by Nicholas Harris Nicolas. 7 vols. London: H. Colburn, 1844–46.

———. *The Letters of Lord Nelson to Lady Hamilton: With a Supplement of Interesting Letters.* 2 vols. London: Macdonald and Son, 1814.

Niles' Weekly Register. Vol. 9 (September 1815–February 1816). Baltimore: H. Niles, 1815–16. HathiTrust Digital Library. https://hdl.handle.net/2027/pst.000055571128?urlappend=%3Bseq=88.

O'Byrne, William R. *A Naval Biographical Dictionary: Comprising the Life and Services of Every Living Officer in Her Majesty's Navy, from the Rank of Admiral of the Fleet to That of Lieutenant, Inclusive, Compiled from Authentic and Family Documents.* London: J. Murray (printed by William Clowes and Sons), 1849. [Available in digital collection, *Sabin Americana: History of the Americas, 1500–1926.* GALE | CY0102755979.]

O'Byrne, William R., and Unspecified Navy of England. "Correspondence and Biographical Notes upon Which William Richard O'Byrne Based His Naval Biographical Dictionary of All Living Officers (1849), Compiled during the Years 1843–1849. 16 vols. Paper. Folio." Unpublished manuscript chapters. BL Add MS 38044, 503.

O'Connor, Erin. *Raw Material: Producing Pathology in Victorian Culture.* Durham, NC: Duke University Press, 2000.

Orde, Denis A. *Nelson's Mediterranean Command: Concerning Pride, Preferment & Prize Money.* Edinburgh: Pentland Press, 1997.

Ortiz, Stephen R., ed. *Veterans' Policies, Veterans' Politics: New Perspectives on Veterans in the Modern United States.* Gainesville: University Press of Florida, 2012.

Ott, Katherine. "Disability and the Practice of Public History: An Introduction." *Public Historian* 27, no. 2 (2005): 9–24. https://doi.org/10.1525/tph.2005.27.2.9.

———. "The Sum of Its Parts: An Introduction to Modern Histories of Prosthetics." In *Artificial Parts, Practical Lives: Modern Histories of Prosthetics,* edited by Katherine Ott, David Serlin, and Stephen Mihm, 1–42. New York: New York University Press, 2002.

"Owen Pell: Profile and Legacies Summary." Legacies of British Slave-Ownership, University College London. https://www.ucl.ac.uk/lbs/person/view/218.

"Parliamentary Paper: Sixth Report from the Select Committee of Finance." *Naval Chronicle* 39 (January–June 1818): 67–71. HathiTrust Digital Library. https://hdl.handle.net/2027/umn.319510007440670?urlappend=%3Bseq=9.

Parker, Johnny. "The Made Whole Doctrine: Unraveling the Enigma Wrapped in the Mystery of Insurance Subrogation." *Missouri Law Review* 70, no. 3 (June 1, 2005). https://scholarship.law.missouri.edu/mlr/vol70/iss3/3.

Parsons, George Samuel. *Nelsonian Reminiscences; or, Leaves from Memory's Log*. Boston: Little, Brown, 1843.

Partridge, Michael. "Luttrell, James (c.1751–1788), Naval Officer and Politician." In *Oxford Dictionary of National Biography*. Oxford: Oxford University Press, 2004-. https://doi.org/10.1093/ref:odnb/17224.

Pearsall, Cornelia D. J. "Burying the Duke: Victorian Mourning and the Funeral of the Duke of Wellington." *Victorian Literature and Culture* 27, no. 2 (1999): 365–93.

Perrett, Bryan. *The Real Hornblower: The Life and Times of Admiral Sir James Gordon*. Illustrated ed. New York: Skyhorse, 2014.

Pettigrew, Thomas Joseph. *Memoirs of the Life of Vice-Admiral, Lord Viscount Nelson, K. B., Duke of Bronté, Etc., Etc., Etc.* 2 vols. London: T. & W. Boone, 1849.

Pocock, Tom. *Remember Nelson: The Life of Sir William Hoste*. London: Thistle, 2013.

Pointon, Marcia R. *Hanging the Head: Portraiture and Social Formation in Eighteenth-Century England*. New Haven, CT: Yale University Press, 1993.

Porter, Roy. *Bodies Politic: Disease, Death and Doctors in Britain, 1650–1900*. London: Reaktion Books, 2001.

"Powerful Incentives to Victory." *The Naval Chronicle, Containing a General and Biographical History of the Royal Navy of the United Kingdom, with a Variety of Original Papers on Nautical Subjects* 15 (January–July 1806): 400. HathiTrust Digital Library. https://hdl.handle.net/2027/uc2.ark:/13960/t16m34z4d?urlappend=%3Bseq=426.

Prentice, Rina. *The Authentic Nelson*. Illustrated ed. London: National Maritime Museum, 2005.

Reynolds, Sir Joshua. "A Discourse Delivered to the Students of the Royal Academy on the Distribution of the Prizes, December 10, 1771, by the President." In *Seven Discourses on Art*. London: Cassell, 1901; Project Gutenberg, 2005. http://www.gutenberg.org/files/2176/2176-h/2176-h.htm.

Richardson, Jonathan. *An Essay on the Theory of Painting*. 2nd ed. London: Printed for A.C. and sold by A. Bettesworth in Pater-noster Row, 1725. Google Books, https://play.google.com/books/reader?id=e9NPAQAAIAAJ&printsec=frontcover&pg=GBS.PA21.

Rodger, N. A. M. *The Command of the Ocean: A Naval History of Britain, 1649–1815*. New York: W. W. Norton, 2005.

———. "Commissioned Officers' Careers in the Royal Navy, 1690–1815." *Journal for Maritime Research 3, no. 1 (December 2001): 85–129. https://doi.org/10.1080/21533369.2001.9668314.

———. *The Wooden World: An Anatomy of the Georgian Navy.* Annapolis, MD: Naval Institute Press, 1986.

Roe, Nicholas. *John Keats: A New Life.* New Haven, CT: Yale University Press, 2012.

Rostker, Bernard D. *Providing for the Casualties of War: The American Experience through World War II.* Santa Monica, CA: RAND, 2013.

Rousseau, Jean-Jacques. *Emile: or, On Education.* 1762; repr., New York: Basic Books, 1979.

"The Royal Hospital for Seamen, Greenwich: 'A Refuge for All.'" Port Cities London, http://www.portcities.org.uk/london/server/show/ConNarrative.148/chapterId/3048/The-Royal-Hospital-for-Seamen-Greenwich-A-Refuge-for-All.html.

Royal Statistical Society of London. "On the Mortality arising from Naval Operations." *Journal of the Royal Statistical Society: General* 18 (September 1855). London: John William Parker and Son, 1855. HathiTrust Digital Library. https://hdl.handle.net/2027/mdp.39015036988460?urlappend=%3Bseq=214.

Rupprecht, Anita. "From Slavery to Indenture: Scripts for Slavery's Endings." In *Emancipation and the Remaking of the British Imperial World,* edited by Catherine Hall, Nicholas Draper, and Keith McClelland, 77–97. Manchester: Manchester University Press, 2014. www.jstor.org/stable/j.ctt18mvmt2.11.

Scull, Andrew, Charlotte MacKenzie, and Nicholas Hervey. "Degeneration and Despair:: Henry Maudsley (1835–1918)." In *Masters of Bedlam: The Transformation of the Mad-Doctoring Trade,* 226–67. Princeton Legacy Library. Princeton, NJ: Princeton University Press, 1996. https://doi.org/10.2307/j.ctt7zvbsw.12.

Seymour, Richard. *Memoir of Rear-Admiral Sir Michael Seymour, Bart., K. C. B.* London: Spottiswoode, 1878; Internet Archive, 2008. http://archive.org/details/memoirrearadmir00seymgoog.

Shakespeare, Tom. "Nasty, Brutish, and Short? On the Predicament of Disability and Embodiment." In *Disability and the Good Human Life,* edited by Jerome E. Bickenbach, Franziska Felder, and Barbara Schmitz, 93–112. New York: Cambridge University Press, 2013.

Siebers, Tobin. *Disability Theory.* Corporealities: Discourses of Disability. Ann Arbor: University of Michigan Press, 2008.

Smith, Adam. *The Theory of Moral Sentiments.* Edited by Dugald Stewart. Edinburgh: A. Miller, A. Kincaid, and J. Bell, 1769.

Smollett, Tobias. "Chapter 34." In *The Adventures of Roderick Random,* edited by James G. Basker, Nicole Seary, and Paul-Gabriel Boucé, 165–71. The Works of Tobias Smollett Series, edited by O. M. Brack Jr. and Alexander Pettit. Athens: University of Georgia Press, 2012. www.jstor.org/stable/j.ctt46nbth.45.

Southey, Robert. *The Life of Nelson.* London: J. Murray, 1813.

Steedman, Carolyn. *Labours Lost: Domestic Service and the Making of Modern England.* Cambridge: Cambridge University Press, 2009.

———. "Servants and Their Relationship to the Unconscious." *Journal of British Studies* 42, no. 3 (July 2003): 316–50.

Stinner, Daniel J., Travis C. Burns, Kevin L. Kirk, and James R. Ficke. "Return to Duty Rate of Amputee Soldiers in the Current Conflicts in Afghanistan and Iraq." *Journal of Trauma and Acute Care Surgery* 68, no. 6 (June 2010): 1476–79. doi:10.1097/TA.0b013e 3181bb9a6c.

Stone, Lawrence. *An Imperial State at War: Britain from 1689 to 1815*. London : Routledge, 1994.

Sugden, John. *Nelson: The Sword of Albion*. Illustrated reprint ed. London: Bodley Head, 2014.

Taylor, Jenny Bourne. "Psychology at the Fin de Siècle." In *The Cambridge Companion to the Fin de Siècle*, edited by Gail Marshall, 13–30. Cambridge: Cambridge University Press, 2007.

"Threatened Invasion." *Naval Chronicle* 6 (July–December 1801): 73–75. HathiTrust Digital Library. https://hdl.handle.net/2027/uc1.b2990327?urlappend=%3Bseq=95.

Thursfield, James Richard. *Nelson and Other Naval Studies*. London: John Murray, 1909; repr., 1920; Internet Archive, 2008. http://archive.org/details/nelsonothernavaloothur.

Tosh, John. *A Man's Place: Masculinity and the Middle-Class Home in Victorian England*. New Haven, CT: Yale University Press, 2007.

Tracy, Nicholas. *Who's Who in Nelson's Navy*. London: Chatham, 2006.

Turner, David M. "Disability and Crime in Eighteenth-Century England: Physical Impairment at the Old Bailey." *Cultural and Social History* 9, no. 1 (March 1, 2012): 47–64. https://doi.org/10.2752/147800412X13191165982953.

———. "Disability History and the History of Emotions: Reflections on Eighteenth-Century Britain." *Asclepio* 68, no. 2 (2016): 146.

United States Department of Labor, Office of Disability Employment Policy. "Focus on Ability: Interviewing Applicants with Disabilities." https://www.dol.gov/odep/pubs/fact/focus.htm.

United States Department of the Interior, National Park Service. "Robert Heriot Barclay: Perry's Victory & International Peace Memorial." Updated February 22, 2019. https://www.nps.gov/people/robert-heriot-barclay.htm.

Walker, R. J. B.. *The Nelson Portraits: An Iconography of Horatio, Viscount Nelson, Vice Admiral of the White*. London: Royal Naval Museum, 1998.

Watt, Sir James. "Naval and Civilian Influences on Eighteenth- and Nineteenth-Century Medical Practice." *Mariner's Mirror* 97, no. 1 (February 2011): 148–66.

———. "Surgery at Trafalgar." *Mariner's Mirror* 91, no. 2 (January 1, 2005): 266–83. https://doi.org/10.1080/00253359.2005.10656949.

White, Colin. *Nelson: The Admiral*. Thrupp, Stroud, Gloucestershire, UK: Sutton, in association with the Royal Navy and the Royal Naval Museum, 2005.

———. *Nelson: The New Letters*. Woodbridge, Suffolk, UK: Boydell Press, 2005.

———. *The Nelson Companion*. Annapolis, MD: Naval Institute Press, 1995.

Wilcox, Martin. "The 'Poor Decayed Seamen' of Greenwich Hospital, 1705–1763." *International Journal of Maritime History* 25, no. 1 (June 1, 2013): 65–90.https://doi.org/10.1177/084387141302500104.

Williams, Kate. "Nelson and Women: Marketing, Representations, and the Female Consumer." In *Admiral Lord Nelson: Context and Legacy,* edited by David Cannadine, 67–89. Basingstoke, UK: Palgrave Macmillan, 2005.

Wilson, Evan. "British Naval Administration and the Quarterdeck Manpower Problem in the Eighteenth Century." In *Strategy and the Sea: Essays in Honour of John B. Hattendorf.,* edited by N. A. M. Rodger, J. Ross Dancy, Benjamin Darnell, and Evan Wilson, 64–75. Rev. ed. Woodbridge, Suffolk, UK: Boydell and Brewer, 2016. http://www.jstor.org/stable/10.7722/j.ctt19x3j3g.13.

———. "Social Background and Promotion Prospects in the Royal Navy, 1775–1815." *English Historical Review* 131, no. 550 (June 2016): 570–95. https://doi.org/10.1093/ehr/cew174.

———. *A Social History of British Naval Officers, 1775–1815.* Woodbridge, Suffolk, UK: Boydell Press, 2017.

Winfield, Rif. *British Warships in the Age of Sail, 1714–1792: Design, Construction, Careers and Fates.* Barnsley, South Yorkshire, UK: Seaforth, 2007.

Wollstonecraft, Mary. *Mary Wollstonecraft's Original Stories.* Edited by E. V. Lucas. 1787; repr., London: Henry Frowde, 1906; Project Gutenberg, 2011. https://www.gutenberg.org/files/36507/36507-h/36507-h.htm.

"Wonderful Preservation of the Meander." *Naval Chronicle* 37 (January–June 1817): 24–26. HathiTrust Digital Library. https://hdl.handle.net/2027/uc1.b2990359?urlappend=%3Bseq=37.

World Health Organization (WHO). "Disabilities." http://www.who.int/topics/disabilities/en/.

INDEX

Italicized page numbers refer to illustrations.

Abbott, Lemuel Francis, 122–23, *123*
ability, modern ideology of, 133
Able-Bodied Seamen (A.B.), 6, 30–32, *33*
abortion, 166–67
Acosta (ship), 92
Active (ship), 67, 100, 110, 139, 175–76, 209, 212
Adams, Sir Thomas, 217
adaptation, 7–8, 89, 91
admirals, 35
Adventures of Roderick Random, The (Smollett), 84
Aeolous (ship), 207
aesthetics, 10, 113, 179–80. *See also* fashion; visual codes, in images of military heroes
Afghanistan, war in, 204–5
aides-du-camp, 107–8
Allen, Tom, 105–6
Amaranthe (ship), 208
Americans with Disabilities Act (U.S.), 5
Amethyst (ship), 64, 136, 208, 215, 219
Amphion (ship), 139, 210
amputee officers, 2; family backgrounds of, 14–16; in modern wars, 205; numbers of and ranks of, 13–20; personal/professional bonds between, 11, 12–13, 132. *See also* Gordon, James Alexander; limb amputation; Nelson, Horatio; Pell, Sir Watkin Owen; Seymour, Sir Michael
amputee officers, personal lives of, 132–73; feuds, 136–37; finances, 142–51; friendship, 47, 133–36, 137–42; marriage, 151–73; sensibility, 132–33, 134–35, 190–91. *See also* father-and-son relationships
amputee officers, representation of, 29, 82–131; and naval uniforms, 83–84; personal assistance, 82, 99–108; prostheses, 82, 88–89, 108–10; self-presentation, 82, 85, 88–97. *See also* portraiture; visual codes, in images of military heroes
Anglesey, Lord. *See* Paget, Henry William, 1st Marquess of Anglesey
Anson (ship), 207
Antigua, 70, 76
Arethusa (ship), 136, 215
Assault on Cádiz (1797), 32, 77
assistive devices, 3, 8–9, 103, 236n150
Aurora (ship), 51, 211
Austen, Jane, 4, 56, 152, 173
authority, 129–30, 159–60, 195–96

{259}

Bacon, Francis, 1
Barclay, Robert Heriot, 15, 18, *180*, 207
Barfleur (ship), 212
Barker, Matthew Henry, 54, 116–17
Barrie, J. M., 1
Battle of Algeziras (1801), 215
Battle of Algiers (1816), 139, 209–10
battle of April 1, 1809 (capture of *La Leda*), 72, 216
Battle of Cape St. Vincent (1797), 54, 66, 77, 133, 137, 214, 218
Battle of Copenhagen (1801), 9, 104, 135, 139, 208, 209, 212, 216
battle of December 12, 1782 (*Mediator* action), 57
Battle of Dogger Bank (1781), 212
battle of February 6, 1800 (capture of *Pallas*), 71, 216
Battle of Groix (1795), 210, 215
battle of July 13, 1795 (Hotham's second partial action), 54, 217
Battle of Lake Erie (1813), 18, 207
Battle of Lissa (March 13, 1811), 67, 133, 175–76, 212
battle of March 14, 1794 (Hotham's action), 217
battle of November 29, 1811 (action at Lissa), 67, 133, 168, 172–73, 212
Battle of San Domingo (1806), 111
Battle of the Nile (1798), 133, 137, 214, 216; in visual images, 115–18, 125–26
Battle of the Nile, The (Cruikshank), 115–16, *116*
Battle of Trafalgar (1805), 32, 54, 85, 207, 208, 218
Battle of Turtle Gut Inlet (1776), 212
Battle of Waterloo (1815), 87, 178
Battle of Yorktown (1781), 41, 136, 215
Baynton, Douglas C., 2
Beatty, James, 104

Beatty, William, 151
beauty. *See* aesthetics
Bedford (ship), 217
Bedford, Frederick, 17, 40, 44
Bedford, John, 15, 208
Berkeley, George Cranfield, 58–61, 62–64, 212
Billy Budd (Melville), 1–2
Bissell, Austin, 51, 211
Blane, Gilbert, 20, 224n61
Bode, Louisa Henrietta, 139
Body and Mind (Maudsley), 192–93
Bold, Edward, 183–84
Bond, John Holmes, 15, 208
boots, 99–100, 104
Boyle, Mary, 108–9, 141
Boys, Charles Worsley, 15, 208
Brilliant, Richard, 113–14
British Journal of Psychiatry, 190
British Royal Navy: documentation through official letters, 26–27; downsizing in Victorian era, 177–78, 185–86; history of, 4; as network of personal bonds, 11, 12–13, 24–25, 47, 132; organizational structure, 55–56; oversupply of officers in, 16, 18, 46; patronage system, 19, 46–50; ranks in, 33–35; retirement from, 46; ships of, 35–36; smart-money system, 27–28, 32, 39–45, 187–89. *See also* hero promotion
British Warship Losses in the Age of Sail (Hepper), 18
Brockliss, Laurence, 151, 178
Bronte, Patrick, 5
Brownlow family, 75
Brydone, Mary (Lady Minto), 107
Bulwark (ship), 208, 218
Burnett, Sir William, 133, 203
Burney, Frances, 141
Bustard (ship), 213

Byron, George Gordon Noel, 6th Baron Byron, 4, 142, 174

Camilla (ship), 215
Canōpus (ship), 216
captains: "description books" of, 31–32; and official letters, 27; post-captains, 35, 53; salaries of, 41
Cardwell, John, 151, 178
caricature, 115–18, *118*
Castor (ship), 213
Cavell, S. A., 48
Censor (ship), 214
Chamberlain, Geoffrey, 166–67
Chartism, 176–77, 178
Chatham (ship), 25, 215
Chest at Greenwich (formerly Chatham Chest), 28, 39
Childers (ship), 136, 208, 215, 216
Christ, comparisons of Nelson with, 128, 134
class, economic: middle-class ideals, 100–103, 194; and officers' pay, 40–41, 46, 56; poor and working-class people, 86–87, 176–77
class, social. *See* social status
clothing. *See* fashion
club life, 136, 139–40
Cochrane, Thomas, 10th Earl of Dundonald, 21, 42
Cockburn, Sir George, 198
Codrington, Edward, 135
Colby, David, *15*, 209
Cole, Francis (Captain), 66
Coleman, Terry, 85, 89, 94
Coleridge, Samuel Taylor, 4, 191
Colley, Linda, 87
Collingwood, Cuthbert, 38–39, 45–46, 47, 72, 190–91
Colossus (ship), 215

comedy, amputees in, 10, 86, 88, 115–18, *118*, 138–39, 141
commanders, 34–35
commemorative goods, 3, 128, 181
Commissioned Sea Officers of the Royal Navy, The, 1660–1815 (DiNardo and Syrett), 28
commissions, 56, 60
commodores, 35
Consolvo, Charles, 18, 19, 46
Cook, Richard, *124*
cooks, amputees as, 32–33
"Correlation of Mental and Physical Force, The: or Man, a Part of Nature" (Maudsley), 192
Cossack (ship), 54, 218
Creole (ship), 51, 211
Cretan (ship), 218
cripple races, 141–42
Cruelty and Laughter (Dickie), 86, 88, 141
Cruikshank, George, 115
Culloden (ship), 214
Culme-Seymour, Sir Michael, 197
Cuppage, William, *15*, 140, 209
Cust, Henry Cockayne, 75
Czisnik, Marianne, 26, 128, 136, 148, 179, 181

damages, compensatory, for loss of earning power due to negligence, 42–43, 188
Dashwood, William Bateman, *15*, 67, *124*, 133, 139, 209–10, 212
Davey, James, 4
Davidoff, Leonore, 103, 145–46
Davis, Lennard, 6–7, 89
Death of Nelson at the Battle of Trafalgar, The, 21 October 1805 (Drummond), 128, *129*
Defiance (ship), 139, 209
"degeneracy," in Victorian medical theories, 174–75, 189–94

"Degeneration and Despair" (Scull), 194
Deustch, Helen, 10
diaries, Watkin Owen Pell's: career in, 70–71; cultural events in, 177, 198; and family memoir, 25; family relations in, 70, 143, 144, 145; Greenwich Hospital in, 145, 184–86; medical events in, 199–202; naval commemoration in, 182–83; and naval history, 23; pension in, 189; social activities in, 96, 139–40; West Indies in, 76
Dickens, Charles, 178
Dickie, Simon, 10, 86, 88, 141
Dido (ship), 209
Diligence (ship), 136, 215
DiNardo, R. L., 28
dinner parties, 133, 135
disability, 2–13; changing ideas about in Victorian era, 187–89; and emotional well-being, 7–8; fictional amputees, 1; identity politics of, 11–12, 203–4; impairment vs., 5–6, 187; modern ideology of ability, 133; modern military disability, 203–4; negative attention to, 10–11; rise of visibility/interest in, 5; stereotypes of disabled poor, 86–87; terminology of, 5–7; visibility of impairments, 2–3. *See also* limb amputation
Disability Discrimination Act (UK), 5
disability rights movement, 5–6, 11–12, 105
Disabled Veterans in History (Gerber), 5
Discourses on Art (Reynolds), 114
diseases, 20, 58, 152
Dixon, Thomas, 132, 194
Douglas, Sylvester, 1st Baron Glenbervie, 65, 69, 155–56, 196, 212
Draper, Nick, 70
Dressed to Kill: British Naval Uniform, Masculinity, and Contemporary Fashion, 1748–1857 (Miller), 83
Druid (ship), 210

Drummond, Samuel, 128, *129*
Duncan, Henry, 48, 71–75, 176

economy, British, and cost of living, 40–41
Edgeworth, Maria and Richard Lovell, 102
Edinburgh Advertiser, 31
Elliot-Murray-Kynynmound, Gilbert, 2nd Earl of Minto, 77, 81
Ellison, Joseph, 15, 42, 210
Emerald (ship), 216
Emile; or, On Education (Rousseau), 102
emotion. *See* amputee officers, personal lives of
Epervier (ship), 212–13
Ephira (ship), 217
Erichsen, John Eric, 193
Essay on the Theory of Painting (Richardson), 113
Evelina (Burney), 141
"Extirpation of the Plagues of Egypt;—Destruction of Revolutionary Crocodiles;—or, ye British Hero Cleansing ye Mouth of ye Nile" (Gilray), 117–18, *118*
eyesight, loss of: Bedford's, 17; Nelson's, 1, 3, 43, 77, 106; Rathbourne's, 217; in seamen, 32, 40

family, navy as extended/alternate, 11, 49. *See also* amputee officers, personal lives of; father-and-son relationships
family memoirs, 25–26; *Letters and Records of Admiral Sir J. A. Gordon*, 65–66, 152, 157–58, 186, 195
Farquar, Arthur, 214
fashion: boots, 99–100, 104; hairstyles, 119–20; legwear, 83–84, 112, 192; naval officers' uniforms, 83–84, 119–20, 191–92; stockings, 9, 84, 104. *See also* sleeves, empty
father-and-son relationships, 11, 196–97; in naval histories, 24–25; and Nelson,

90, 107, 142, 150; and promotions/
  patronage, 48–49
Favret, Mary, 26, 114
femininity, 175
First Battle of Ushant (1778), 213
Flaxman, John, 179
Foley, Thomas, 66
Formidable (ship), 31, 64
Forte (ship), 75, 120
Fragments of Voyages and Travels (Hall),
  30–31
Freemantle, Elizabeth, 79, 89, 147–48
Freemantle, Thomas, 80
friendship, 12–13, 47, 132–36, 137–42
Furneaux, Holly, 202

gallantry, 38–39, 50–51, 52, 53–54, 72–73,
  77–78, 95. *See also* hero promotion
Ganges (ship), 58, 219
Garland-Thomson, Rosemarie, 11, 89
Garrety, James Henry, 15, 210–11
gender roles: femininity, 175; in James and
  Lydia Gordon's relationship, 152, 159–61;
  and medical profession, 202–3; in Nelson's relationship with Emma Hamilton,
  148; polarization of in Victorian era, 174,
  189–94; in service profession, 233n76. *See
  also* masculinity
Gentleman's Magazine, 43
George III, King of England, 57–58, 90, 97
Georgiana (ship), 214
Gerber, David A., 5, 204
Gill, Ellen, 26, 142, 156, 157
Gill, Thomas, 14, 15, 51–52, 68, 211
Gillray, James, 117–18, *118*
Glenbervie, Lord. *See* Douglas, Sylvester,
  1st Baron Glenbervie
Glorious First of June, 1794 (battle), 25,
  61–62, 208, 214, 219
Glory (ship), 212, 215
Goliath (ship), 66

Gordon, Adelaide, 26, 88
Gordon, Elizabeth, 26
Gordon, Frances, 68, 154–55, 167
Gordon, Hannah, 165, 194
Gordon, James Alexander, 15, 65–70, 209,
  211, 212; anecdotes about, 88; appearance, 110, *119*, 119–20; children, 145–46,
  147; death of, 139, 167, 194–95; early
  career at sea, 65–66; as family patriarch,
  195–96; finances, 143, 147; friendships
  of, 133–34; and Greenwich Hospital, 182,
  186; and hero promotion, 38; injury, 67–
  68; leadership of, 14; marriage, 69, 156;
  medical care toward end of life, 202–3;
  and Pell, 71, 73, 76, 139–40, 141–42, 216;
  performance of fitness, 82, 93–94, 96–97,
  130; on physical impairment, 167–70;
  portraiture of, 118–19, *119*, 129–30, *130*,
  158; and prosthetics, 9, 13, 108–10, 167–
  68; relationship with Lydia, 129–31, 151–
  73; and Seymour, 137–39; temperament
  of, 159, 162–63, 167; and Victorian era,
  194–96. *See also* letters, James and Lydia
  Gordon's; *Letters and Records of Admiral
  Sir J. A. Gordon, G.C.B., 1782–1869*
Gordon, James Alexander, Jr., 197
Gordon, Lydia (Ward), 69, 93–94, 110,
  139, *153*; concern for propriety, 158–59;
  courage of, 162–63; courtship with
  James, 151–55; death, 167; and gender
  roles in relationship with James, 159–61;
  and portrait of James, 129–30, *130*, 158;
  pregnancy and childbirth, 163–67; relationship with James, 151–73; responsibility for financial and other public affairs,
  159–62; writing style of, 158
Gordon, Maria, 133
Gordon, Pryse Lockhart, 148
Gordon, Sophia, 26
Graeme, Alexander, 15, 73, 212
Grampus (ship), 136, 215

Greatbatch, William, 129, *130*
Great Exhibition of 1851, 197–98
Greenwich Hospital: Bedford at, 17, 40; charter, 6, 115, 187; directors of, 210, 218; Gordon at, 212; Painted Hall at, 122, 182–83; Pell and Gordon at, 140, 182; prostheses at, 108; and smart-money, 28, 40; in Victorian era, 184–86, 189
Greenwich Hospital: A Series of Naval Sketches, Descriptive of the Life of a Man-of-War's Man (Barker), 54, 116–17
Guadeloupe (ship), 136, 214–15
Gustav IV Adolf, King of Sweden, 214, 220

Hackett, John, *15*, 212–13
half-pay, 46, 56
Hall, Basil, 30–31, 32–33
Hall, Catherine, 103, 145–46
Hamilton, Charles Powell, 52
Hamilton, Emma, 104, 107, 126, 147–49, 150, 151, 190
Hamilton, W. A. B., 110
hand-in-waistcoat pose, 181
hands and arms, in portraiture, 126
Hardy, Thomas Masterman, 9, 104–5, 151
Harpy (ship), 208
Harrington, Peter, 126–27
Harrison, James, 43
Hawkins-Whitshed, James, 65, 66, 119
Hay, Kate, 198
Hay, Lord John, 8, *15*, 213
Haydon, William Phippard, 23–24
Head, Guy, 125–26, *127*
Hepper, David J., 18
heroes, portraiture of. *See* portraiture
hero promotion, 37–81; Gordon, 65–70; and loss of limb as mark of honor, 19–20, 29, 37–38; Nelson, 76–81; Pell, 70–76; practices of, 45–55; Seymour, 55–65; smart-money, 39–45

Holles, Frescheville, 120–21, *121*
Hood, Sir Samuel, *15*, 124, *125,* 213–14
Hoppner, John, 124, *125*
Horatio Nelson: A Controversial Hero (Czisnik), 26
horses, 158, 166
Hoste, William, 67, 68, 90, 95, 175, 212
Houghton, Walter, 177
Hughes, Thomas, 194–95

Immortality of Lord Nelson, The (West), 127
independence, 100–103. *See also* personal assistance with everyday tasks
injuries, as significant but not disabling, 39–46, 50–55, 187–89
interest, relating to patronage/promotions, 46–48
Iphigenia (ship), 207
Iraq, war in, 204

Jamaica, 169, 176
James, William, 67, 148
Jaseur (ship), 213
Java (ship), 140, 209
Jenks, Timothy, 5, 43, 114
Jervas, Charles, 121, *122*
Jervis, John, 1st Earl of St. Vincent, 210; and attack on Tenerife, 77, 80; and Nelson, 78–79, 81; on promotions, 47, 48, 49
Johnson, Joshua, *15*
Journal of Medical Science, 194
Journal of the Royal Statistical Society, 40
Jubilee Sailing Trust, 3

Kafer, Alison, 7
Keats, John, 5
Keats, Richard Godwin, 111
Kennedy, Catriona, 86
Kingfisher (ship), 51, 211, 212

Kneeshaw, Joshua, 14, *15*, 214
Knight, R. J. B. (Roger), 4, 95, 106
Kurzman, Steven L., 8, 88–89, 112

"lameness," meanings of, 86–87, 155, 157
Latona (ship), 209
Lavery, Brian, 18, 31–32
Lely, Peter, 120–21, *121*
Lemire, Beverly, 83, 113
Le Nieman (ship), 136, 219
letters, James and Lydia Gordon's, 147; contributions to family in, 110, 132, 159–60, 162; emotion in, 158–59; impairment in, 110, 168–73, 199; James' performances of able-bodiedness in, 93–94, 96–97, 98, 170–71; personal assistance in, 99–100; portraiture in, 129–30, 158; relationship in, 153, 156–57, 159–62, 163–66; writing styles in, 158. See also *Letters and Records of Admiral Sir J. A. Gordon, G.C.B., 1782–1869*
letters, official, 23, 26–27, 72, 78, 104
letters, personal, 23, 25–26; and construction of identity, 142, 156–57; Luttrell's letters to Seymour, 59; Nelson's, 14, 78–80, 103, 104, 106–7, 135, 149, 150. See also family memoirs; letters, James and Lydia Gordon's
Letters and Records of Admiral Sir J. A. Gordon, G.C.B., 1782–1869 (family memoir), 65–66, 152, 157–58, 186, 195
LeVesconte, Phillip, 25, 214
Lewis, Michael, 20
Licorne (ship), 210
Liddell, Sir John, 185, 202–3
lieutenants, 14, 22–23, 34, 41, 53, 60
Life of Nelson (Southey), 43
Life of the Right Honorable Horatio Viscount Nelson, The (Harrison), 43
limb amputation: ages at, 16; among modern U.S. soldiers, 205; Gordon's, 67–68; loss of a limb in battle as mark of honor and not disability, 37–39, 77, 80–81, 154–55; Mends's, 136; Nelson's, 77–78; Pell's, 71; Peyton, 92; risks of, 16–17; Seymour's, 62–63; and social status, 86–88; and spasms/pain, 30, 175, 193, 195, 199, 201; as standard of value, 20–22; Victorian ideas about masculinity and, 193
Lincoln, Margarette, 5, 50, 115
literacy, 65–66
Locker, William, 122, 182
Loire (ship), 70, 216
London Gazette, 52
loneliness, 133
Lonsdale, James, 124
Lord Nelson (ship), 3
L'Orient (ship), 118, 126
love. See amputee officers, personal lives of
Lucas, John, *120*
Luttrell, James, 55, 56–58, 59, 219

Madagascar (ship), 217
Magnificent (ship), 51, 59, 60, 211, 219
Marlborough (ship), 61–62, 210, 219
marriage, 151–73
Marshall, John, 22–23, 24, 25, 48, 72, 74, 92, 136, 177, 207
Martial (ship), 214
Martin, Sir Byam, 198–99
masculinity: and gallantry, 38–39; and heroic military portraiture, 114–15, 126–27, 128; middle-class, 100–101, 194; and naval officers' uniforms, 83–84, 191–92; proper men for the service, 38–39; and providing for one's children, 196–97; and sensibility, 132–33, 159, 190–91; in Victorian era, and "wholeness," 179, 193; and vulnerability, 86, 114–15, 125–27, *127*, 132–33, 152

master's mates, 14
Maudsley, Henry, 174–75, 179–80, 190, 192–94
Meander (ship), 163
Mediator (ship), 57, 219
medical care, naval vs. civilian surgeons, 16–17
medical science, in Victorian era, 174–75; degeneracy and ideas of gender difference, 189–94; medical care received by amputee officers, 199–203; and "wholeness," 179
Melville, Herman, 1–2
Memoirs of Lady Hamilton (anonymous), 148
Mends, Robert, 14, 15, 41–42, 136–37, 214–15
mental illness, 20
Mercury (ship), 71–72, 216
Merlin (ship), 55, 56, 219, 220
Meyer, Arline, 118, 120, 124–25
Micale, Mark S., 132, 191
middle-class ideals, 100–103, 194
midshipmen, 14, 34, 41
Military Men of Feeling: Emotion, Touch, and Masculinity in the Crimean War (Furneaux), 202
Miller, Amy, 83, 84
Minto, Lady (Mary Brydone), 107
Minto, Lord. *See* Elliott-Murray-Kynynmound, Gilbert, 2nd Earl of Minto
money/finances, 40–42, 142–51; prize money, 45, 136–37; smart-money system, 27–28, 32, 39–45, 187–89. *See also* pensions
monuments, 3, 127–28, 178–79, 181, 182, 183–84
Morton, Andrew, 119
Moss, Michael, 151, 178

Namur (ship), 66, 218
National Archives (formerly Public Records Office), 27–28
National Gallery of Naval Art, 182
National Maritime Museum, Caird Archive, 25, 26
Naval Biographical Dictionary (O'Byrne), 22–24, 25, 54, 207
Naval Chronicle, 107–8, 163
Naval Gallery, 122
naval history, 4, 11, 22–23
Naval History of Great Britain, The (James), 67, 148
needlework/sewing, 152
negligence, 42–43, 188
Nelson, Frances, 106–7, 150
Nelson, Horatia, 150
Nelson, Horatio, 15, 76–81; affair with Emma Hamilton, 147–49; anecdotes about, 43; on aristocrat naval officers, 47–48; assistive devices of, 8–9, 103, 236n150; and attack on Tenerife, 77–78; attitude toward body of, 149; bonds with other amputee officers, 12–13; caricatures of, 117–18; correspondence of, 26; death of, 126–27, 151, 191; dressing for battle, 84; and emotion/sensibility, 132, 134–35; family, 149–50; finances, 147, 150–51; as Jekyll/Hyde, 189–90; leadership of, 14, 135; loss of arm, 77–78; monuments to, 3, 127–28, 178–79, 181, 182, 183–84; patronage of seamen by, 32, 216; personal assistance to, 9, 13, 103–8; portraits of, 3, 111, 121–23, 123, 124–27, 127; promotion of his officers, 50; public image of, 1–2, 2–3, 4, 5, 89–91, 94–95, 181; "Sketch of My Life," 134; as standard for professional excellence, 134; and St. Vincent, 77, 78–79
Nelson, Maurice, 150
Nelson and Other Naval Studies (Thursfield), 189–90
Nelsonian Reminiscences: Leaves from Memory's Log (Parsons), 148

INDEX 267

Nelson Monument, Edinburgh, 127–28, 182
Nelson's Mediterranean Command (Orde), 38
Newman, James, 71
Niger (ship), 217
Nightingale, Florence, 202, 203
Nisbet, Josiah, 48, 77–79, 95, 150, 197
Nore, mutiny at (1797), 41, 77
North, Catherine Anne, 65, 212
Northcote, James, 123, 180
North Star (ship), 213
Northumberland Records Office, 26
Notes on Nursing (Nightingale), 202
Nussbaum, Felicity, 10

O'Byrne, William, 22–24, 25, 54, 207
occupational injuries, 22
O'Connor, Erin, 179, 193, 197
"Of Deformity" (Bacon), 1
officers: commissions, 56, 60; rankings of, 33–35; salaries of, 40–41. *See also* amputee officers; promotion and patronage
Opossum (ship), 213
Orde, Denis, 38
Orde, Sir John, 215
Original Stories from Real Life (Wollstonecraft), 103
Orpheus (ship), 208
Ott, Katherine, 3, 50, 108
Otter (ship), 52, 218, 219
Owen, Sarah Dorothea. *See* Pell, Sarah Dorothea (Owen)
Owen Glendower (ship), 137, 215
Oxford Dictionary of National Biography, 66

Packwood, Joseph, 14, 15, 215–16
Paget, Henry William, 1st Marquess of Anglesey, 87, 198, 199
pain: Gordon on, 167, 169–70; mental/emotional as higher order than physical, 115; popular images of sailors' indifference to, 45; self-reporting of, 199; and spasms, 30, 175, 193, 195, 199, 201; Victorian ideas about masculinity and, 193. *See also* smart-money system
Painted Hall (at Greenwich Hospital), 122, 182–83
parenting, 101–2
Parker, Edward Thornborough, 107
Parker, Peter, 38, 47
Parsons, George Samuel (Lieutenant), 148
Parthian (ship), 211
patronage system, 19, 46–50
Pell, Edwin, 144, 145
Pell, Owen, 70, 73, 145, 198
Pell, Sarah Dorothea (Owen), 76, 143–44, 145
Pell, Sir Watkin Owen, 15, 70–76, 216; appearance, 109; club life and friendships, 139–40; on curtailing of Chartism, 177; family, 70; family memoir/correspondence of, 25–26; finances, 143, 145; and Gordon, 71, 73, 76, 133, 139–40, 141–42; and Great Exhibition of 1851, 197–98; and Greenwich Hospital, 182, 184–86; injuries, 16, 71, 72, 189; leadership of, 14; marriage, 76, 143–44; and Marshall's naval history, 23; and Nelson memorials, 181–83; pension, 74, 189; performance of fitness, 91–92, 96; portraiture of, 120; and promotion, 38, 72–74, 75; and prosthetics, 13, 108, 109; retirement, 140; temperament of, 8; and Victorian era, 175, 199. *See also* diaries, Watkin Owen Pell's
Pell, Watkin Owen Spencer, 70, 143, 197
Pellew, Edward, 67–68
Pellew, Fleetwood, 134
Penguin (ship), 208
pensions, 21; cutting in Victorian era, 186–87; and loss of earning power, 42–44; and smart-money, 28, 40, 41; and supporting officers' families, 142

Pepys, Samuel, 36
Perdrix (ship), 215
performances of mock-pity (comedy/humor related to disability), 138–39
performing able-bodiedness, 88–96, 133–34
Perrett, Bryan, 65, 88, 157
personal assistance with everyday tasks, 9, 13, 99–108
Persuasion (Austen), 152, 173
petty officers, 33–34
Peyton, John Strutt, 8, *15*, 92, 216–17
Phoenix (ship), 213
physical stature/appearance, prejudices based on, 30–32, 38
Piercer (ship), 214
Pique (ship), 213
Plumper (ship), 210
Pointon, Marcia R., 112
police force, professionalization of, 177, 185–86
political influence, relating to promotion and patronage, 38–39, 46–48
poor and working-class people, 86–87, 176–77
Porter, Roy, 202
Portland (ship), 57, 219
portraiture, 3, 82; amputation made invisible in, 118–21, 127, 128; as collaboration between sitter and artist, 112–13; empty sleeves in, 121–24; hand-in-waistcoat pose, 124–25; and private life, 129–30; and visual codes of heroism, 111–12, 113–15; vulnerability in, 125–27, *127*
post-captains, 35, 53
Practical Education (Edgeworth and Edgeworth), 102
pregnancy and childbirth, 163–67, 192–93
Preston (ship), 73, 212
Princess of Orange (ship), 54, 218
prize money, 45, 136–37
promotion and patronage, 38–39, 46–50. *See also* hero promotion
property damage, 188
prostheses: choices of, 13, 108–10; and managing other people's perceptions, 88–89; in Victorian era, 197; and visibility of battle injuries, 50–51
Prudente (ship), 42, 210
psychiatry, 174–75, 189–90, 192–94, 201

quarterdecks, 85

Racoon (ship), 51, 67, 68, 211, 212, 217
Raisonnable (ship), 212, 218
Rathbourne, Sir Wilson, 217
Raw Material: Producing Pathology in Victorian Culture (O'Connor), 179
Real Hornblower, The: The Life and Times of Admiral Sir James Gordon (Perrett), 66
Regulus (ship), 208
reproductive choice, 166–67
retirement, 46, 140
Reynolds, Joshua, 114
Richardson, Jonathan, 113
Rivers, William, 14, *15*, 53–55, 217–18
Roberts, Thomas Cadman, 211
Robertson, J. Culp, 74–75
Robinson, George, 218–19
Robust (ship), 209
Rodger, N. A. M., 4, 18–19, 40–41, 46, 61, 85
Roebuck (ship), 215
Rosamond (ship), 53, 219
Rousseau, Jean-Jacques, 102
Rowley, Sir Charles, 67, 218
Royal George (ship), 208
Royal Naval Biography (Marshall), 22–23, 24, 25, 48, 72, 74, 92, 136, 177, 207
Royal Naval College, 56
Royal Navy. *See* British Royal Navy
Royal William (ship), 25, 214

San Josef (ship), 140, 209
Santa Margaritta (ship), 217
Science and Art of Surgery, The (Erichsen), 193
Scull, Andrew, 194
Sea Fencible service, 215, 217
Seahorse (ship), 69, 156, 212, 213
sensibility, 132–33, 134–35, 190–91
servants, 9, 41, 100, 102, 105–6, 196, 233n76
"services and sufferings," 28, 41–42, 44, 73
Seymour, Edward, 146
Seymour, John, 55, 219
Seymour, Richard, 26, 146
Seymour, Sir Michael, 15, 55–65, 208; and Berkeley, 58–61, 63–64; children, 101, 145–47, 196–97; family, 55, 57; family memoir of, 26, 37, 146; feud with Mends, 136–37; finances, 143, 146; first years at sea, 55, 57–58; and Gordon, 133, 137–39; injured at Glorious First of June, 61–63; and Luttrell, 55–58, 59; pension, 42, 43; performance of fitness, 91, 95–96; and personal assistance with daily tasks, 9, 13, 99, 100–101; portraiture of, *124*, 180–81, *181*; and Princess Victoria, 174; and promotions, 37, 38, 49, 63–64; retirement, 146
Seymour, Sir Michael, Jr., 146–47, 196–97
Shakespeare, Tom, 7
ships, 35–36
Siebers, Tobin, 10, 12, 99, 133, 172
Siege of Cádiz (1810–12), 209
slavery, 2, 58, 70, 76, 176
sleeves, empty: adaptations to clothing, 9, 103; Nelson's, 2–3; in portraits, 112, 121–24, 126–27, *127*, 180–81
smart-money system, 27–28, 32, 39–45, 187–89
Smith, Adam, 115
Smollett, Tobias, 84

Snap (ship), 139, 209
sociability. *See* friendship
Social History of British Naval Officers, A, 1775–1815 (Wilson), 10
social management (managing other people's reactions), 88–89, 97–98, 133–34
social status: and amputation, 86–88; and naval officers' backgrounds, 16, 19; and naval officers' uniforms, 83–84; and personal assistance, 100–103; self-reporting of, in naval histories, 23; and sensibility, 191; and smart-money/ officers' pensions, 41, 43
Southey, Robert, 43
Sparrowhawk (ship), 51, 211
spasms and pain, 30, 175, 193, 195, 199, 201
Spencer, George John, 2nd Earl Spencer and First Lord of the Admiralty, 64, 70, 143, 216
Spencer, Lavinia, 107
Spitfire (ship), 64, 91, 137, 219
Spithead, mutiny at (1797), 41, 77, 210
Standard (ship), 210
Statira (ship), 208
steam power, 176
Steedman, Carolyn, 102, 233n76
Stevenson, Robert Louis, 1, 33
St. George (ship), 213
stigma, about personal assistance, 9, 101–4
stockings, 9, 84, 104
Stopford, Edward, 15, 52–53, 219
St. Vincent, Lord. *See* Jervis, John, 1st Earl of St. Vincent
Suckling, Maurice, 50, 121
Sugden, John, 4, 94–95, 103, 105
Superb (ship), 111
surgeons, naval vs. civilian, 16–17
Swallow (ship), 208
Swan (ship), 211
Swiftsure (ship), 207

Sykes, John, 32
Syrett, David, 28

Taylor, Jenny Bourne, 193–94
Temple (ship), 212
Tenerife, attack on (July 24, 1797), 77–78, 80, 84, 94–95, 214
Thames (ship), 218
Theory of Moral Sentiments, The (Smith), 115
Thompson, Henry Clements, 15, 220
Thompson, Thomas B., 135
Thunder (ship), 75
Thursfield, James Richard, 189–90
Times, 128
Tonnant (ship), 208
tort law, 42, 188
Tosh, John, 100–101, 178, 190, 194
Tracy, Nicholas, 24–25
Trafalgar Square, monument to Nelson at, 3, 128, 178–79, 181, 183–84
Treasure Island (Stevenson), 33
Turner, David M., 7, 12, 86–87

uniforms, naval officers', 9, 83–84, 119–20, 191–92
U.S. Department of Labor, 9
U.S. National Park Service, 18

Venerable (ship), 213
Victoria, Queen of England, 96, 174
Victorian era, 174–205; centralization of state power, 177, 184–85, 187; changes in, 174, 176–78; changing ideas about disability and impairment, 187–89; degeneracy and ideas of gender difference, 189–94; professionalization of domestic security forces, 177, 185–86
Victory (ship), 36, 52, 53–54, 85, 151, 216, 217–18
Virginia (ship), 215

visibility. *See* amputee officers, representation of
visual codes, in images of military heroes, 111–30; amputation made invisible in, 118–21, 127, 128, 180–81; caricature, 115–18, *118*; commemorative goods, 3, 128, 181; empty sleeves in portraits, 121–24; hand-in-waistcoat pose, 124–25, 181; monuments, 3, 127–28, 178–79, 181, 182, 183–84; portraits as collaboration between sitter and artist, 112–13; portraits of Nelson, 3, 111, 121–23, 124–27, *127*; and private life, 129–30; in Victorian era, 179–81; and visual codes of heroism, 111–12, 113–15; vulnerability in, 114–15, 125–27, *127*
vulnerability, 86, 114–15, 125–27, *127*, 132–33, 152

Walcheren Expedition (1809), 208, 214, 217
Walpole, Galfridus, 121, *122*
War at a Distance (Favret), 114
Ward, Lydia. *See* Gordon, Lydia (Ward)
Ward, Rawdon, 154–55, 165
warrant officers, 33–34
Warspite (ship), 213
Wasp (ship), 215
Weazle (ship), 217
Weeping Britannia (Dixon), 194
Wellesley, Arthur, 1st Duke of Wellington, 21, 178, 198, 199
West, Benjamin, 127
West Indies, 58, 70, 76, 96, 169, 176, 215
White, Colin, 80, 90, 150
White Jacket (Melville), 1–2
wholeness/dismemberment, 179
William IV, King of England, 79–80
Williams, Kate, 5
Williams, Richard, 25
Williams, Sir Thomas, 54, 218

Williams, Thomas (Lieutenant, pension 1783), 25
Williams, Thomas (Lieutenant, pension 1816), 8
Wilson, Evan, 10, 16, 18, 19, 37–38, 47, 142, 225n66
Wollstonecraft, Mary, 103
women: as servants, 233n76; Victorian ideas of gender difference, 191–93. *See also* Gordon, Lydia (Ward)

Woodyear, Lumley, 217
workers' compensation, 45
working-class movement, 176–77
World Health Organization, 167
World War II, 204
Wynne, Betsey, 149
Yorke, Charles Phillip, 75

Zealous (ship), 213–14

Peculiar Bodies: Stories and Histories

Beyond the Moulin Rouge
WILL VISCONTI

Sapphic Crossings: Cross-Dressing Women in Eighteenth-Century British Literature
ULA LUKSZO KLEIN

Sight Correction: Vision and Blindness in Eighteenth-Century Britain
CHRIS MOUNSEY

www.ingramcontent.com/pod-product-compliance
Lightning Source LLC
Chambersburg PA
CBHW021349300426
44114CB00012B/1142